Cruise Tourism in Polar Regions

Cruise Tourism in Polar Regions

Promoting Environmental and Social Sustainability?

Edited by
Michael Lück, Patrick T. Maher and Emma J. Stewart

publishing for a sustainable future

London • Washington, DC

First published in 2010 by Earthscan

Earthscan Ltd, Dunstan House, 14a St Cross Street, London EC1N 8XA, UK
Earthscan LLC, 1616 P Street, NW, Washington, DC 20036, USA

Earthscan publishes in association with the International Institute for Environment and Development

For more information on Earthscan publications, see www.earthscan.co.uk or write to earthinfo@earthscan.co.uk

ISBN 978-1-84407-848-6

Typeset by Safehouse Creative
Cover design by Susanne Harris

A catalogue record for this book is available from the British Library

Library of Congress Cataloging-in-Publication Data

Cruise tourism in polar regions : promoting environmental and social sustainability? / edited by Michael Lück, Patrick T. Maher and Emma J. Stewart.
   p. cm.
 Includes bibliographical references and index.
 ISBN 978-1-84407-848-6 (hardback)
  1. Tourism--Polar regions. 2. Ocean travel--Environmental aspects--Polar regions. 3. Sustainable tourism--Polar regions. 4. Polar regions--Environmental conditions. I. Lück, Michael. II. Maher, Patrick T. III. Stewart, Emma J.
 G155.P65C78 2010
 910.911--dc22
       2010003070

Mixed Sources
Product group from well-managed forests and other controlled sources
www.fsc.org Cert no. SGS-COC-2482
© 1996 Forest Stewardship Council

Contents

List of Figures, Tables and Boxes

Figures

Tables

Boxes

List of Contributors

Bas Amelung, Universiteit Maastricht, The Netherlands
Bas is an associated researcher at the International Centre for Integrated Assessment and Sustainable Development (ICIS) at Maastricht University, The Netherlands. He received his PhD from Maastricht University in March 2006 with a study on the linkages between climate change and tourism.

Arthur Asa Berger, San Francisco State University, US
Arthur is professor emeritus of broadcast and electronic communication arts at San Francisco State University. He has published more than 100 articles and more than 60 books on media, popular culture, humour, cultural studies and tourism. Among his books on tourism are *Deconstructing Travel* (AltaMira), *Ocean Travel and Cruising* (Haworth), *Vietnam Tourism* (Haworth), *Thailand Tourism* (Haworth), *The Golden Triangle* (Transaction), *Bali Tourism* (Routledge) and *Japan Tourism* (Channel View). He is married, has two children and four grandchildren and lives in Mill Valley, California.

Jackie Dawson, University of Guelph, Canada
Jackie is a postdoctoral fellow in the Global Environmental Change Group (GECG) at the University of Guelph, Department of Geography. Her PhD was completed at the University of Waterloo, Canada, in the Department of Geography and Environmental Management and her MA was completed at Otago University, New Zealand, in the Department of Tourism. Her research focuses on the human dimensions of global environmental change, social–ecological systems, and environmental values and behaviour.

Ngaire Douglas, Bond University, Australia
Ngaire holds a PhD and was associate professor and head of school in Southern Cross University's School of Tourism and Hospitality and also lectured in special interest tourism at the University of Stavanger, Norway. She is author, co-author or

editor of a dozen books, numerous journal articles and chapters on various aspects of tourism in the Pacific Asia region. She is co-author, with Norman Douglas, of *The Cruise Experience: Global and Regional Issues in Cruising* (Pearson Hospitality Press). She is currently with Bond University on Australia's Gold Coast where she teaches cruise management.

Norman Douglas, Pacific Profiles, Australia
Norman holds a BA (Hons) from Newcastle University and a PhD from the Australian National University. He has taught at universities in Australia, Fiji, Norway and the US in subjects that include modern history, Pacific studies, tourism and media studies. He is author, co-author or editor of 15 books and scores of articles in both academic and popular publications on topics ranging from history to tourism and film analysis. He is co-author, with Ngaire Douglas, of *The Cruise Experience: Global and Regional Issues in Cruising* (Pearson Hospitality Press).

Dianne Draper, University of Calgary, Canada
Dianne is a professor in the Department of Geography, University of Calgary, and has authored numerous publications on environmental management, sustainable tourism and coastal zone management. Her current research focuses on governance and quality-of-life issues in communities working towards sustainable tourism, and on managing tourism growth and its impacts on communities, water resources, and parks and protected areas.

Neil Gilbert, Antarctica New Zealand, New Zealand
Neil has worked on polar matters for the last 24 years. In 1985, he joined the British Antarctic Survey as a research scientist, completing his PhD on near-shore marine ecology in 1991. Neil joined Antarctica New Zealand as environmental manager in 2003. In this capacity, he attends meetings of the Committee on Environmental Protection (CEP) to the Antarctic Treaty as New Zealand's representative and was elected to the chair of the CEP in 2006.

Geoff Green, Students on Ice, Canada
Geoff is the founder and executive director of Students on Ice (www.studentsonice. com), an award-winning educational organization based in Gatineau, Quebec, Canada. Now in its tenth year, the programme has taken over 1200 students from 40 different countries on expeditions to the Arctic and Antarctic. The goal of this unique project is to give the world's youth a heightened understanding and respect for the planet, and the inspiration to protect it. Geoff has led over 100 expeditions to the polar regions and, in the past two decades, has inspired thousands around the world by sharing his passion for Planet Earth. Learn more about Geoff at www. GeoffGreen.ca.

Robert K. Headland, University of Cambridge, UK
Bob is a senior associate of the Scott Polar Research Institute of the University of Cambridge where he has worked for 30 years. His principal interests are the historical geography of the Arctic and Antarctic, and current human effects on

both polar regions. He has lectured extensively to passengers visiting these areas, particularly when on voyages reaching several of the islands. He is a fellow of the Royal Geographical Society and a member of the Institute of Historical Research of the University of London. In 1984 he was decorated with the Polar Medal and is a member of the Arctic Club and the Antarctic Club.

John S. Hull, Auckland University of Technology, New Zealand
John is senior lecturer in the School of Hospitality and Tourism, and associate director at the New Zealand Tourism Research Institute, based at Auckland University of Technology (AUT), New Zealand. In 1998, John completed his PhD at McGill University in Montreal, Canada. His present research addresses tourism development issues in peripheral regions with a specific focus on community-based tourism and strategic planning and development. John has worked on tourism projects in North America, Europe, South America, the Middle East, Africa and Asia. Past clients include the United Nations World Tourism Organization (UNWTO), United Nations Convention on Biological Diversity (UNCBD), United Nations Environment Programme (UNEP), *United Nations Educational, Scientific and Cultural Organization* (UNESCO), World Bank, Nordic Council, European Tourism Research Institute, Commission on Environmental Cooperation, Canadian Tourism Commission, Tourism Atlantic, and Parks Canada. John is also a guest professor at the Icelandic Tourism Research Centre, Iceland.

Ross A. Klein, Memorial University of Newfoundland, Canada
Ross is an internationally recognized authority on the cruise ship industry. The Memorial University of Newfoundland professor of social work has published four books on the industry, was commissioned to write four reports for the Canadian Centre for Policy Alternatives and two reports for Bluewater Network/Friends of the Earth, and has more than a dozen articles and book chapters in academic and non-academic publications. He maintains www.cruisejunkie.com and the International Centre for Cruise Research; his work is equally academic and applied. He has given invited lectures at international conferences, universities, and to community organizations in the UK, across Canada and the US, across the Caribbean, and in Mexico, Australia and New Zealand. In addition, Klein is often quoted in media around the world, is frequently interviewed on television and radio, and has been/is an expert witness in a range of lawsuits against the cruise industry. He has given invited testimony to the San Francisco Board of Supervisors, Hawai'i County Council, US House of Representatives and the US Senate.

Ross received his BSc from Arizona State University, MSW from University of Maryland, and MA and PhD from Syracuse University. His books include *Death by Chocolate: What You Must Know before Taking a Cruise* (2001); *Cruise Ship Blues: The Underside of the Cruise Industry* (2002); *Cruise Ship Squeeze: The New Pirates of the Seven Seas* (2005); and *Paradise Lost at Sea: Rethinking Cruise Vacations* (2008).

Machiel Lamers, Universiteit Maastricht, The Netherlands
Machiel is a researcher at the International Centre for Integrated Assessment and Sustainable Development (ICIS) at Maastricht University, The Netherlands. His

PhD research was on the strategic challenges of tourism development in Antarctica, which he received from the same university in November 2009. His research interests include polar tourism, sustainable development, climate adaptation and participatory research approaches.

Daniela Liggett, University of Canterbury, New Zealand
Daniela has an MSc in Environment and Development (University of Manchester, UK) and a PhD in Antarctic Studies (University of Canterbury, New Zealand). Her recent research focuses on polar tourism regulation and management. Other research interests include tourism and development and interdisciplinary research methodologies.

Michael Lück, Auckland University of Technology, New Zealand
Michael is associate professor and head of the Department of Tourism and Events in the School of Hospitality and Tourism and associate director of the New Zealand Tourism Research Institute, both at Auckland University of Technology, New Zealand. He received his PhD from the University of Otago in Dunedin. Michael has more than ten years work experience in the tourism industry, having worked for a large package tour operator, travel agencies, a campervan rental company, and as tour guide in Belize. He taught at universities in Germany, New Zealand, Scotland and Canada. Michael's research interests lie in the areas of marine tourism (particularly marine wildlife tours and the cruise industry), ecotourism, sustainable tourism, the impacts of tourism, gay tourism and aviation. He has published in a number of international journals, is founding editor-in-chief of the academic journal *Tourism in Marine Environments*, and associate editor of the *Journal of Ecotourism*. Michael edited or co-edited two volumes on ecotourism, two on marine tourism, one on polar tourism and the *Encyclopedia of Tourism and Recreation in Marine Environments* (CABI).

Patrick T. Maher, University of Northern British Columbia, Canada
Pat is an associate professor in the Outdoor Recreation and Tourism Management Program at the University of Northern British Columbia. His PhD research, funded by a Commonwealth Scholarship and an Antarctica New Zealand/New Zealand postgraduate scholarship, examined the notion of visitor experience in the Ross Sea region. In the Arctic, Pat has planned, implemented and led a number of extensive paddling expeditions, been active in the University of the Arctic curriculum development regarding tourism, and helped to found the International Polar Tourism Research Network. He has taught at three universities in New Zealand and three universities in Canada, and led field courses to both polar regions. Pat has chaired and organized sessions at a number of international conferences and symposiums, sits on the scientific committee for TÉOROS (Revue de Recherche en Tourisme), is book review editor for the *Journal of Experiential Education*, has contributed to a number of books, and has published in or reviewed for a variety of international journals, including *Tourism in Marine Environments*, *Annals of Tourism Research*, *Arctic*, *Polar Geography*, *Human Dimensions of Wildlife*, *Current Issues in Tourism*, *International Journal of Tourism Research*, *Scandinavian Journal of Hospitality and Tourism*, *International Journal of Wilderness* and *Journal of Sustainable Tourism*.

Alison McIntosh, University of Waikato, New Zealand
Alison is professor of tourism at the University of Waikato, New Zealand. Her main research interests are in tourists' experiences of heritage and culture, and sustainable tourism development. Alison has published in leading journals such as *Annals of Tourism Research*, *Journal of Travel Research* and *Tourism Management*.

Simon Milne, Auckland University of Technology, New Zealand
Simon is professor of tourism at Auckland University of Technology, where he directs the New Zealand Tourism Research Institute. Simon completed his PhD in economic geography at Cambridge in 1989 and taught at McGill University, Montreal, until 1998. Simon's research interests focus on the links between tourism, information technologies and sustainable economic development. Simon has worked as a consultant to a number of international agencies, including the United Nations Economic and Social Commission for Asia and the Pacific (UNESCAP), the United Nations Development Programme (UNDP), the Canadian International Development Agency (CIDA), the European Union and the Organization of American States.

Mark B. Orams, Auckland University of Technology, New Zealand
Mark is professor of tourism at Auckland University of Technology and associate director of the New Zealand Tourism Research Institute. His work has focused on coastal and marine tourism and he has a particular interest in marine mammal tourism, extreme risk tourism, yachting, surfing and other marine recreational activities. Mark founded and directed the Coastal-Marine Research Group at Massey University at Albany in New Zealand before moving to take up a position at AUT. He is an experienced offshore yachtsman, having sailed over 60,000 nautical miles offshore, including winning the Whitbread Round the World Yacht Race in 1989/1990.

Greg Ringer, Royal Roads University, Canada
Greg is associate professor in the School of Tourism and Hospitality Management, Royal Roads University, Canada, and an adjunct professor in International Studies, University of Oregon, US. He also serves as visiting professor at universities in Montenegro and Vietnam, and as a sustainable tourism consultant to the National Geographic Society, the World Wide Fund for Nature (WWF), the US Bureau of Land Management, and the US State Department. Greg is the editor of *Destinations: Cultural Landscapes of Tourism* (Routledge), and the author of numerous book chapters and journal articles on protected area management and heritage tourism in post-conflict countries in Europe, Asia, Africa and Latin America.

Valerie Sheppard, University of Victoria, Canada
Valerie is an associate faculty member in the School of Tourism and Hospitality Management at Royal Roads University and is currently undertaking PhD studies in International Management and Organization at the University of Victoria. Valerie has an Honours Bachelor's degree in Tourism Studies (2003) and an MA, with distinction, in Recreation and Leisure Studies (2005) from Brock University,

Canada. Her research interests include business and community sustainability, tourism and ethics.

Emma J. Stewart, Lincoln University, New Zealand
Emma is a senior lecturer in tourism and parks at Lincoln University, New Zealand, and a research associate at the Arctic Institute of North America (AINA). She completed her PhD in the Department of Geography, University of Calgary, with support from the Pierre Elliot Trudeau Foundation. Her doctoral research used a community-based methodology to explore resident attitudes towards tourism development in three Arctic communities. This builds on research experience in Antarctica and New Zealand where she completed her Masters degree at Lincoln University. Emma's research interests include polar tourism, cruise tourism, climate change and tourism, environmental interpretation, and participatory research methodologies.

Bryan Storey, University of Canterbury, New Zealand
Bryan received his BA from Trinity College Dublin (1974) and his PhD from the University of Birmingham (1979), was a fellow of the Geological Society of London, Polar Medal (1987), a professor of Antarctic studies (2000), and is currently director of Gateway Antarctica, Centre for Antarctic Studies and Research (2000 to present). He has 24 years of experience as an Antarctic researcher and programme leader at the British Antarctic Survey. His research interests include earth system science, human impacts on Antarctica and policy issues.

Anna Thompson, University of Otago, New Zealand
Anna is the co-director of the Centre for Recreation Research and a senior lecturer at the Department of Tourism, University of Otago, New Zealand. Prior to academia she worked for the Department of Conservation for nine years and worked a summer season at Scott Base with Antarctica New Zealand. Her research interests include ecotourism and adventure tourism operations management, wilderness management, environmental certification systems, and visitor interpretation/education.

Acknowledgements

We were fortunate to receive enthusiastic support for this book, and we must acknowledge a number of individuals. We are grateful for the contributing authors, who have taken time out of their very busy schedules to write chapters for this volume: Alison McIntosh, Anna Thompson, Arthur Asa Berger, Bas Amelung, Bryan Storey, Daniela Liggett, Dianne Draper, Geoff Green, Greg Ringer, Jackie Dawson, John S. Hull, Machiel Lamers, Mark B. Orams, Neil Gilbert, Ngaire Douglas, Norman Douglas, Robert K. Headland, Ross A. Klein, Simon Milne and Valerie Sheppard. Their dedication and professionalism were instrumental in this book becoming reality.

Tim Hardwick, Anna Rice, Claire Lamont, Hamish Ironside and Rachel Butler at Earthscan have greatly facilitated the publication process. It has been a pleasure working with such a professional and friendly team! We would particularly like to acknowledge Shawn Mueller, assistant professor of information design at Mount Royal University in Calgary, for his exceptional cartographic skill. Shawn suggested a Molleweide projection of the Earth to help illustrate the introductory chapter, providing a view of both polar regions on one map, and something that more conventional projections do not allow. Shawn's map provides a unique contribution because it draws the polar regions into a central position on the world map – a theme, and a critical need, which we hope is also conveyed by the words in this book.

Many thanks also to those photographers who have generously provided the part title page photos. These are Patrick T. Maher (Parts IV and V), Jan-Eric Österlund (Part I), Greg Ringer (Part III) and Emma J. Stewart (Part II).

Michael would like to thank his colleagues at the School of Hospitality and Tourism and the New Zealand Tourism Research Institute, both at Auckland University of Technology. Linda O'Neill (head of school), Simon Milne (director, New Zealand Tourism Research Institute), and Nigel Hemmington (dean, Faculty of Applied Humanities, and pro vice-chancellor) continue to support his endeavours, and give him the time and freedom to do so. Any work is easier when you have a supportive and loving home environment. Michael's families in Germany and New

Zealand are always there for him, and Neil makes sure he has a healthy balance between work and leisure. Thank you all!

Pat would first like to thank all those who have professionally supported his interest in the polar regions and the tourism that occurs there. A specific list is far too long to elaborate upon, but includes colleagues and mentors near and far; funding agencies in Canada, New Zealand and Norway; various tour operators; many community members; and at least a few tourists themselves. Thank you all! The support shown to Pat by students, faculty and administration at the University of Northern British Columbia is exceptional. Every inquisitive question, engaging discussion and congratulatory remark is appreciated. Friends and family complete the sphere of support – there is truly no real measure to how much their positive 'vibes' help him to feel balanced when the weight of academia seems unbearable.

Emma would like to thank her colleagues, funding organizations, students and loved ones across the world who have provided support in her pursuit to understand the complex relationships between communities and tourism in polar places. To her young family, Emma would like to say thank you for enduring her absences to polar locations, and she truly hopes the separation is forgotten, and that all is remembered is a mother who returned (as she promised she would each time she left you) inspired and invigorated.

Foreword

Norman Douglas and Ngaire Douglas

It should no longer surprise anyone that cruise tourism is a global pursuit, despite the apparent obstacles and limitations it once faced. In the few decades since the 'revival' of cruising during the late 1960s, what was once regarded as a recreational activity under threat of extinction has grown to such an extent that there is barely a waterway on Earth that does not provide the location for a cruise vessel of some kind, from the extravagantly large (Royal Caribbean's *Oasis of the Seas*, which hit the water in late 2009 and carries 5400 passengers and 2165 crew) to the modestly small. However, modesty may be related only to limited passenger capacity; some of today's smallest cruise vessels are among the most luxuriously appointed. *Prince Albert II* (capacity 132 passengers), the most recent addition to the fleet of Silversea Cruises, is equipped, say its owners, to navigate both polar regions, while guests enjoy 'a privileged lifestyle that is simply second-to-none... The *Prince Albert II* even features The Humidor, where connoisseurs can enjoy the finest cigars and cognacs – a diversion offered by no other expedition ship' (Silversea Cruises, 2009). The expression 'luxury expedition vessel', which at one time may have seemed an oxymoron, is now applied freely to a number of new builds or recent conversions that seek to combine extremes of client comfort with extremes of environment. Environmental extremes are nowhere on Earth better represented than in the polar regions.

It can be claimed that polar cruising is not new – one researcher has traced the origin of cruise ship tourism to the Arctic to 1875 (Barthelmess, 2007); but the rate of growth in the popularity of cruising in polar regions in less than a decade is without precedent. Antarctic cruise tourism is generally considered to have had a far more recent origin (the 1950s) and to have been given a particular boost in 1969 by the efforts of Lars-Eric Lindblad with the construction of *Lindblad Explorer*, a vessel that embodied Lindblad's wish to combine exploration with education. There is some irony in the fact that this celebrated ship, renamed simply *Explorer*, sank in November 2007 after being holed by ice, as the debate about the future of Antarctic cruising was gaining additional momentum. Opponents of tourism in any form to the Antarctic are inclined to view this – and other marine mishaps in the region – as portentous, along with various evidences of climate change.

The Antarctic attracted more than 46,000 visitors during the 2007 to 2008 season, according to the International Association of Antarctica Tour Operators (IAATO, 2009a). The great majority of them were, of course, seaborne, and most of these are from the US. This last detail may be partly explained by the fact that the US ships included three visits from Holland America's *Rotterdam* and two from Princess Cruises' *Star Princess*, which between them contributed 8602 visitors. Not all visitors made landings, a detail often omitted in media comments on Antarctic tourism. The Arctic Region, with a greater number of accessible sites and widespread human populations, receives a far greater number of tourists. In 2006, cruise tourism to Svalbard alone accounted for 52,540 visitors (including crews) from overseas cruise ships and expedition cruise vessels (Governor of Svalbard, 2007).

Compared with the millions who visit recognized tourist destinations elsewhere on Earth by air, or the fewer millions who travel to them by ship, the numbers of visitors to polar regions may appear inconsequential. But in the rapidity of their increase they appear nothing short of alarming. There are many reasons for the upsurge in numbers, some evident, others less so, and they are dealt with in detail elsewhere. However, in addition to the general reasons for the expansion of cruising, at least a couple are specifically polar – the greater availability of ice-breakers or ice-strengthened vessels, and the worldwide popularity of films such as *Happy Feet*, the brilliantly animated film in which a dancing penguin saves the Antarctic from predatory developers and exploiters by attracting tourists.

Readers who regard this observation as frivolous should note that the film *Titanic*, which depicted one of the greatest of all maritime disasters, was credited by cruise industry sources with greatly stimulating popular interest in cruising. The idea that tourism may be the solution to all the world's social and economic problems has been voiced frequently – though often unconvincingly. In the case of Antarctica, it is offered as a possible solution to the problems of the environment. As stated by the IAATO: 'While growing numbers of passengers could present environmental challenges, the opportunity for the world's citizens to see Antarctica also solidifies popular support for preserving the continent's environmental integrity' (IAATO, 2009b). How does it achieve that? Out of sheer human goodwill? We are not told. But this affirmation of faith has something of a *Happy Feet* quality about it. Unfortunately, serious goodwill is in somewhat short supply all around the world.

Cruise tourism brochures, as we have suggested elsewhere, while attempting to evoke the sublime, are sometimes written in language bordering on the ridiculous. This can be as true of polar cruising as of any other kind. 'Have you ever wanted to meet a polar bear, spring across the tundra, watch shimmering ice floes, or explore native cultures in colorful and remote villages?' asks Polar Cruises' online brochure (Polar Cruises, 2009). 'If the answer is yes, then the Arctic has an iceberg with your name on it.' Like *Titanic*, perhaps? It continues: 'Just take the first iceberg on your left and follow that polar bear.' A great deal is made of the transcendental (mystical?) quality of the Earth's two extreme regions, of their ability to inspire feelings close to religious reverence. For example, the Captain's Choice Tour 2009–2010 (Captain's Choice, 2009) on the Antarctic itinerary of the 'luxury expedition vessel' *Orion* states: 'Antarctica is truly awe inspiring … and evokes a feeling of complete humility in each person who experiences this land.' In other brochures visitors are said to be 'transfixed' – or 'transformed' – by the all-enveloping silence.

This is not an experience shared by all. 'I thought it was going to be eerily quiet', wrote a woman friend who visited Antarctica recently:

> ... *but it's bloody noisy. What with the penguins yelling their heads off, the seals grunting, the whales blowing water out of their spouts, which sounds like a bear growling, ice cracking and birds calling – it's all very noisy. I took some photos of grubby penguins as all you ever see are pristine penguins. That's all poo they're standing on as well. It stinks.*

Fortunately there were other awe-inspiring attractions on this cruise, not the least of them the vessel's first officer, 'a big Russian with a voice from the depths of the sea', who charmed passengers daily by encouraging everyone to hold his sextant. The novelty quickly became 'come and have sextent [sic] with Sergey.'

While cruise tourism is the subject of this volume and the topic of much concern at present, there are other visitor activities which perhaps should not go unnoticed. In the online edition of the Canadian journal *Sudbury Star* (Veilleux, 2009) we are told that the difficulties of polar travel would not deter one Sudburian explorer (is there more than one?). This is Meagan McGrath who, having 'figured out the high altitude world' by climbing Mount Everest, seeks to test her limits in a polar environment, using her assault on the North Pole as a proving ground for an expedition to the South Pole. The ultimate aim of this? 'I'll be going to Antarctica in an attempt to become the first Canadian to solo from the coast of Antarctica, at Hercules Inlet, to the South Pole.'

Is it likely that this effort will be followed by the first Croatian, then the first Cambodian, then perhaps the first Corsican ... until Antarctica or at least large parts of it become adult adventure playgrounds for enthusiasts of extreme sports? Lamers et al (2007) note: 'Adventure tourism in the Antarctic interior is a very small niche market... Nevertheless, the trend has been upwards over the last few years.' This observation is not irrelevant here: something very similar was once said about cruising to the Antarctic. Indeed, cruising was itself thought a niche market for many years. Niche markets, as we have seen, have a habit of blowing out, even with sacred sites, which the polar regions represent for many.

The IAATO may take comfort from the fact that the recent Antarctic Treaty meeting provided regulatory endorsement to guidelines proposed by the organization in 1991 that prevent landings from ships carrying more than 500 passengers and limit the number of passengers ashore at any given time. Actual enforcement of these well-meaning measures, however, is still some distance in the future. Moreover, the increasing size of vessels that come to look rather than land does not yet appear to be a very serious topic of the 'how many is too many' debate. But any discussion concerning restrictions is likely to provoke disagreement, even between members of the IAATO, at least one of whom objected recently to the limitation on numbers when the matter was raised by US Secretary of State Hilary Clinton (Wilson, 2009). It was described as 'unfair' if it did not also limit government vessels. An opposing view was offered by another Australian operator, who agreed with the proposed reforms, saying that the region's major problem was one of greed. 'There's big money in it [Antarctic cruise tourism]. Every Tom, Dick and Harry wants to go down there.'

He could well be right. Royal Caribbean and Silversea, with whom we began this preface, are members of the IAATO already, although at this stage the former is a B1 (cruise only) member. Silversea's ice-strengthened *Prince Albert II* is scheduled to make many Antarctic cruises out of Ushuaia in the forthcoming season. The prospect of *Oasis of the Seas* turning up in Antarctic waters seems remote, but so would have been the prospect of the vessels of Holland America, Princess Cruises, Celebrity and Crystal at one time. The increasing number of large vessels must surely make the monitoring of each of them more difficult and, thus, the possibility of accident and environmental pollution more likely. There may still be too much reliance on honesty and good faith, both of which can be easily side-stepped. Consider merely one example, that of a Crystal Cruises executive who, faced with explaining why his company had not reported a discharge of waste into Monterey Bay, responded that the company had not broken the law, merely its own word (Klein, 2003).

It is appropriate that this valuable work is being published soon after the International Polar Year (2007 to 2009), and in the 50th anniversary year of the signing of the Antarctic Treaty, as the debate over the future of tourism – particularly cruise tourism – to Antarctica is gathering momentum and the issue of placing limits on tourist numbers continues to be vigorously discussed. This is not the first book published on the subject of polar tourism, but it is the first to deal extensively with what is probably polar tourism's most debatable aspect: the sustainability of cruising. The contributors represent a wide range of interests; their expertise is unquestionable and is already represented by their previous publications. Several are known for their controversial views. The approach is comprehensive; the many dimensions of cruise tourism examined in its pages include those that relate to social, ethical, environmental and regulatory factors, many of which have received relatively scant examination until now. It seems unlikely that the controversy over cruise tourism in the polar regions will abate in the near future or that issues concerning sustainability and best practice will ever be completely resolved. That being so, this book will maintain its value for quite some time.

References

Barthelmess, K. (2007) 'The commencement of regular Arctic cruise ship tourism: Wilhelm Bade and the *Nordische Hochseefischerei Gesellschaft* of 1892/1893', *Tourism in Marine Environments*, vol 4, nos 2–3, 113–120, p113

Captain's Choice (2009) *The Captain's Choice Tour 2009–2010, Antarctica Cruise aboard Orion*, www.captainschoice.com.au/cpa/htm/htm_tours, accessed 12 April 2009

Governor of Svalbard (2007) *Tourism Statistics for Svalbard 2006*, Sysselmannen Pa Svalbard, Longyearbyen, Norway, pp5–6

IAATO (International Association of Antarctica Tour Operators) (2009a) 'Tourism statistics', www.iaato.org/tourism_stats.html

IAATO (2009b) 'Tourism overview', www.iaato.org/tourism_overview.html, accessed 12 April 2009

Klein, R. A. (2003) *The Cruise Industry and Environmental History and Practice: Is a Memorandum of Understanding Effective for Protecting the Environment?* Bluewater Network, San Francisco and Ocean Advocates, Seattle, US, p16

Lamers, M., Stel, J. H. and Amelung, B. (2007) 'Antarctic adventure tourism and private expeditions', in J. M. Snyder and B. Stonehouse (eds) *Prospects for Polar Tourism*, CAB International, Wallingford, Oxfordshire, pp170–187

Polar Cruises (2009) 'Cruising in the Arctic', www.polarcruises.com/arctic/articles/cruising_ arctic_12, accessed 12 April 2009

Silversea Cruises (2009) Silversea Cruise Fleet – Prince Albert II', www.silverseaships.com/ cruiseships/silversea_albertcruise.html, accessed 12 June 2009

Veilleux, E. (2009) 'McGrath prepares for Antarctica trek', *The Sudbury Star* (online edition), www.thesudburystar.com/ArticleDisplay.aspx?e=1215636, accessed 12 April 2009

Wilson, L. (2009) 'US bid to cap Antarctic tourism 'unfair' says explorer', *The Australian*, 8 April 2009, www.theaustralian.news.com.au/business/story/0,,25306184-5018012,00. html?from=public_rss, accessed 9 April 2009

List of Acronyms and Abbreviations

ACIA	Arctic Climate Impact Assessment
ACSI	Alaska Cruise Ship Initiative
ADEC	Alaska Department of Environmental Conservation
AECO	Association of Arctic Expedition Cruise Operators
AFS Convention	International Convention on the Control of Harmful Anti-Fouling Systems on Ships
AINA	Arctic Institute of North America
AMSA	Arctic Marine Shipping Assessment
ASMA	Antarctic Specially Managed Area
ASPA	Antarctic Specially Protected Area
ATCM	Antarctic Treaty Consultative Meeting
ATCP	Antarctic Treaty Consultative Party
ATIA	Alaska Travel Industry Association
ATOS	Antarctic Tourism Opportunity Spectrum
ATS	Antarctic Treaty System
AUT	Auckland University of Technology
AWPPA	Arctic Waters Pollution Prevention Act
B&B	bed and breakfast
CANAL	Cruise Association of Newfoundland and Labrador
CEP	Committee on Environmental Protection
CIDA	Canadian International Development Agency
CLIA	Cruise Lines International Association
CO_2-e	carbon dioxide equivalent
DEC	US Department of Environmental Conservation
EPA	US Environmental Protection Agency
FPSO	floating production storage and off-loading unit
FSU	floating storage unit
GECG	Global Environmental Change Group
GRP	glass-reinforced plastic

IAATO	International Association of Antarctica Tour Operators
ICIS	International Centre for Integrated Assessment and Sustainable Development
ICSU	International Council for Science
IMO	International Maritime Organization
IPCC	Intergovernmental Panel on Climate Change
IPY	International Polar Year
km	kilometre
m	metre
MARPOL	International Convention for the Prevention of Marine Pollution from Ships
MES	Multidimensional Ethics Scale
MGO	marine gas oil
MOU	memorandum of understanding
MW	megawatt
NGO	non-governmental organization
NORDREG	Northern Canada Traffic Regulation System
NPS	National Park Service
NWCA	North West Cruise Ship Association
NZTRI	New Zealand Tourism Research Institute
ppm	parts per million
RGO	regional governmental organization
SCUBA	self-contained underwater breathing apparatus
SOI	Students on Ice
SWOT	strengths, weaknesses, opportunities and threats
TBT	tributyltin
UK	United Kingdom
UNCBD	United Nations Convention on Biological Diversity
UNDP	United Nations Development Programme
UNEP	United Nations Environment Programme
UNESCAP	United Nations Economic and Social Commission for Asia and the Pacific
UNESCO	United Nations Educational, Scientific and Cultural Organization
UNWTO	United Nations World Tourism Organization
US	United States
WCED	World Commission on Environment and Development
WMO	World Meteorological Organization
WWF	World Wide Fund for Nature (*formerly* World Wildlife Fund)

Setting the Scene:
Polar Cruise Tourism in the 21st Century

Michael Lück, Patrick T. Maher and Emma J. Stewart

Introduction

The polar regions have long fascinated explorers and researchers, from the early adventures of explorers, such as Shackleton, Scott and Amundsen, to modern day scientists who have access with modern military aircraft to research stations such as McMurdo Station and Scott Base in Antarctica, and Alert and Ice Station Barneo in the Arctic. Tourism to these remote and hostile environments has a much shorter history; however, the polar tourism sector has increased rapidly over the past two decades. Climate change is affecting these regions to a large extent and, in turn, has repercussions for tourism (Maher, 2008). In fact, some argue that tourism will increase in the form of 'last chance tourism' or 'doom tourism', where people rush to see places before they disappear. A particular case in point is polar bear viewing in Churchill, Manitoba, where polar bear populations are feared to rapidly decline due to the effects of climate change (Lemelin et al, in press). On the other hand, tourism to the polar regions may become easier due to a lack of ice and generally milder conditions – so much so that some of the main attractions, such as icebergs and wildlife that are dependent upon them, are not guaranteed to be seen at all times (Schwabe, 2008). This may have an adverse effect on visitor satisfaction (Maher, in press) and demand (Stewart et al, 2007). In order to raise awareness, and better understand the climatic processes in the polar regions, the Fourth International Polar Year (IPY) was proclaimed by the International Council for Science (ICSU) and the World Meteorological Organization (WMO) as a large scientific programme focused on the Arctic and the Antarctic from March 2007 to March 2009 (ICSU and WMO, 2009). As we have commented elsewhere (Maher et al, in press; Maher and Stewart, 2007), unfortunately there was an overall lack of tourism-related research projects under the auspices of the IPY; but as the collection of chapters in this book indicates, critical issues about polar tourism, and polar cruise tourism in particular, are becoming important and active areas of research.

Polar tourism is defined as 'tourism that occurs in the polar regions' (Maher et al, in press, p1); however, defining the polar regions is more difficult and ambiguous. Delineating Antarctica is relatively easy, as Figure 1.1 shows, with land and sea south of 60°S considered Antarctica, as outlined by the Antarctic Treaty System. Subsequently, the sub-Antarctic is land and sea between 60°S and 45°S, including all the islands of the Southern Ocean, and the tip of South America (Maher et al, in press). In contrast, the Arctic and sub-Arctic are much more difficult to define. This can be done by either political boundaries (e.g. the three northern Canadian territories at 60°N, or the Arctic Circle) or by biophysical boundaries, such as the tree line or the July 10°S isotherm (Maher et al, in press). Maher (2007) suggests that because large parts of the Arctic are dependent on the marine environment, a marine delineation of the Arctic would be useful and appropriate. In addition, there are different terms used interchangeably by different authorities, such as the 'High North', 'North', Circumpolar North' and the 'Arctic'. The *Arctic Human Development Report* defines the Arctic as encompassing:

> ... *all of Alaska, Canada north of 60°N together with northern Québec [Nunavik] and Labrador [Nunatsiavut], all of Greenland, the Faroe Islands, and Iceland and the northernmost counries of Norway, Sweden and Finland ... [in Russia], the Murmansk Oblast, the Nenets, Yamalo-Nenets, Taimyr, and Chukotka autonomous okrugs, Vorkuta City in the Komi Republic, Norilsk and Igsrka in Krasnoyarsky Kray, and those parts of the Sakha Republic whose boundaries lie closest to the Arctic Circle.* (Stefansson Arctic Institute, 2004, pp17–18)

The cruise industry and the polar regions

The cruise industry has seen phenomenal growth rates over the past few decades. Some sources contend that it is the fastest growing sector of the tourism industry (Dowling, 2006; Lück, 2007; CLIA, 2009), with growth rates of up to 1800 per cent since 1970 (CLIA, 2006). Table 1.1 illustrates the growth of the industry for the 25 member cruise lines of the Cruise Lines International Association (CLIA), which account for approximately two-thirds of the total market. Thus, it is estimated that, overall, close to 20 million people took a cruise in 2009 (R. Klein, pers comm). Despite the fact that the cruise industry accounts for only 0.6 per cent of all hotel beds offered worldwide (Dowling, 2006), it is a significant player in the tourism industry.

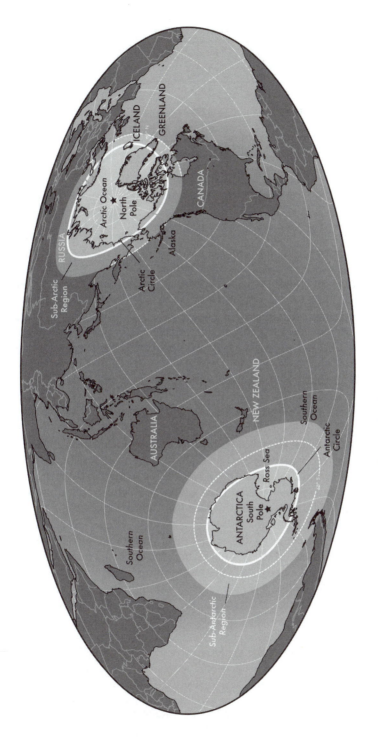

Figure 1.1 *The polar regions*

Source: Shawn Mueller, University of Calgary, Canada

Table 1.1 *Passenger numbers on CLIA member cruise lines*

Year	Passengers (000s)
1990	3774
1995	4721
2000	7214
2005	11,180
2008	13,008

Source: CLIA (2009)

The growing trend in the cruise industry is equally reflected in a rapidly growing cruise activity in the polar regions. The majority of tourists to these regions are cruise ship-based, with Antarctica's tourism almost being entirely ship-based. CLIA member lines saw an increase in capacity from approximately 4.2 million bed-days in 2000, to just under seven million bed-days in 2009 for Alaska-bound cruises. For Antarctica cruises, the number of bed-days increased from 49,000 in the year 2000 to 217,000 in 2009 (CLIA, 2009). Antarctica also sees a small number of small private yachts (estimated at about 1000 people), and a number of passenger over-flights (not landing on the continent) from Australia and, to a lesser extent, from Chile (Higham, 2008). Lemelin and Johnston (2008) contend that Arctic tourism is mostly based on wildlife (e.g. polar bears and whales) and landscape (e.g. fjords, glaciers and icebergs) as attractions. Due to the fact that the Arctic is more difficult to define and that not all tourists are ship-based, it is much more difficult to obtain reliable data about tourism activities in the Arctic. Data compiled from various sources are shown in Table 1.2. Numbers for Sweden, Finland and Norway (excluding Svalbard), and Alaska are assumed to be quite large; but statistics separating Arctic/sub-Arctic tourism from general tourism in these countries/states do not exist. Similarly, there is modest cruise ship activity in Russia, but data is not available (Lemelin and Johnston, 2008).

Given the steadily increasing demand for polar tourism, tour operators are reacting accordingly. Skagway in Alaska, for example, experienced growth to an extent that this small town now receives daily cruise ship visits from mid May to mid September, with four to five ships almost daily during the summer months of July and August (Cruise Line Agencies of Alaska, 2009). On a busy day in July, this means that up to 10,000 passengers would disembark in a town with a population of approximately 800. Similarly, in the Canadian Arctic, the number of cruise ships doubled to 22 cruises during 2006 (Stewart et al, 2007) and by 2008 six vessels carried approximately 2400 passengers on 26 separate cruises representing the busiest ever cruise season in Nunavut (Stewart et al, 2010). More dramatically, Antarctica has seen large increases in cruise ship activity, and especially in the size of ships. During the 2008 to 2009 season, 37,858 passengers (plus 24,579 staff and crew) visited Antarctica on a number of ships (IAATO, 2009). While the ratio of ship-based passengers decreased slightly due to the success of air/ship operations, the vast

Table 1.2 *Estimated tourist numbers in the Arctic and sub-Arctic regions*

Country/region/ province	Tourist numbers (estimates)	Sources/notes
Canada		
Northwest Territories	33,000–40,000 62,045	Lemelin and Johnston (2008) Northwest Territories Industry, Tourism and Investment (2007); 2006–2007 data for all non-resident travellers to the entire territory
Yukon	8049	Yukon Department of Tourism and Culture (2006); 2004 data – covers only Northern Yukon tourism region
Nunavut	13,000 33,000 9323	Buhasz (2006) Milne (2006) Datapath (2006); summer only
Northern Manitoba	2100–3000	Lemelin (2005); specific visitors to the Churchill Wildlife Management Area
Nunavik (northern Quebec)	25,000	Tourisme Quebec (2004); in 2004, Nord du Quebec statistics included both the Nunavik and James Bay regions
Nunatsiavut (northern Labrador)	565 21,000	Maher and Lemelin (in press); 2008 visitors to Torngat Mountains National Park Hull (2001); adventure tourists to all of Labrador
US (Alaska)	1,631,500	State of Alaska (2007); summer 2006 data for all out-of-state visitors
Greenland	33,000 (air arrivals) 22,051 (cruise arrivals)	Kaae and Raahede (in press)
Iceland	277,800	Lemelin and Johnston (2008)
Norway (Svalbard)	40,000 (ship-based) 10,000 (air based) 77,926 (guest nights in Longyearbyen) 27,296 (cruise tourists)	Lemelin and Johnston (2008) Viken (2006)

Country/region/ province	Tourist numbers (estimates)	Sources/notes
Norway (Finnmark)	2,420,959	Viken (2008); data from 2002
Sweden (Norrbotten county)	1,700,000	Zillinger (2007); data from 2001 tourist overnight stays
Finland (Finnish Lapland)	2,117,000	Hakkarainen and Tullentie (2008); 2006 data for the number of registered tourist overnights
Russia	Estimated at a few tens of thousands and growing steadily – data difficult to obtain	See Pisarev (2008) and Tsekina (2008) for general descriptions

majority (96 per cent during the 2004/2005 season) of tourists to Antarctica are still ship-based, with growth rates in excess of 400 per cent between the 1992/1993 and the 2005/2006 seasons (Bertram, 2007; Higham, 2008).

As the sinking of the *Explorer* in November 2007 off the Antarctic Peninsula illustrates, there are concerns associated with the enormous growth rates of polar tourism (Stewart and Draper, 2008). Key stakeholders, including national programme managers, tour operators and tourists themselves have to adapt to situations previously unheard of. In 2008, for example, a passenger who was booked on a cruise via the Northwest Passage successfully sued the tour operator for a shortcoming of his trip: the brochure of the operator promised 'meter-thick pack ice'. During the journey in July 2007, there was no 'meter-thick pack ice' to be seen (attributed to the effects of climate change), and the court agreed that this was a shortcoming of the journey and a broken promise of the tour operator, despite the tour operator's brochure advising that schedules may have to be changed due to extreme weather (Schwabe, 2008). In contrast to not having enough ice, in November 2009, the Russian icebreaker *Kapitan Khlebnikov* was stuck in ice around Antarctica with 101 passengers, 23 staff and 60 crew on board (Associated Press, 2009; Shaw, 2009). The return to Ushuaia, Argentina, was delayed by eight days, and in order to pass the time in the ice, the operator organized tours to spend time at the Snow Hill Island Emperor Penguin Rookery (Shaw, 2009). While there was no obvious risk for an icebreaker like the *Kapitan Khlebnikov* in such a situation, there is concern about the increasing number of regular large cruise liners visiting the polar regions, which are not ice-strengthened. A potential rupture of the hull, or even a sinking, could result in the leaking of oil and other hazardous liquids, which would be a disaster for fragile polar environments (O'Grady, 2006). In addition, a search and rescue mission to such remote areas, and in adverse weather conditions, is very difficult at best. With a capacity of more than 3500 passengers and crew on board, and often adverse weather conditions, an aerial rescue mission is next to impossible. Response capabilities of Australia and New Zealand, for example, are very limited (Jabour, 2007).

Sustainable tourism and the polar regions

After the World Commission on Environment and Development (WCED) published the report *Our Common Future*, also commonly referred to as the Brundtland Report in 1987, sustainable tourism became the lofty goal of many tour operators, regional governmental organizations (RGOs) and non-governmental organizations (NGOs), as well as pressure groups and various industry organizations (Lück, 1998). Sustainability is defined as 'development that meets the needs of the present without compromising the ability of future generations to meet their own needs' (WCED, 1987, p43). It is the WCED's goal to have all forms of tourism develop sustainably, from mass tourism to special interest tourism. However, Weaver (2008) notes that there is an area of contention with the inclusion of environmental and social sustainability. While there are good intentions to include both in development plans, problems become apparent when the implementation of tourism development provides the basis for conflicts between the two. In that case, the question is which should take priority over the other.

According to Walker and Moscardo (2006), expedition cruise ships carry up to 120 passengers, offering an educational experience with teams of environmental and cultural guides on board. Thus, many of the cruises in polar waters would qualify as expedition cruises, nature-based tourism or even as ecotourism (Dawson, 2001). However, the sections above contain examples that illustrate that there are a number of issues and questions about the credibility of polar cruises as sustainable tourism. These range from the negative social and environmental impacts related to tourist and operator behaviour, problems and pollution related to incidents and accidents (such as groundings, collisions and sinkings), crowding of remote peripheral communities by cruise passengers, and the sheer size of modern (non-ice-strengthened) cruise liners plying the polar waters. Such issues raise the question at the heart of this book: can cruise activities in the polar regions ever be synonymous with environmental and social sustainability?

Thus, this book was conceived during the International Polar Year (2007 to 2009), and is the only volume to address a variety of concerns and issues related to polar cruising to date. Part I introduces the market dimensions of polar cruising, including yacht cruising, cruises on icebreakers and an ethnographic report of polar adventure cruisers. Safety and security, ethical standards of passengers, and educational cruises are covered in Part II, which deals with human dimensions. The environmental dimensions of Part III introduce general environmental impacts of polar cruises, monitoring issues and the implications of climate change. Part IV, which examines governance and policy dimensions, addresses stakeholder perspectives, port readiness and policy issues. The intention of this volume is to raise awareness of some subjects, that have previously been neglected, in the hope that it will create some action on solutions. As with many books, *Cruise Tourism in Polar Regions: Promoting*

Environmental and Social Sustainability? will undoubtedly raise more questions than it provides answers. It is our hope that this will result in healthy debates about the issues raised and stimulate more research on these important topics.

References

Associated Press (2009) 'Cruise ship with 100 tourists stuck in Antarctica', *The Sydney Morning Herald*, 18 November, www.smh.com.au/travel/travel-news/cruise-ship-carrying-100-tourists-stuck-in-antarctic-ice-20091118-iknl.html

Bertram, E. (2007) 'Antarctic ship-borne tourism: An expanding industry', in J. M. Snyder and B. Stonehouse (eds) *Prospects for Polar Tourism*, CABI, Wallingford, pp149–169

Buhasz, L. (2006) 'Northern underexposure', *Globe and Mail*, 1 July

CLIA (Cruise Lines International Association) (2006) *Profile of the US Cruise Industry*, www.cruising.org/press/sourcebook2006/profile_cruise_industry.cfm, accessed 1 June 2006

CLIA (2009) *2009 CLIA Cruise Market Overview: Statistical Cruise Industry Data through 2008*, Cruise Lines International Association, Fort Lauderdale

Cruise Line Agencies of Alaska (2009) *Cruise Ship Calendar for 2009*, www.skagway.com/09calendar.pdf, accessed 27 November 2009

Datapath (2006) *Nunavut Exit Survey*, Marsh Lake

Dawson, C. P. (2001) 'Ecotourism and nature-based tourism: One end of the tourism opportunity spectrum?', in S. F. McCool and R. N. Moisey (eds) *Tourism, Recreation and Sustainability: Linking Culture and the Environment*, CABI, Wallingford, pp41–53

Dowling, R. K. (2006) 'The cruising industry', in R. K. Dowling (ed) *Cruise Ship Tourism*, CABI, Wallingford, pp3–17

Hakkarainen, M. and Tullentie, S. (2008) 'Tourism's role in rural development of Finnish Lapland: Interpreting national and regional strategy documents', *Fennia*, vol 186, no 1, pp3–13

Higham, J. (2008) 'Antarctic tourism', in M. Lück (ed) *The Encyclopedia of Tourism and Recreation in Marine Environments*, CABI, Wallingford, pp18–21

Hull, J. S. (2001) 'Opening up the big land to the world: The role of the public sector in adventure tourism development in Labrador', in B. Sahlberg (ed) *Going North: Peripheral Tourism in Canada and Sweden*, European Tourism Research Institute, Östersund, Sweden

IAATO (International Association of Antarctica Tour Operators) (2009) *2008–2009 Summary of Seaborne, Airborne, and Land-based Antarctic Tourism*, International Association of Antarctica Tour Operators, Providence, RI

ICSU and WMO (International Council for Science and World Meteorological Organization) (2009) *About IPY*, www.ipy.org/about-ipy, accessed 27 November 2009

Jabour, J. (2007) 'Underneath the radar: Emergency search and rescue insurance for east Antarctic tourism', *Tourism in Marine Environments*, vol 4, no 2–3, pp203–220

Kaae, B. C. and Raahede, M. K. (in press) 'Governance dimension: Tourism strategies and environmental labelling in Greenland', in P. T. Maher, E. Stewart and M. Lück (eds) *Polar Tourism: Human, Environmental and Governance Dimensions*, Cognizant Communication, Elmsford, NY

Lemelin, R. H. (2005) 'Wildlife tourism at the edge of chaos: Complex interactions between humans and polar bears in Churchill, Manitoba', in F. Berkes, R. Huebert, H. Fast, M. Manseau and A. Diduck (eds) *Breaking Ice: Renewable Resource and Ocean Management in the Canadian North*, University of Calgary Press, Calgary

Lemelin, R. H. and Johnston, M. E. (2008) 'Arctic tourism', in M. Lück (ed) *The Encyclopedia of Tourism and Recreation in Marine Environments*, CABI, Wallingford, pp32–33

Lemelin, R. H., Dawson, J., Stewart, E. J., Maher, P. T. and Lück, M. (in press) 'Last-chance tourism: The boom, doom, and gloom of visiting vanishing destinations', *Current Issues in Tourism*

Lück, M. (1998) 'Sustainable tourism: Do modern trends in tourism make a sustainable management more easy to achieve?', *Tourismus Jahrbuch*, vol 2, no 2, pp141–157

Lück, M. (2007) 'The cruise ship industry: Curse or blessing?', in M. Lück (ed) *Nautical Tourism: Concepts and Issues*, Cognizant Communication, Elmsford, NY, pp75–82

Maher, P. T. (2007) 'Arctic tourism: A complex system of visitors, communities, and environments', *Polar Geography*, vol 30, no 1–2, pp1–5

Maher, P. T. (2008) 'International polar years', in M. Lück (ed) *The Encyclopedia of Tourism and Recreation in Marine Environments*, CABI, Wallingford, pp243–244

Maher, P.T. (in press). 'Cruise tourist experiences and management implications for Auyuittuq, Sirmilik and Quttinirpaaq National Parks, Nunavut, Canada', in C. M. Hall and J. Saarinen (eds.), *Tourism and Change in the Polar Regions: Climate, Environments and Experiences*, Routledge, Abingdon, UK

Maher, P. T. and Lemelin, R. H. (in press) 'Northern exposure: Opportunities and challenges for tourism development in Torngat Mountains National Park, Labrador, Canada', *Polar Record*

Maher, P. T. and Stewart, E. J. (2007) 'Polar tourism: Research directions for current and future possibilities', *Tourism in Marine Environments*, vol 4, no 2–3, pp65–68

Maher, P. T., Stewart, E. and Lück, M. (in press) 'An introduction to polar tourism: Human, environmental and governance dimensions', in P. T. Maher, E. Stewart and M. Lück (eds) *Polar Tourism: Human, Environmental and Governance Dimensions*, Cognizant Communication, Elmsford, NY

Milne, S. (2006) 'Baffin Island, Nunavut, Canada', in G. Baldacchino (ed) *Extreme Tourism: Lessons from the World's Cold Water Islands*, Elsevier, Oxford

Northwest Territories Industry, Tourism and Investment (2007) *Canada's Northwest Territories: Tourism & Parks: Tourism Research and Statistics*, www.iti.gov.nt.ca/parks/tourism/research_and_statistics.htm, accessed 28 September 2007

O'Grady, R. (2006) 'Cruise ships threaten disaster in Antarctic', *The New Zealand Herald*, 13 September, pA21

Pisarev, S. V. (2008) 'Tourism in polar oceans: Advantages and disadvantages of cooperation with marine investigations', in M. Breiling (ed) *The Vienna Symposium on Polar Tourism*, 22–25 October 2008, Vienna University of Technology – Technology, Tourism and Landscape Centre, Vienna, Austria

Schwabe, W. (2008) 'Klage gegen Packeis: Klimawandel begründet "Mangel" im Sinne des Reiserechts', *Kölner Stadtanzeiger*, 24 November, www.ksta.de/html/artikel/1226655119168.shtml

Shaw, P. (2009) *Icebreaker Successfully Navigates Antarctic Pack Ice and Enters Open Water*, Quark Expeditions, Waterbury, VT

State of Alaska (2007) *Alaska Visitor Statistics Program: Summer 2006*, State of Alaska, Department of Commerce, Community and Economic Development, Juneau

Stefansson Arctic Institute (2004) *Arctic Human Development Report*, Stefansson Arctic Institute, Akureyri, Iceland

Stewart, E. J. and Draper, D. (2008) 'The sinking of *MS Explorer*: Implications for cruise tourism in Arctic Canada', *Arctic (InfoNorth)*, vol 61, no 2, pp224–231

Stewart, E. J., Howell, S. E. L., Draper, D., Yackel, J. and Tivy, A. (2007) 'Sea ice in Canada's Arctic: Implications for cruise tourism in the Northwest Passage', *Arctic*, vol 60, no 4, pp370–380

Stewart, E. J., Howell, S. E. L., Draper, D., Yackel, J. and Tivy, A. (2010) 'Cruise tourism and sea ice in Canada's Hudson Bay region', *Arctic*, vol 63, no 1, pp57–66

Tourisme Québec (2004) *Tourisme en chiffres 2004 – version finale*, Gouvernement du Québec, Québec

Tsekina, M. V. (2008) 'The usage of the tourist potential of the Northern and Southern Poles', in M. Breiling (ed) *The Vienna Symposium on Polar Tourism*, 22–25 October 2008, Vienna University of Technology – Technology, Tourism and Landscape Centre, Vienna, Austria

Viken, A. (2006) 'Svalbard, Norway', in G. Baldacchino (ed) *Extreme Tourism: Lessons from the World's Cold Water Islands*, Elsevier, Oxford

Viken, A. (2008) 'The nature of Arctic tourism', presentation to the initial meeting of the University of the Arctic Thematic Network on Northern Tourism, Gjesvaer, Norway, 24 May 2008

Walker, K. and Moscardo, G. (2006) 'The impact of interpretation on passengers of expedition cruises', in R. K. Dowling (ed) *Cruise Ship Tourism*, CABI, Wallingford, pp105–114

WCED (World Commission on Environment and Development) (1987) *Our Common Future*, Oxford University Press, Oxford

Weaver, D. B. (2008) *Ecotourism*, 2nd edition, John Wiley & Sons, Milton, UK

Yukon Department of Tourism and Culture (2006) *2004 Visitor Exit Survey: Klondike Region*, Government of Yukon, Whitehorse, Canada

Zillinger, M. (2007) 'Organizing tourism development in peripheral areas: The case of the Subarctic project in northern Sweden', in D. K. Müller and B. Jannson (eds) *Tourism in Peripheries: Perspectives from the Far North and South*, CABI, Wallingford, UK

Part 1
MARKET DIMENSIONS

2

Polar Yacht Cruising

Mark B. Orams

Introduction

Our planet's polar regions have fascinated humans for centuries. The extreme conditions, the flora and fauna and the dramatic geography have created ecosystems in the Arctic and Antarctic that are unique, almost to a point where they are considered otherworldly – that is, they are places that are the most far removed from the day-to-day living conditions of most people as is possible. It is this contrast and the challenges associated with the travel to these locations that, for some, have proved irresistible. For over a century these challenges have meant that travellers (for they never thought of themselves as tourists) were a few determined explorers and adventurers who had the skill, determination and fortitude to venture into these regions. Advances in technology over the past three decades, increased media attention and profile and, most recently, climate change-induced changes have dramatically transformed visitation to polar regions. An increasing number of both commercial charter yachts and privately owned vessels are venturing to the Arctic and Antarctic and this trend is highly likely to continue. The implications of such growth in visitation are multifaceted and will be a significant management challenge over the coming years.

The past: Adventurers and explorers

With the exception of the indigenous peoples of the Arctic, early visitors to polar regions were European explorers and adventurers (Headland, 1998). They mounted major expeditions that were supported by private donors and public fundraising campaigns. These expeditions achieved significant attention, particularly in the countries of origin, and they were strongly associated with nationalistic pride and ambition. The early explorers of both the Arctic and Antarctic became legends in their own lifetimes and their names, exploits and stories defined the so-called 'heroic age'. Bering, Hudson, Franklin, Ross, Scott, Shackleton, Amundsen, Nansen, Peary, Cook and Fiennes (amongst others) are names strongly associated with this era and their legacy remains tremendously influential today, over a century after their expeditions began.

While these explorers and adventurers accessed the polar regions via sea (for there was no alternative), their purpose was specific (i.e. exploration and science) and they cannot be considered to be 'polar cruising tourists'. However, for many who visit the Arctic and Antarctic today, including tourists, there is a strong awareness of that legacy and a desire to engage with it, to pay respect to it and to vicariously experience something of the trials, successes and 'heroism' of those days.

An example of this interest is the increasing demand for visits to the huts of Scott and Shackleton on Ross Island, Antarctica. These huts formed the base for the expeditions to reach the South Pole in 1901 to 1904 (led by Scott), 1907 to 1909 (led by Shackleton) and 1910 to 1913 (led by Scott). The huts are managed (and are being restored) by the Antarctic Heritage Trust (see www.heritage-antarctica.org), which is also managing requests and applications for visits to the huts from cruise ship-based tourists and a limited number of yacht-based tourists. Thus, the legacy of the polar explorers remains a strong influence on those who venture to the Arctic and Antarctic onboard yachts today.

Figure 2.1 *Shackleton's hut, Cape Royds, Ross Island, Antarctica*
Source: Mark B. Orams

The present: The polar regions and yachts

Over the past three decades a new means of visiting and experiencing the polar seas has emerged. The growth of ship-based tours to Antarctica and the Arctic has been significant over the past 30 years (covered in detail in other chapters in this book) and a similar pattern is emerging with regard to tours based on sailing vessels (and some 'motor yachts'). This type of tourism can be divided into two main types: those yachts that operate as commercial tours with fee-paying passengers, and those that are private expeditions or cruises onboard privately owned vessels. Both types have become increasingly part of the tourism activity in polar regions; however, there is little verified and reliable data with regard to the numbers and types of yachts cruising to and within these polar regions.

Geographically, the polar regions are delineated by the impact of the seasons and the presence and absence of sunlight related to those seasons. The Arctic and Antarctic circles are generally considered bounded by the latitude of 66° 33' 39" (North and South, respectively), this latitude being where, for at least one day each summer, the sun is visible for an entire 24-hour period. For the Antarctic Circle there are no land masses (with the exception of Antarctic scientific bases) where humans permanently reside. Furthermore, all land within the Antarctic Circle is part of Antarctica and, as a consequence, is managed via the multinational Antarctic Treaty. This treaty applies to all land, sea and sea ice (including the permanent and seasonal sea ice) south of the 60° latitude meridian. As a consequence, a number of sub-Antarctic islands are also subject to the provisions of the treaty.

In contrast to the Antarctic, there are a number of permanent human settlements and independent sovereign nations that exist inside the Arctic Circle. Countries that have part of their land and territorial waters inside the Arctic Circle include the US, Canada, Greenland (Denmark), Iceland, Norway, Sweden, Finland and Russia. For a number of these areas, yachts and marine tourism activities have a long and established history. Activities such as whale-watching, scenic cruises, wildlife-viewing, fishing and, in winter, ice-skate touring on the sea ice are popular. There are a number of sea ports and numerous anchorages, moorings and some marinas inside the Arctic Circle. Details of these are contained in the popular yacht-cruising guides that have been produced for Norway (Harries and Nickel, 2009), Sweden (Saunders et al, 2005) Finland (Saunders and Saunders, 2005), Russia (Glaister and Ivankiv, 2005), and Alaska, US (Terdal, 2000; Ludmer, 2001).

There are no summative data regarding the number of yachts cruising the Arctic Circle region, but there is little doubt that it is substantial and would number in the thousands each year. With few exceptions, this cruising activity is concentrated during the summer months (June, July and August). The attractions of 24-hour daylight, usually more settled weather, spectacular scenery, encounters with marine and terrestrial wildlife, and protected anchorages in fjords, harbours and inlets are significant for both smaller cruising yachts (as small as 10m in length) and large 'super-yachts' (in excess of 30m in length).

In contrast, cruising to Antarctic waters remains a significant and challenging voyage which is rarely attempted by less experienced recreational sailors (Rolfo and Ardrizzi, 2006). The Southern Ocean is infamous amongst sailors throughout history for its extremes of wind and sea conditions and the monikers; 'Roaring Forties', 'Furious Fifties' and 'Screaming Sixties' refer to the often life-threatening conditions that occur in these latitudes. As a consequence of these challenging conditions, the significant distances from protected ports to Antarctic waters and the lack of facilities and anchorages in Antarctica, few cruising yachts attempt the voyage.

Table 2.1 *Summary of cruising yacht visits to Antarctic waters during the 20th century*

Decade	Number of voyages	Country of yacht registration	Comments
1940s	1	UK	Niall Rankin's *Albatross* visited South Georgia Island
1950s	2	Australia, UK	Both were visits to sub-Antarctic islands
1960s	2	Australia, UK	Visits to sub-Antarctic islands
1970s	24	Australia, Belgium, France, Italy, New Zealand, Poland, UK, US	First private yacht to Antarctica itself was David Lewis's *Ice Bird* to the Antarctic Peninsula in 1972 First private yacht to visit the Ross Sea region was David Lewis's *Solo* in 1977/1978.
1980s	77	Argentina, Australia, Belgium, Brazil, France, Germany, Italy, Japan, The Netherlands, New Zealand, Panama, South Africa, Sweden, Switzerland, UK, US	Nearly half of these vessels visited the Antarctic Peninsula
1990s	217	Argentina, Australia, Brazil, Canada, Croatia, Czechoslovakia, Denmark, Estonia, Finland, France, Germany, Ireland, Italy, Japan, The Netherlands, New Zealand, Norway, Russia, Spain, Switzerland, Sweden, UK, US	France was the most frequent nation of yacht registration with 86 Jerome Poncet (France and UK) was the most frequent vessel master, with nine separate voyages during this decade

Source: Boris Baltzer (see www.sy-lundi.de)

Because Antarctica is managed under the Antarctic Treaty System for peaceful and scientific purposes, all vessels entering Antarctic waters require a permit and clearance before doing so. As a consequence, there is a register of vessels that have visited Antarctica and a summary of this has been compiled by Boris Baltzer (see Table 2.1 and www.sy-lundi.de). This summary shows that the first private cruising yachts to undertake the voyage did not do so until after World War II and Rankin's *Albatross* from the UK was actually transported to South Georgia onboard a whaling ship in 1946. During the 1950s, two vessels sailed to Antarctic waters and two further vessels did so during the 1960s. Thus, prior to the 1970s, only five separate private voyages are recorded for Antarctic waters. However, during the 1970s the number of voyages increased dramatically and the interest in and confidence to sail to Antarctic waters increased rapidly. Particular individuals started to become regular visitors from this time and these yacht skippers became well known for their exploits via books and television documentaries. For example, during the 1970s, Frenchman Jerome Poncet sailed to Antarctica on four separate occasions and subsequently he has made dozens of further voyages visiting the continent multiple times in every decade since. Similarly, New Zealander David Lewis made a number of voyages to Antarctic waters (including an attempt at a solo circumnavigation of Antarctica) and the stories of his adventures, accidents and challenges became well known through his many books (e.g. Lewis, 2002). In more recent times, American Skip Novak has made many trips to Antarctic waters and now runs a successful charter yacht operation which specializes in polar cruising, exploration and adventures (see www.pelagic.co.uk).

From the 1970s, when 24 separate voyages by private yachts are recorded, visits to Antarctica increased exponentially. The decade of the 1980s saw 77 separate voyages and the 1990s 217 (see Table 2.1 for a summary of yacht visits to Antarctica).

Increasing interest, confidence and the growing opportunities to use technology for yacht design, construction, navigation, communication, safety and weather forecasting have all contributed to the growth in private (and now commercial charter) yacht voyages to Antarctica (Poncet and Poncet, 2007).

The influence of technology

Prior to 1970 almost all cruising yachts (sail or power) were built from either wood or steel (although sailing yachts were almost exclusively wood construction). This construction provided significant challenges in terms of strength, durability, cost and safety. Furthermore, sailing vessels' super-structure (namely, rigging such as masts, booms and other sail-related hardware) were also mostly wooden, and reliability in extreme wind and sea conditions and durability over long periods of time compromised the conditions that vessels could safely handle.

In addition to construction-related issues, yachts were relatively slow, meaning that long-distance passages of over 1000 nautical miles were weeks in duration, and if adverse weather was encountered, such voyages could stretch to months at sea. Weather forecasting and communication were rudimentary, and navigation required significant skill and experience in celestial navigation using a sextant. The reality of open-ocean cruising during the 1950s and 1960s, particularly to the poles, was that it was often arduous, fraught with risk, difficult and relatively expensive. Not surprisingly, few undertook these journeys and those who did were very experienced hardy sea-farers who were expecting and looking for adventure.

The advent of new lighter, stronger construction materials and their application to yacht design and construction revolutionized sail and power boats from the 1970s onwards (Orams, 1999). A wide range of materials became available and were applied to vessels. These included glass-reinforced plastic (GRP, also known as fibre-glass) construction, aluminium spars and hulls, dacron sails, ferro-cement, kevlar, mylar, carbon fibre, aramid fibres, titanium and so on, which provided opportunities for designers and builders to create new vessels that were faster, stronger, more reliable, more sea worthy and far more durable. The technology provided by satellites and computers also revolutionized long-distance cruising (and racing). Satellite-based navigation and communication, the ability to receive up-to-date, localized and accurate weather forecasts while at sea, electronic charts, sonar, and satellite imagery for ice monitoring and modelling have all made polar yacht cruising safer, more comfortable and far easier than it ever has been before.

Demand

The demand for new and exciting experiences has always existed; however, the growth of interest in experiencing high-quality natural environments and iconic wildlife as a mass tourism attraction is more recent (Grenier, 2004). Wildlife and nature-based tourism has become a specialist and rapidly growing sector within tourism globally (Newsome et al, 2005), and the opportunities offered for this kind of experience in polar regions are widely known. Television documentaries and specialist nature-based television channels, popular movies (e.g. *March of the Penguins*), including animated films (e.g. *Happy Feet*), books, websites and specific promotions have all contributed to a rise in awareness of, and interest in, the poles, particularly Antarctica. In addition, the opportunity to visit previously inaccessible areas via cruise ships and commercial tourism operators has contributed to this demand. A visit to Antarctica, previously only available to a few select scientists and experienced adventurers, is now widely available, particularly via dedicated cruise ship voyages (Bauer, 2001). Thus, polar regions have become an accessible destination for a number of travellers who wish to experience the attributes of these locales (Maher, in press a). Cruising yacht tourism is part of this wider demand, where there is increasing recognition that cruising the polar regions is now possible.

A related influence which contributes to demand is the 'prestige value' of having conducted such a trip. For many long-term travellers and off-shore cruisers there is a sense of wanting to have done things that others have not. This creates a sense of 'kudos' or perhaps even superiority over fellow cruisers and travellers who, when comparing experiences, are unable to 'match' the stories from Antarctica and the Arctic. The 'one-upmanship' of travellers and tourists is frequently evident at social gatherings, and when sharing and comparing stories (author's personal observation). The relative rarity of polar cruisers adds prestige value to such experiences (Maher, in press b).

Activities

While scenery and wildlife viewing remain preeminent activities for tourists to polar areas, related activities are also popular. For example, photography and publishing, particularly via the World Wide Web, are increasingly an important activity for polar yacht cruisers. Many establish their own websites and blogs and encourage friends, family and others to follow their expeditions (e.g. see www.taraexpeditions.com). A number of vessels now carry specialist scuba diving capability to allow for underwater viewing and photography, and all vessels carry a tender or tenders which allow crew members to go ashore and to view shore-based attractions, such as penguin and seal rookeries, and to hike and climb to vantage points and lookouts. Shore-based sites of historic significance, such as whaling stations, expedition bases and cemeteries, are also popular stop-off points. In some cases, yacht cruisers seek to contribute to research efforts by reporting sitings of particular species or by contributing fluke identification photographs of whales to research catalogues. For some vessels, hospitality and hosting are important activities and occasions where crew members from other vessels are invited onboard or when guests from elsewhere fly in to join the boat for a period of time.

A number of visitors to polar regions undertake voyages to explore, discover and undertake extreme adventure activities. For example, the expedition yacht *Tara* deliberately spent the northern winter of 2007/2008 trapped in the Arctic ice pack to undertake an Arctic drift across the top of the world reminiscent of the voyage of

Figure 2.2 *Sea kayakers from Adventure Philosophy circumnavigated South Georgia Island in 2007*

Source: Mark Jones

the *Fram* over 100 years ago (see www.taraexpeditions.com). Similarly, three New Zealand sea kayakers mounted an expedition in the Antarctic Peninsula during the southern summer of 2000/2001 (see www.adventurephilosophy.com). These kinds of more extreme small vessel-based expeditions are becoming more prevalent as polar tourism expands (Lamers et al, 2007).

Thus, the use of small vessels (not just yachts) is expanding in polar regions. In a similar pattern to other remote destinations which have experienced growing tourism, Antarctica and the Arctic are being utilized more than ever for tourism. Visitors are going further afield than ever before, undertaking a more diverse range of activities, and their impacts are becoming more widespread.

Important issues regarding impacts

Cruising yachts have the potential to produce similar environmental impacts as cruise ships, albeit on a smaller scale. Almost all cruising yachts are covered below the waterline with an anti-fouling paint. This coating is designed to reduce the attachment of algae and micro-organisms that will eventually establish on the underwater surfaces of any vessel. These organisms will eventually grow to adult stage as barnacles and other crustaceans, and weed and other marine plants, rendering the underside of the vessel a veritable marine food chain. This adds significant drag, resulting in slower speeds and less fuel efficiency, and burrowing organisms can damage vessels' outer surfaces. As a consequence, minimizing the 'fouling' of the bottom of a boat is an important objective. Currently, the most cost-effective way of doing this is by painting the surfaces of a boat that will remain under water with an ablative anti-fouling paint. These paints deliberately contain chemicals that are toxic to marine organisms as a means of discouraging their attachment to the vessel. In addition, the paints are created to slowly leach or ablate into the sea in order to ensure that the outer surface still attached to the hull is clear of fouling organisms. Historically, anti-fouling paints contained significant amounts of toxic biocides such as mercury, lead, arsenic and tin. These highly toxic chemicals were found to have long-term detrimental effects on marine ecosystems due to their tendency to persist in the marine food chain and to bio-accumulate. As a consequence, these additives have been banned from anti-fouling paints in most developed countries – although 'tin-boosters' are widely available in the Caribbean. Most anti-fouling paints now use copper as an active biocide: copper, while toxic to marine organisms, does not tend to persist and bio-accumulate; therefore, it is considered less environmentally damaging. Nevertheless, anti-fouling paints do leach toxic chemicals into the marine environment, and in the relatively pristine ecosystems of the Arctic and Antarctic this issue may become significant.

Conversely, the tendency of organisms to attach to the hull of vessels presents another problem for remote locations. The introduction of alien and invasive species via transport on the bottom of cruising yachts has become a major concern for remote destinations such as New Zealand, so much so, that all cruising yachts arriving in New Zealand are carefully inspected to ensure that they have an adequate coating of anti-fouling paint and are carrying no organisms on the hull. Similar risks exist for Arctic and Antarctic waters where cruising yachts arriving from other destinations could introduce foreign invasive plants and animals into the ecosystem which could have significant long-term detrimental consequences.

While cruising yachts primarily use sail for propulsion when transiting oceans, when in enclosed bays, fjords and harbours, or when conditions are not conducive for sailing, they use engines. The great majority of motors found in cruising yachts (and powerboats) are water-cooled diesel engines. These engines, while petro-chemical-based internal combustion engines, extract sea water from the sea for cooling purposes. The sea water is passed through a heat exchanger and then exhausted together with fuel combustion-derived gases back into the sea. Depending on the efficiency of the engine and the systems used, these exhausted gases and water have varying quantities of diesel residue in them. It is not uncommon to see a slick on the water surface immediately adjacent to a diesel exhaust on a cruising yacht. Furthermore, diesel- and petrol-fuelled engines create noise, and combined with the sound created by propellers turning in the water, vessels do emit noise into the marine environment. Thus, the use of engines on cruising yachts has impacts upon marine ecosystems.

While there is an increasing installation and use of wastewater-holding tanks onboard cruising yachts, they are not universal (thus, wastewater, including sewage, is flushed straight into the sea) and are seldom large enough to store significant quantities of wastewater. As a consequence, cruising yachts must regularly empty their wastewater-holding tanks, including sewage into the sea. While small quantities on an irregular basis are unlikely to have long-term detrimental impacts, the increasing number of cruising vessels visiting remote polar areas may have impacts as a consequence of these discharges.

The disposal of other waste is also an issue. While the great majority of vessels will retain non-biodegradable waste (such as plastic wrapping and tins and cans) onboard for disposal on land at a suitable facility, it is common practice to dispose of biodegradable waste overboard. In polar regions this can be problematic: first, because that waste is seldom material naturally found in those ecosystems; and, second, because the biodegrading of waste is often slower and sometimes incomplete in colder polar regions. Because of the extreme cold and the isolation of the Arctic and particularly the Antarctic, bacterial levels (needed for biodegradation) are low in both abundance and diversity. Thus, disposal of food waste into polar waters can result in unintended consequences.

Other issues well detailed with regard to more general polar tourism activities (see other chapters of this volume), such as wildlife disturbance, removal of material for souvenirs, litter, vegetation trampling and noise pollution, are also relevant for polar yacht cruising.

It would be remiss not to point out that polar yacht cruising, as with other tourism, can also have positive benefits. Remote communities in the Arctic Circle receive important economic stimulus from yacht-based tourists. Similarly, yacht-based tourists provide assistance with search and rescue efforts and are often able to provide assistance with medical advice and supplies (to one another and for remote communities). The passion of cruising yachties for the protection of polar ecosystems areas and their experiences in these remote, mostly pristine, locations shape the attitudes of cruising sailors and is an important political force that can assist with decision-making in terms of the future management of these areas.

Conclusions

The future: Super-yachts, soft adventurers and rallies?

It is highly likely that the increases seen over the past two decades in polar yacht cruising will continue. The profile of these destinations is growing, the demand is strong and the technology is now available that allows for relatively safe, comfortable access to these regions, rendering polar cruising more attractive than ever. In particular, the growth of interest in 'soft adventure' – travel to 'adventurous' locations in comfort and safety – and the significant social and psychological benefits that accrue to polar yacht cruisers exacerbate the rapid growth trend.

The massive increase in the numbers of super-yachts (greater than 30m in length) over the past decade is also resulting in a change in vessel type and activity in polar regions. These luxury vessels often carry with them significant technology and equipment such as helicopters, scuba diving equipment, submarines, personal water craft and elaborate security systems. Historically, these vessels have frequented the Mediterranean and the Caribbean seas; but more and more are venturing further afield, with the polar regions becoming preferred destinations. For example, the 180 foot ketch *The Adèle* voyaged to both the Arctic and Antarctic during 2005 to 2007 (Österlund, 2008).

A popular means of cruising is for private cruise sailors to join cruising 'rallies'. These are organized cruising events where a group of yachts leave from a common area for a common destination or series of destinations. Rallies are valuable for safety, social contact and, in some cases, discounts, and immigration assistance is organized for rally participants. Almost all popular cruise sailing destinations have such events

Figure 2.3 *The super-yacht The Adèle explored both the Arctic and Antarctic in 2006 and 2007*
Source: Jan-Eric Österlund

now. Perhaps it will not be long before the first cruising yacht rally to a polar destination is organized?

Climate change

The impacts of human-induced climate change on the poles are dramatic and this will increasingly be the case in the future. The most significant change for cruising yachts is the 'opening up' of the Northwest Passage between the North Atlantic and the North Pacific (Stonehouse and Snyder, 2007). During the northern summer of 2009, four yachts are reported to have successfully transited the passage and it is highly likely that this route will become regularly navigable and more popular over the next few years. This will present a dramatic change for the Arctic and likely drive a significant increase in visitation of cruising yachts from Europe and North America. Similar opportunities are likely to occur in the Antarctic as the permanent sea ice retreats and areas, particularly in the Antarctic Peninsula, that were previously inaccessible become open for vessels to explore.

Management challenges

The current tools for management which include international agreements, such as the International Convention for the Prevention of Pollution from Ships, the Convention of the Conservation of Antarctic Marine Living Resources, the Antarctic Treaty System and the United Nations Convention on the Law of the Sea, were not created with marine tourism in mind. Thus, they are relatively 'blunt' tools under which polar yacht cruising can be managed.

Similarly, the organizations related to tourism in these areas such as the International Association of Antarctica Tour Operators (IAATO) and the Association of Arctic Expedition Cruise Operators (AECO) are not specifically focused on yacht cruising (especially private yacht cruising). As a consequence, development and growth of yacht-based tourism in polar regions is occurring in the absence of an adequate management regime. The risk of negative consequences is exacerbated by the paucity of information on yacht cruising to these remote areas. It is time for more research attention to be directed at this tourism activity and for the resulting increased understanding to be used to inform management.

References

Bauer, T. G. (2001) *Tourism in the Antarctic: Opportunities, Constraints and Future Prospects,* Haworth Hospitality Press, New York, NY

Glaister, R. and Ivankiv, V. (2005) *Cruising in and Through Russia,* Cruising Association Information Series, Cruising Association, London

Headland, R. K. (1998) *Antarctic Chronology,* unpublished revision of *Chronological List of Antarctic Expeditions and Related Historical Events,* Cambridge University Press, Cambridge, UK

Lamers, M., Stel, J. H. and Amelung, B. (2007) 'Antarctic adventure tourism and private expeditions', in J. M. Snyder and B. Stonehouse (eds) *Prospects for Polar Tourism,* CABI, Wallingford, Oxon, UK

Lewis, D. (2002) *Ice Bird: The Classic Story of the First Single-Handed Voyage to Antarctica*, Sheridan House, New York, NY

Ludmer, L.H. (2001) *Cruising Alaska*, Hunter Publishing, Walpole, MA

Maher, P. T. (in press a) 'Ambassadors for the experience: Perspectives from the Ross Sea region', in P. T. Maher, E. J. Stewart and M. Lück (eds) *Polar Tourism: Human, Environmental and Governance Dimensions*, Cognizant Communications Corp, Elmsford, New York

Maher, P. T. (in press b) '"Awesome size … magnitude of the place … the incredible beauty": Visitors' onsite experiences in the Ross Sea region of Antarctica', in C. M. Hall and J. Saarinen (eds) *Tourism and Change in the Polar Regions: Climate, Environments and Experiences*, Routledge, Oxford

Newsome, D., Dowling, R. and Moore, S. (2005) *Wildlife Tourism*, Channel View, Clevedon Hall, UK

Orams, M. B. (1999) *Marine Tourism: Development, Impacts and Management*, Routledge, London

Österlund, J. E. (2008) *Exploring with Adele*, Duncan Baird Publishers, UK

Poncet, S. and Poncet, J. (2007) *Southern Ocean Cruising*, Environmental Research and Assessment, Cambridge, UK

Rolfo, M. and Ardrizzi, G. (2006) *Patagonia and Tierra del Fuego Nautical Guide*, Editrice Incontri Nautici, Italy

Saunders, R. and Saunders, K. (2005) *Cruising in Finland*, Cruising Association Information Series, Cruising Association, London

Saunders, R., Saunders, K., Firth, T., Thorne, D, Thorne, P., Cattell, F. and Cattell, G. (2005) *Cruising in Sweden*, Cruising Association Information Series, Cruising Association, London

Stonehouse, B. and Snyder, J. M. (2007) 'Polar tourism in changing environments', in J. M. Snyder and B. Stonehouse (eds) *Prospects for Polar Tourism*, CABI, Wallingford, UK

Terdal, L. G. (2000) *Small-Boat Cruising to Alaska*, Hara Publishing Group, Bothell, WA

3

Cruising to the North Pole aboard a Nuclear Icebreaker

Robert K. Headland

Introduction

Russia, and previously the Soviet Union, has by far the largest and most efficient icebreaker fleets. Indeed, Russians are also the oldest and most experienced icebreaker operators. The reason for this is purely geographical because Russia has 164° of longitude facing the Arctic Ocean, and the Northeast Passage has become a major commercial waterway (in contrast to the Northwest Passage, where only two commercial cargoes have ever made a transit). Political and military considerations have also applied, which were, for a long period, why nearly all the Soviet Arctic was effectively a closed territory (until 1991 only three foreign ships had made a transit, and very few others had entered its waters). There have been many rapid changes in Russia from 1990: the consequences of several made tourist voyages to the North Pole a practical proposition. There are many aspects of these voyages that, with one exception, were aboard atomic-powered icebreakers (the Russian term is *atomic ledokol* – 'icebreaker' – rather than a nuclear one). These are described by a series of separate themes. The author has accompanied 18 North Pole voyages to 2008, lecturing on historical geography, thus most of this chapter reports direct personal experience. The role of Russian icebreakers in polar tourism, more generally, is discussed by Splettstoesser and Headland (2009).

Logistics

Even during the height of summer, the Arctic Ocean has never been less than half covered by pack ice well over 1m thick. Much of it is the multiyear, or palæocrystic, ice, which is hard and consolidated, thus presenting particularly difficult problems for navigation. The determinants for passage through the pack ice are: area covered (measured in tenths), thickness (metres), form (first year to multiyear), surface (wet snow vastly increases friction), and pressure (ridges especially). All may be adverse on the central Arctic Ocean; thus, only the most powerful classes of icebreakers have been able to penetrate these regions, and those that do it most effectively are powered by nuclear reactors. By 2008, 77 surface vessels had reached the North Pole, of which 62 were atomic powered. Of the 15 others, with two exceptions, they either travelled in pairs or went with an atomic escort. The exceptions, both by the Swedish icebreaker *Oden*, took advantage of times when conditions were known to be comparatively favourable.

Of all voyages to the North Pole 58, or 75 per cent, have carried tourist passengers. Table 3.1 lists the Russian atomic icebreaker fleet, three of which have been adapted to accommodate passengers on North Pole voyages (*Sovetskiy Soyuz, Yamal* and *50 Let Pobedy*). Table 3.2 lists all surface voyages to the North Pole and indicates which were tourist based. Table 3.3 gives an approximate analysis of the number of people who have stood on the ice of the North Pole, from which it is seen that 44 per cent of the tourists arrived aboard icebreakers, and about 66 per cent in other capacities.

Table 3.1 *Nuclear icebreakers*

Name	Launched	Engine power	Class
Ленин (*Lenin*)	1959	32.4MW	Lenin (out of service)
Арктика (*Arktika*)	1975	55.3MW	Arktika I
Сибирь (*Sibir'*)	1977	55.3MW	Arktika I (out of service)
Россия (*Rossiya*)	1985	55.3MW	Arktika II (Rossiya)
Таймы (*Taymyr*)	1989	32.4MW	Taymyr
Вайгач (*Vaygach*)	1990	32.4MW	Taymyr
Советский Союз (*Sovetskiy Soyuz*)*	1990	55.3MW	Arktika II (Rossiya)
Ямал (*Yamal*)*	1992	55.3MW	Arktika II (Rossiya)
Пятдесять Лет Победы* (*50 Let Pobedy*)	1993 (entered service 2007)	55.3MW	Arktika III (Ural)

Note: * Indicates that the icebreaker has been adapted to take passengers to the North Pole.

Source: Robert K. Headland, compiled 1 January 2009

A few explorers and scientists, many naval men, a range of tourists and adventurers, and various others have reached the ice surface at the North Pole (90°N). Some of these attainments have received much publicity, while others have been accomplished discreetly. Table 3.3 provides an analysis of the ways in which the pole has been reached, with an estimate of the total number of people involved. As well as those who have landed, people in submarines or aboard balloons and other aircraft have reached the position of 90°N but have not stood on the ice. This data varies in precision, depending on variable sources, but comprises generally recent and reliable estimates.

Table 3.2 *Ships that have reached the North Pole*

	Name (14)	Captain (24)	Date	Flag (6)	Fuel
1	Arktika[1]	Yuriy Kuchiyev	17 August 1977	Soviet Union[1]	Uranium
2	Sibir'	Zigfrid Vibakh	25 May 1987	Soviet Union[2]	Uranium
3*	Rossiya[1]	Anatoly Lamehov	8 August 1990	Soviet Union[3]	Uranium
4*	Sovetskiy Soyuz[1]	Anatoly Gorshkovskiy[1]	4 August 1991	Soviet Union[4]	Uranium
5	Oden[1]	Anders Backman[1]	7 September 1991	Sweden[1]	Oil
6	Polarstern[1]	Ernst-Peter Greve	7 September 1991	Germany[1]	Oil
7*	Sovetskiy Soyuz[2]	Anatoly Gorshkovskiy[2]	13 July 1992	Russia[5]	Uranium
8*	Sovetskiy Soyuz[3]	Anatoly Gorshkovskiy[3]	23 August 1992	Russia[6]	Uranium
9*	Yamal[1]	Andrey Smirnov[1]	21 July 1993	Russia[7]	Uranium
10*	Yamal[2]	Andrey Smirnov[2]	8 August 1993	Russia[8]	Uranium
11*	Yamal[3]	Andrey Smirnov[3]	30 August 1993	Russia[9]	Uranium
12*	Yamal[4]	Andrey Smirnov[4]	21 July 1994	Russia[10]	Uranium
13*	Kapitan Dranitsyn	Viktor Terekhov	21 July 1994	Russia[11]	Oil
14*	Yamal[5]	Andrey Smirnov[5]	5 August 1994	Russia[12]	Uranium
15*	Yamal[6]	Andrey Smirnov[6]	21 August 1994	Russia[13]	Uranium
16	Louis S. St Laurent	Philip Grandy	22 August 1994	Canada	Oil
17	Polar Sea	Lawson Brigham	22 August 1994	US[1]	Oil
18*	Yamal[7]	Andrey Smirnov[7]	12 July 1995	Russia[14]	Uranium
19*	Yamal[8]	Andrey Smirnov[8]	28 July 1995	Russia[15]	Uranium
20*	Yamal[9]	Andrey Smirnov[9]	12 July 1996	Russia[16]	Uranium
21*	Yamal[10]	Andrey Smirnov[10]	27 July 1996	Russia[17]	Uranium
22*	Yamal[11]	Andrey Smirnov[11]	14 August 1996	Russia[18]	Uranium
23	Oden[2]	Anders Backman[2]	10 September 1996	Sweden[2]	Oil
24*	Sovetskiy Soyuz[4]	Stanislav Shmidt[1]	12 July 1997	Russia[19]	Uranium
25*	Sovetskiy Soyuz[5]	Stanislav Shmidt[2]	25 July 1997	Russia[20]	Uranium
26*	Sovetskiy Soyuz[6]	Yevgeniy Bannikov[1]	10 July 1998	Russia[21]	Uranium
27*	Sovetskiy Soyuz[7]	Yevgeniy Bannikov[2]	23 July 1998	Russia[22]	Uranium
28*	Yamal[12]	Stanislav Rumantsev[1]	25 July 1999	Russia[23]	Uranium
29*	Yamal[13]	Aleksandr Lembrik[1]	29 July 2000	Russia[24]	Uranium
30*	Yamal[14]	Aleksandr Lembrik[2]	11 August 2000	Russia[25]	Uranium
31*	Yamal[15]	Aleksandr Lembrik[3]	12 July 2001	Russia[26]	Uranium
32*	Yamal[16]	Aleksandr Lembrik[4]	24 July 2001	Russia[27]	Uranium
33	Oden[3]	Mats Johansen	31 July 2001	Sweden[3]	Oil
34*	Yamal[17]	Aleksandr Lembrik[5]	5 August 2001	Russia[28]	Uranium

Name	Captain	Date	Flag	Fuel
35* Yamal[18]	Aleksandr Lembrik[6]	23 August 2001	Russia[29]	Uranium
36 Healy[1]	David Vizneski	6 September 2001	US[2]	Oil
37 Polarstern[2]	Jurgen Keil	6 September 2001	Germany[2]	Oil
38* Yamal[19]	Aleksandr Lembrik[7]	11 July **2002**	Russia[30]	Uranium
39* Yamal[20]	Aleksandr Lembrik[8]	24 July 2002	Russia[31]	Uranium
40* Yamal[21]	Aleksandr Lembrik[9]	12 August 2002	Russia[32]	Uranium
41* Yamal[22]	Aleksandr Lembrik[10]	25 August 2002	Russia[33]	Uranium
42* Yamal[23]	Stanislav Rumantsev[2]	25 July **2003**	Russia[34]	Uranium
43* Yamal[24]	Stanislav Rumantsev[3]	10 August 2003	Russia[35]	Uranium
44* Yamal[25]	Stanislav Rumantsev[4]	24 August 2003	Russia[36]	Uranium
45* Yamal[26]	Aleksandr Lembrik[11]	8 July **2004**	Russia[37]	Uranium
46* Yamal[27]	Aleksandr Lembrik[12]	21 July 2004	Russia[38]	Uranium
47* Yamal[28]	Aleksandr Lembrik[13]	7 August 2004	Russia[39]	Uranium
48* Yamal[29]	Aleksandr Lembrik[14]	28 August 2004	Russia[40]	Uranium
49 Sovetskiy Soyuz[8]	Stanislav Shmidt[3]	7 September 2004	Russia[41]	Uranium
50 Oden[4]	Tomas Årnellon[1]	7 September 2004	Sweden[4]	Oil
51 Vidar Viking	Jörgen Haave	7 September 2004	Norway	Oil
52* Yamal[30]	Aleksandr Lembrik[15]	11 September 2004	Russia[42]	Uranium
53* Yamal[31]	Stanislav Rumantsev[5]	7 July **2005**	Russia[43]	Uranium
54* Yamal[32]	Stanislav Rumantsev[6]	20 July 2005	Russia[44]	Uranium
55* Yamal[33]	Stanislav Rumantsev[7]	7 August 2005	Russia[45]	Uranium
56* Yamal[34]	Stanislav Rumantsev[8]	19 August 2005	Russia[46]	Uranium
57 Akademik Fedorov[1]	Mikhail Kaloshin[1]	29 August 2005	Russia[47]	Oil
58 Arktika[2]	Dmitry Lobusov	1 September 2005	Russia[48]	Uranium
59* Yamal[35]	Stanislav Rumantsev[9]	1 September 2005	Russia[49]	Uranium
60 Healy[2]	Daniel Oliver	12 September 2005	US[3]	Oil
61 Oden[5]	Tomas Årnellon[2]	12 September 2005	Sweden[5]	Oil
62* Yamal[36]	Aleksandr Lembrik[16]	8 July **2006**	Russia[50]	Uranium
63* Yamal[37]	Aleksandr Lembrik[17]	19 July 2006	Russia[51]	Uranium
64* Yamal[38]	Aleksandr Lembrik[18]	7 August 2006	Russia[52]	Uranium
65* Yamal[39]	Aleksandr Lembrik[19]	18 August 2006	Russia[53]	Uranium
66* Yamal[40]	Stanislav Rumantsev[10]	2 July **2007**	Russia[54]	Uranium
67* Yamal[41]	Stanislav Rumantsev[11]	14 July 2007	Russia[55]	Uranium
68* Yamal[42]	Stanislav Rumantsev[12]	27 July 2007	Russia[56]	Uranium
69 Rossiya[2]	Aleksandr Spirin	1 August 2007	Russia[57]	Uranium
70 Akademik Fedorov[2]	Mikhail Kaloshin[2]	1 August 2007	Russia[58]	Oil[15]
71* Yamal[43]	Stanislav Rumantsev[13]	11 August 2007	Russia[59]	Uranium
72* Yamal[44]	Stanislav Rumantsev[14]	23 August 2007	Russia[60]	Uranium
73* 50 Let Pobedy[1]	Valentin Davydyants[1]	29 June **2008**	Russia[61]	Uranium
74* 50 Let Pobedy[2]	Valentin Davydyants[2]	12 July 2008	Russia[62]	Uranium

	Name	Captain	Date	Flag	Fuel
75*	50 Let Pobedy[3]	Valentin Davydyants[3]	25 July 2008	Russia[63]	Uranium
76*	Yamal[45]	Aleksandr Lembrik[20]	28 July 2008	Russia[64]	Uranium
77*	Yamal[46]	Aleksandr Lembrik[21]	8 August 2008	Russia[65]	Uranium[62]

Note: Dates given are those kept aboard the ship; Russian ships are on Moscow time and others are on Greenwich mean time. * Indicates a tourist voyage. Superscript numbers are cumulative numbers of voyages, commands, flags, etc.

Source: Robert K. Headland, compiled 1 January 2009

Table 3.3 *Estimate of the number of people who have stood on the ice at the North Pole*

Arrived by surface vessel (first in 1977, *Arktika*):
64 Soviet Union or Russian voyages aboard icebreakers and 1 other vessel (1977 to 2008)

Officers and crew (120), 61 voyages of 6 atomic vessels, 75% repeating	2370
Officers and crew (90), 3 voyages of 2 diesel vessels, 1 with 75% repeating	153
Passengers carried by 58 of these voyages, average 90	5220
Passenger staff (16) from 2 companies aboard these vessels, 40% repeating	570

12 other icebreakers (Canada: 1; Germany: 2; Norway: 1; Sweden: 5; US: 3),

8 with average complement of 50 (4 with 50% repeating)	275
4 with average complement of 130 (50% repeating on one ship)	390
Subtotal	8978

Arrived by submarine (first in 1959, USS *Skate*):
Average complement 100, repeats 20%

49 United States boats	3940
20 Soviet Union or Russian boats	1620
12 British boats	980
Subtotal	6540

Arrived by fixed wing aircraft (first in 1948, Aleksandr Kuznetsov):
From Canada (usually Twin Otters with 8 passengers and 2 crew who repeat 80%)

10 flights a year, 1988–2008	1764
6 flights a year, 1983–1987	242

From Russia (usually an Antonov 2 with 2 crew and 6 passengers)

First landing at the North Pole	23
Flights from 1948 to 2008	576
From Alaska (1952)	4
Subtotal	2609

Arrived by helicopter (first in 1952, Joseph Fletcher):
50 flights from Severnaya Zemlya or 'Borneo', 1995, 1996, 1999–2008

3 crew who repeat 80%	75
8 passengers	400
1 flight from Canada	4
1 flight from ice station T-3	4
Subtotal	483

Arrived by surface traverse: (first in 1968, Ralph Plaisted):	
Complete traverses (from a coast to the North Pole and return to a coast)	34
Incomplete traverses (aircraft or other transport to or from the North Pole)	
One way (coast to pole only)	132
Partial (short distances to the pole, 'the last degree', etc.), 1995, 1996, 1999–2008	1220
Subtotal	1386
Arrived aboard a drift station (on СП-15 in 1967 and СП-21 in 1972):	
Subtotal	36
Arrived by parachute (first in 1949, Vitaliy Volovich; annual events from 1997):	
Subtotal	430
Grand total	**20,462**

Source: Robert K. Headland, calculated 1 January 2009

Navigation to the North Pole is practicable between late July and early September, the period when an icebreaker could be spared from normal service. Conveniently, this is the period of constant daylight. In the spring and autumn most icebreakers are in service to open the Northeast Passage (the Northern Sea Route) early in the year, keeping it open as late as practicable. In summer some are stationed at the few choke points to assist cargo ships, if needed, and any can be available at any time for emergencies, such as during the disastrous 1983 season when masses of palæocrystic ice trapped many ships along the east Siberian coast (Armstrong, 1984). During the Arctic winter, ocean navigation is exceptional and is for emergencies only. In theory, an atomic icebreaker could reach almost anywhere at any season – but the effort has not been worth the cost in winter.

As well as the emphasis on the North Pole, tourist voyages usually visit some of the Russian Arctic archipelagos during the southbound or return journey. This is for two reasons: the fascination of these previously prohibited regions in their own right is strong, and it is desirable to provide a 'buffer' as timings can never be certain when navigation through ice is involved (especially the first voyage of a summer). Zemlya Frantsa-Iosifa (Franz Josef Land) is the principal destination, and about three days are usually spent there if conditions are favourable.

The icebreakers

Three atomic icebreakers, *Sovetskiy Soyuz*, *Yamal* and *50 Let Pobedy*, have made most North Pole tourist voyages and two others, atomic-powered *Rossiya* and conventional *Kapitan Dranitsyn*, have each made one. The first three vessels, all Arktika class, are the world's most powerful icebreakers, which develop 75,000 shaft horsepower (55.3MW) and have broken pack ice up to 6m thick. The ships are working icebreakers, which when not carrying passengers are used to keep the Northeast Passage open. One consequence of this is that accommodation, although quite adequate, is not luxurious; a compensating advantage is that they are exceptionally interesting ships. The uranium fuel lasts for about four years and refuelling takes several months as it is combined with maintenance operations while the reactors are out of commission; thus, different icebreakers have been used sequentially. All but the newest, *50 Let Pobedy* (in service from 2007; see Figure 3.1), have the classic icebreaker hulls with an ice-knife in a forward position. The latest design has an experimental spoon-shaped bow, which, although effective in ice, is less efficient in open water as it develops a large bow wave.

In 1991 the latest atomic icebreaker, *Sovetskiy Soyuz* (launched in 1990), was adapted for a tourist North Pole voyage. Subsequently, similar modifications were made aboard more recent icebreakers. These involved doubling accommodation in many cabins with improved berths and other facilities, enhancing the dining saloon, library and lounge areas, provision of a bar, and many similar modifications to adapt the vessel for passengers. More improvements, notably in communications, were introduced over subsequent years. The icebreakers, even before conversions, are generally more comfortable than most Russian ships because their crews tend to serve for longer periods at sea than any other modern services.

Figure 3.1 50 Let Pobedy *in open water of the Barents Sea, returning to Murmansk from her first season of passenger voyages to the North Pole, August 2007*

Source: Robert K. Headland

There was a problem in accommodating approximately 100 passengers, as well as the tour operators' staff with lecturers, logistic assistants, cooks and others involved (another 20 people). The Russian crew were increased with stewards and catering staff, but were also reduced as the division which attended to towing and convoy operations was not aboard. Most cabins, for all ranks, were normally single. Crew moved to occupy cabins as doubles or, for some, triples. Most officers moved down into petty-officers' cabins and this process made not only about 40 standard cabins available, but also provided for a few larger ones, including several senior officers' cabins, described as state rooms, to accommodate passengers. The icebreakers became crowded – but it was to be for only a little more than a month.

There is always a potential incompatibility between icebreaker operations and tourist voyages. Difficulties are rare; but icebreaking work is not accustomed to close constraints of time and is ready to wait in adverse conditions for these to change and to eventually become propitious. In contrast, tourist voyages, especially when sequential, are tightly constrained by time; outgoing and incoming passengers have complex itineraries involving flights that are rarely flexible and that involve expense. If time is becoming scarce the icebreaker will need to be worked much harder than in normal operations, and occasional damage to propeller blades occurs. In open water an icebreaker is not a comfortable vessel in rough conditions. In ice, the sensation of movement is distinct and there is much persistent vibration. When the ice-knife does its work, a powerful jolt is felt throughout the forward parts of the vessel (where the dining saloon, bar and lecture theatre are situated). This is especially so when backing and ramming manoeuvres are necessary to break floes and ridges in severe ice. The air curtain, supplied by centrifugal compressors near the lecture theatre, blasts air through ice-rubble when operating so that faster progress, but accompanied by a loud persistent roar, results.

All Russian atomic icebreakers are owned by the government and were leased to the Murmansk Shipping Company. In 2009 this changed for economic reasons and a separate company, Rosatom, was established to operate them. During the same year construction of a new class of atomic icebreaker, to be launched in 2012, was announced.

Inception

Russian circumstances began to change rapidly during the late 1980s as *perestroika* and *glasnost* developed, which was at a time when the stability of the rouble became dubious and, conversely, Russian need for convertible currency increased. These circumstances were taken advantage of by two entrepreneurs, Lars Wikander from Sweden and Mike McDowell from Australia, who negotiated an unprecedented contract with the Murmansk Shipping Company. In the west of Arctic Russia this company operates the atomic icebreaker fleet, as well as several conventional icebreakers (the Far East Shipping Company, in Vladivostok, was the eastern equivalent, but had conventional icebreakers only). Thus, in 1990, an experimental passenger voyage to the North Pole was made with 50 selected and invited guests aboard the atomic icebreaker *Rossiya* to see how such an enterprise might operate. This was only the third voyage to the North Pole, which was reached on 8 August 1990 (*Arktika*, on 17 August 1977, was the first and *Sibir*, on 25 May 1987, the second) (Brigham, 1999). The experiment was successful and the company, Quark Expeditions, arranged a major tourist voyage from Murmansk to the North Pole, continuing across the Arctic Ocean to reach the Pacific Ocean during the summer of 1991.

The first full-scale voyage

The first full-scale passenger voyage was advertised at the high end of tourism for it was to be unique: the first Atlantic to Pacific crossing over the North Pole by any surface vessel. The contrast in wealth between the passengers and the ship's complement was very noticeable (high capitalism versus communism in its decline). Nevertheless, both sides were very interested in the voyage and a surprising degree of camaraderie developed – especially as the competency of the icebreaker operations became apparent. The voyage began in Murmansk, as did the majority of the subsequent ones, and finished in Provideniya, the eastern port of the Northern Sea Route in the Pacific Ocean.

The northbound voyage

There are (as a result of logistics, ice conditions and other reasons) significant differences between all the North Pole voyages. Most begin from Murmansk; but Longyearbyen in Svalbard has also been used to embark passengers. Russian administrative procedures, for passengers and cargo, have always been complicated and, at times, obstructive. It was for this reason that, for several years, embarking passengers and loading supplies were conducted at Longyearbyen, which is logistically more difficult but, because of simple procedures and the absence of corruption, had advantages. There are normally several hours available in the departure ports and both Murmansk and Longyearbyen have much of interest. This time also enables luggage to precede passengers and to be stowed in cabins. The Murmansk Shipping Company's icebreaking museum is particularly good and *Lenin*, the first atomic icebreaker, is being converted into a museum and hotel in the Murmansk docks.

Boarding in Murmansk is at Atomflot, about 4km north of the city centre. This port is a restricted area where security requirements, especially prohibition of photography, are enforced. Upon boarding the icebreaker, the traditional Russian welcome with bread and salt is presented as passengers are directed to their cabins. In Longyearbyen, a series of long helicopter flights was necessary, which takes several hours to board passengers and luggage, as the Norwegian authorities do not permit Russian atomic-powered vessels in their territorial waters.

In Atomflot, other atomic icebreakers are docked, often including *Arktika*, the first surface ship to have reached the North Pole. These are seen early during about the two hours needed to reach the mouth of the Kola Fjord, and subsequently there are views of the Russian surface and submarine fleets. The voyage begins near high tide (the fjord has depth limits and the icebreaker draws 11.5m), and after entering the Barents Sea the icebreakers make about 18 knots (33 kilometres per hour).

The North Pole

To stand at the North Pole, at the Earth's axis of rotation, is a very strong attraction for passengers; but the concept is not entirely simple. Sir Wally Herbert, writing after reaching the position on 5 April 1969, observed: 'Trying to set foot upon it is like trying to step on the shadow of a bird that was circling overhead. The surface across which we were moving was itself moving on a planet that was spinning around an axis' (Herbert, 1969, p174). The circumstances are that the icebreaker approaches through variable ice conditions, the most difficult having taken hours of patient navigation and manoeuvring. A helicopter is often dispatched to indicate the position as the last few kilometres are broken through successive pressure ridges.

Historical attainment of the North Pole is contentious – a matter of much interest to passengers. Despite assertions in 1908 (Frederick Cook) and 1909 (Robert Peary), it was first definitely seen in 1926 from an airship; but it was not until 1977 that a ship broke through to it on the surface. Flights (first in 1948), submarines (first in 1958 submerged, and in 1959 surfaced), and surface traverses (first in 1968) have reached it. Although remote, the North Pole is not without other visitors; on several occasions surfaced submarines, all from the US, have been seen there by tourists. Communications, however, have consisted only of very terse radio signals. Tourist voyages have rescued adventurers and assisted aviators in the central Arctic. Where this does not involve a lot of lost time, it is a fascinating operation, particularly for the passengers.

In all voyages, during easy and difficult approaches, announcements of progress are made and when the North Pole is close, passengers gather on the bridge or bow to wait for the moment of attainment when the engines stop and powerful foghorns are sounded. The precision of modern global positioning systems is such that the main system on the bridge is used exclusively. Many passengers carry handheld instruments, which rarely read 90°N as their position aboard and their accuracy do not coincide with the main system.

After celebrations aboard, a search is made to find a safe location for landing on the ice as close as practicable to the North Pole. Usually this is easy and might occur where the icebreaker has halted. Normally some time is needed to find and dock the vessel in a floe large and strong enough for a party. A gangway is then lowered, trestle tables and benches with a barbecue and bar are deployed on the ice, and all aboard are invited 'ashore'. The crew set up a pole flying flags of all countries represented aboard (which may be difficult as some passengers come from unexpected places, such as Saudi Arabia, Papua New Guinea or Guatemala). Activities then include commemorative speeches (sometimes remembering those who strove to reach this position and who did not return), descriptions of the region's geographical significance, icebreaking data and logistics, and a general appreciation of the environment and other circumstances. Food and refreshments flow freely and as the party goes on, increasing numbers of the officers and crew join in (indeed, by the time of departure these form the majority 'ashore'). A 'polar plunge' is usually arranged with the crew, providing steps and a safety harness, with the medical officer in attendance (the ocean is 4197m deep and the water temperature about −1.8°C at the pole). The pack ice is constantly drifting and has been measured at as much as 22km a day. On one occasion, after a few hours, this caused the icebreaker to move across the geographical position of the North Pole as it continued through the vessel and across the barbecue area at a speed which could easily be walked by a person holding a global positioning instrument (claimed as 'a second visit to the North Pole, at no extra charge').

The return voyage from the North Pole, unless a crossing of the Arctic Ocean is intended, starts by following the channel used on arrival. This appears to be different on the chart owing to displacement by the constant drift of the ice. Usually it is easy to let the icebreaker follow the 'tram lines', with minimal navigation for as much as a day, before the channel becomes obliterated. Should the ice be under severe pressure, this, of course, happens much earlier and difficult icebreaking resumes.

Ice and weather conditions

For logistical reasons tourist voyages are made only during the summer. In 2005, under separate charters by two companies, *Yamal* made five tourist voyages to the North Pole, taking an average of about two weeks each, the largest annual number of tourist voyages. This was during an easy ice year, but was, nevertheless, an onerous duty for the ship. As well as a progressive reduction in ice cover and thickness of the central Arctic pack ice during many decades, there is a tendency for it to become more variable (Stroeve, 2008). Thus, some voyages have been slowed by thick multiyear ice with numerous pressure ridges. Conversely, large extents of open water have been found near the North Pole (often giving rise to exaggerated ideas of global warming). The opportunity of measuring ice and conducting other research is taken by the Arctic and Antarctic Research Institute in Saint Petersburg that usually has an observer aboard. Similarly, other organizations have been able to take advantage of the possibilities for ice research in remote areas (Toomey, 2001).

The ice conditions in early July 2003 for the earliest voyage towards the North Pole were exceptionally severe: ice thickness exceeded 3m with much pressure and ridging as far south as 84°N. Despite both reactors operating at full power, and much backing and ramming, *Yamal* had averaged only 2.7 knots (5 kilometres per hour) in thick pressure ice. Scout flights indicated that these conditions persisted as far north as could be examined. To reach the North Pole in the time available would not have been possible; thus, after a full explanation to the passengers, the attempt was abandoned at 86°05' N. The icebreaker turned with some difficulty and went south, keeping to the northbound track as far as practicable. This also was difficult because the pressure had closed the channel relatively quickly. This is the only failed voyage; but others have demonstrated the importance of having a 'buffer' of time to be spent at the islands if not used later on the voyage to the pole.

Weather may be severe in the central Arctic. Among the main problems are fog and mist, which, although thick, rarely extend vertically (indeed, sometimes it is bright and sunny on the topmost deck, while elsewhere there is fog). Snow and strong winds may occur at any time and rapid changes are not uncommon. Thus, passengers are issued with parkas and advised before departure of the other appropriate clothing necessary. Amazing phenomena may be seen in the frigid atmosphere, such as diamond dust, fog bows, solar haloes or corona, parhelia, mirages, *fata morgana*, whiteout, ice blink and water sky. Pack ice vastly attenuates any wave action of the sea; thus, after the icebreaker reaches its element, seasickness becomes a minor problem (indeed, the motion of the vessel feels more like moving on a fast train along a badly ballasted railway). Conversely, on the way to and from the ice, an icebreaker may be very uncomfortable on a rough sea; icebreakers have no external stabilizers as these would slow the vessel in ice until they became avulsed. The specialized hull shape, especially the absence of a protruding keel, is such that rolls have exceeded 40° on exceptional occasions.

Environmental considerations

Environmental considerations of using the atomic icebreakers have been contentious. A strong lobby against anything involving radioactivity has been critical of their use for tourism or any for other purpose. Doubt about their use caused a North Pole voyage organized by Friends of the American Museum of Natural History to charter *Kapitan Dranitsyn*, a diesel-electric vessel, to take them to the pole in 1994. Although escorted by *Yamal*, this was dubiously successful because ice conditions were severe during that summer. The conventionally powered icebreaker had much difficulty following the channel broken by the atomic-powered one. A cloud of thick black smoke from heavy oil was emitted by *Kapitan Dranitsyn* all the way through the ice as her six engines worked at full power for long periods. The atomic-powered vessel had no emissions, while the reek of sulphur and soot permeated the conventional one, which followed behind. It has also been noted that no carbon dioxide is emitted from atomic reactors and associated propulsion systems. The reprocessing of fuel rods, after about four years of service when the radioactive isotopes are depleted, is undertaken by a specialized facility that deals with similar products from power stations, submarines and other reactors (Nilsen and Bøhmer, 1994).

The Association of Arctic Expedition Cruise Operators (AECO) was founded in 2003 and has developed a series of guidelines for sustainable Arctic tourism that are applied during the voyages. Similarly, various national and local regulations are followed, which, in some places, may require a local inspector to be present. Obtaining the necessary permits from Russian authorities is a complex matter, largely because the rate of change is great – new reserves for conservation and other purposes are being established at a surprising pace. Occasionally an area may be closed for military operations at short notice. A large proportion of passengers have had previous experience in polar regions and, for instance, are already familiar with the conservation, safety and other requirements of similar groups, particularly those of the International Association of Antarctica Tour Operators (IAATO), founded in

1991. To a large extent, after explanations are given, the passengers are self-policing, with only a small degree of control needing to be exercised by staff and Russian authorities.

Wildlife records and observations

Observations on wildlife, particularly birds, provide additional information that, in some cases, might be attributed to sea ice presence or thinning, such as sightings of seabirds at the geographic North Pole (Todd et al, 1992), nesting reports on remote islands (Vuilleumier, 1995), and sightings of a polar bear (*Ursus maritimus*) only 13 nautical miles (24km) from the pole (van Meurs and Splettstoesser, 2003). Later, on 11 August 2007, a polar bear approached the ship during a barbecue at the North Pole, presumably being attracted by the smell of cooking meat. Its approach was sighted by the watch from a distance, allowing for a timely tactical withdrawal aboard (Sísteních, 2007). Paw prints of bears, often accompanied by those of the Arctic fox (*Alopex lagropus*), have also been seen on drifting ice near the pole. On several occasions bearded seals (*Phoca hispida*) have surfaced in open water or through brash ice astern of the icebreaker (this open area was also used by people indulging in the 'polar plunge'). Species of Arctic cod (*Boreogadus saida*) are commonly reported throughout ice-covered waters and seen when a floe is overturned as they wriggle to get back below the surface.

Polar bears are a major sight for passengers and a bear watch is maintained, especially when near Zemlya Frantsa-Iosifa, a major denning area. Mothers with twin cubs are seen almost as often as solitary bears. Occasionally they have the remains of a recent seal kill and on rare occasions a kill has been witnessed. Bears present no problems when seen from the decks of the icebreaker and many come close, presumably attracted by smell as well as innate curiosity. Some adult bears are cautious, especially where cubs are present (although the cubs rarely show fear); in these instances, approach by the icebreaker is slow and careful, and the voyage is resumed after a brief halt to limit any adverse effects to the animals.

When passengers are off the ship a careful lookout is maintained: even in the best circumstances, a polar bear could approach, camouflaged, over snow and not be detected until inconveniently close. Russian hunters, who know the behaviour of bears and carry appropriate weapons, are aboard as a precaution. This is particularly significant during landings on the islands. In suitable flying conditions helicopters are also useful as bear deterrents.

Passengers

Most passengers have adequate time and money for such voyages and thus may not be young. The companies arranging voyages provide information about the physical attributes necessary (such as the ability to use steep gangways and stairs, noting the absence of lifts between the many decks). A medical questionnaire is included with the booking forms and information. The range of nationalities is extensive and includes many people who have travelled previously in other Arctic and Antarctic regions. Most have English as a first language, followed by German and French. Groups from Japan and China are usually accompanied by a specialized translator. Incidentally, translators for communicating with the officers and crew are also aboard (although the fluency in English of many Russian staff has increased enormously during successive voyages).

At the North Pole, records are kept of the youngest, oldest, first from a particular country, first to bicycle or hit a golf ball (not to play golf!), and other similar facts. Marriages are occasionally solemnized. A few of these events are of sufficient significance to appear in the *Guinness Book of Records*; most are not.

Lectures and other activities

The days to and from the North Pole may include at least a week of breaking ice. While this is a fascinating procedure, it may become repetitive, and even monotonous, for a proportion of passengers. Thus, a programme of other activities is organized, as is usual aboard many tourist vessels in polar regions. Lecturers usually cover the subjects of ornithology, marine mammals, geology, glaciology, history and geography. In addition, a lecture on icebreaking is very relevant after a period in severe ice. A review of the day's activities is often done as a 'recap' before dining. The opportunity of giving passengers introductions to the vessel and the expedition staff, lifeboat drill, and similar requirements is taken before the pack ice is encountered. From then on some activities may become problematic: the passage is not rough, but lurches and other sudden movements may be frequent in difficult ice.

Ice conditions and weather are always variable; thus, a *carpe diem* philosophy applies during the period in ice. There are, of course, limited opportunities for some activities, as reaching the pole takes precedence. The operation of the icebreaker passing through the pack ice, often upending pieces of floes many cubic metres in volume, is best seen from helicopters; thus, when a bright sunny period occurs and progress is good, groups of passengers can enjoy 'flight-seeing' for a period of about 15 minutes. With two aircraft each carrying only six passengers so that all individuals may benefit from a window view, the flights take several hours in total; but this does not slow the voyage down. About halfway through the pack ice towards the pole, if good strong, wide floes are found and time is available, the icebreaker halts in an 'ice-dock', a gangway is lowered and passengers go onto the ice. This enables the specialized hull and other attributes to be seen and provides an example of the thickness of the ice where floes are tipped against the hull.

The Russian complement is well aware of many ancient and modern maritime customs; thus, a Neptune party is arranged. Although usually associated with the Equator, there is also a tradition for this going back to the period of the Arctic whalers and sealers during the 1700s. It also provides another excellent opportunity for crew and passengers to mix. Lectures on icebreaker operations form a prelude to tours of the engine rooms, although insurance and safety considerations have increasingly limited these excursions. A view of the reactors is possible through thick high-density glass-viewing ports – again an interesting diversion during several days at sea.

Recreational facilities used by the complement are generally available to passengers. Thus, the latter may enjoy a swimming pool (about 4m by 9m), a sauna, a gymnasium with many facilities, table tennis, and even a chess room for those who might be equal to the crew. A library is usually in what was the *priroda* room, or nature room, where a variety of plants is grown, pictures of rural scenes displayed, and water features operated to produce an impression of a warm, humid rural environment. The captain's welcome and departure parties are common to all such voyages; but receptions for successive small groups are also frequent which allow many questions to be answered. Translators have also contributed to the voyage by providing basic lessons in Russian. Occasionally a voyage coincides with Russian Navy Day, in late summer, which passengers are invited to celebrate (it dates from the reign of Peter the Great).

Helicopters

Helicopters are essential equipment for icebreakers as frequently the quickest and most efficient way through the pack ice is not the shortest one and scouting for easier passages is important. For normal operations only one is carried; but on passenger voyages two are necessary for safe operations (the comment that, with passenger flights, 'one helicopter is no helicopters' has obvious safety implications). The aircraft are usually Mi-2, although others have been used. These carry eight passengers, but usually fly with six so that everyone has a window (and bulky polar clothing occupies more space than usual). The aircraft are used for landings on ice and on islands visited; in addition, they have proved very useful as a deterrent to polar bears, with the ability to fly low over them if a confrontation is likely to occur.

Other locations: Eurasian Arctic archipelagos and the Northeast Passage

Most voyages are to the North Pole and back to Murmansk or, rarely, Longyearbyen. Two have gone all the way across, reaching the Bering Strait. Several of the truly fascinating, and almost unknown, series of Arctic archipelagos are usually visited during the voyages. These are replete with wildlife and historical sites, and have much of scientific interest. The most commonly visited archipelago, Zemlya Franstsa-Iosifa, (of 191 islands) provides a 'buffer' should a voyage be delayed by severe ice. Most voyages see some of the world's most spectacular bird colonies, especially at the huge volcanic plug Rubini Rock. Bears, foxes, walrus and seals are usually sighted. Historical remains from the discovery of the archipelago in 1873 to comparatively recent polar stations abound. The geology includes rare and exceptional phenomena such as the 'Devil's Marbles', spheroidal concretions over 2m in diameter, and much else (indeed, discussion of the islands could fill several chapters). The botany, at the height of summer, easily explains the name Cape Flora, with its several historical sites.

Other islands visited include Novaya Zemlya, with the site of Willem Barents's 1597 wintering, although parts of the island are restricted as nuclear weapons test sites. Severnaya Zemlya, the largest major land discovered (in 1913) has much to offer with its geology and ice domes. Mammoth remains are commonly found on the New Siberian Islands, where ruins of the buildings of hunters and trappers survive. Large populations of polar bears, seals and walrus inhabit Wrangel Island, where introduced musk oxen flourish. Bird cliffs, such as on Ostrov Kolyuychin, the Stone Forests near Mys Shaularova Izba, as well as the most northern and eastern points of continental Asia (Mys Chelyuskin and Mys Dezhnev, respectively), are various other places visited during some North Polar voyages. Specialist lecturers, often Russian, describe these and many other sites when the icebreaker is able to make visits.

Pole of relative inaccessibility

North Pole voyages have many unexpected occurrences; an example of an unprecedented one is described here. Four poles may be defined in the Arctic and Antarctic; those of the axis of rotation of the Earth are the best known. Two of the other pairs, the magnetic poles and the geomagnetic poles, are less familiar. The Northern and Southern Pole of Inaccessibility mark the distinct positions on the Earth's surface most distant from land (Arctic) or from sea (Antarctic). Since they are more remote than either geographic pole, they are more difficult to attain and are thus a desirable objective. During a voyage, in 1996, from Murmansk to the North Pole and onwards to Alaska, the Northern Pole of Inaccessibility was attained. This was a historic occasion: although aircraft had been there, this was the first time that any ship had reached this point. By fortunate coincidence, it was on an important Russian anniversary: Navy Day. The following signal was received by *Yamal* from the president of the Murmansk Shipping Company and is translated in its entirety to illustrate the event:

STF HTGD0801002 08011921 MPMHTGD (892) PST O009 080020008 /UCJT

STF MPM UCJT

MURMANSK, I AUGUST [1996] 19:00

TO YAMAL CAPT. SMIRNOV

TO THE CAPTAIN, CREW AND PASSENGERS, TO ALL PARTICIPANTS OF THE MEMORABLE EVENT IN THE HISTORY OF ARCTIC NAVIGATION; THE FIRST TRANSIT ALONG THE TRANS-ARCTIC VOYAGE OF THE NORTHERN SEA ROUTE FROM MURMANSK TO THE NORTH POLE, TO THE POLE OF INACCESSIBILITY, AND TO THE CHUKCHI SEA, IMPLYING THAT YOU MADE THE SHORTEST POSSIBLE TRANSIT BY A SURFACE SHIP BETWEEN NORTHERN EUROPE AND THE EXIT TO THE NORTH PACIFIC OCEAN.

THIS MEANS THAT THE CENTURY-LONG ASPIRATIONS OF THOSE WHO PRECEDED US HAVE ULTIMATELY BEEN FULFILLED. YOU SHOULD BE PROUD OF THIS EVENT, WHICH SIGNIFICANTLY COINCIDED WITH THE 300TH ANNIVERSARY OF THE RUSSIAN NAVY AND WHICH IS AN IMPORTANT CONTRIBUTION TO THE HISTORY OF GREAT GEOGRAPHICAL DISCOVERIES.

BY THIS COMMUNICATION WE OFFICIALLY CONFIRM YOUR PRECEDENCE IN THIS ACCOMPLISHMENT. IT IS ALSO A DEMONSTRATION OF THE HIGH PROFESSIONALISM OF THE OFFICERS AND CREW, AS WELL AS OF THE TECHNICAL PERFECTION OF OUR ICEBREAKER FLEET.

CONGRATULATIONS, MY BEST WISHES FOR YOUR WELL-BEING AND FOR GREAT NEW ACHIEVEMENTS.

ALEXANDROVICH

NNNN

Operating companies

Quark Expeditions, with headquarters in the US, was the company that pioneered North Polar voyages in 1990 and has organized the vast majority of them (42 in all) subsequently. A Russian company, Poseidon, which was formed in 2002, has also organized others, and the Murmansk Shipping Company took one passenger group to the pole in 1995. Several other companies arrange sub-charters from Quark with various numbers of cabins, and occasionally an entire voyage. The expertise in running such a voyage is distinctly specialist, with experience derived over many years. It is unlikely that other companies will be involved unless logistic arrangements become substantially simpler. In 2009 there were five voyages planned to the North Pole; at the time of writing, only two are expected to sail (world economic circumstances having adversely affected much of the travel industry). Global economic circumstances have profoundly affected polar tourism, but are not expected to last. Demand for North Polar voyages may be expected to be strong and to persist.

Conclusions

Attaining the North and South Poles has been a perennial fascination for humanity. This has become a practicable object within only the last two decades (1987 for the South Pole and 1990 for the North Pole). Their geography, however, make the logistics vastly different. Economic constraints will always be serious: the use of atomic-powered icebreakers through the pack ice of the Arctic Ocean will remain essential and their fuel is not cheap. Even if conventionally (and less reliable) powered vessels are deployed, fuel is still very expensive. Fiscal costs are the intrinsic limiting factor. Those advertised in recent brochures range from 16,000 Euros to 28,000 Euros per person, depending on class of cabin selected. In contrast to travel elsewhere, there are very few extrinsic social considerations – apart from the fact that no local inhabitants are to be adversely affected when docking at ports. Environmentally, the use of uranium fuel is a global issue and, in this case, may be contrasted with the adverse consequences of burning hydrocarbons. The sustainability of North Polar cruises mainly depends upon economics, rather than the use of other resources. Fewer tourist voyages are now planned for the coming summers following the economic depression of 2008 – but the companies involved expect a return to average numbers when this ameliorates. Such voyages are, of necessity, specialist operations and comparatively new ones, about which much detailed information is available.

References

Armstrong, T. E. (1984) 'The Northern Sea Route, 1983', *Polar Record*, vol 22, no 137, pp173–198

Brigham, L. W. (1999) 'Soviet-Russian polar icebreakers: Changing fortunes', *U.S. Naval Institute Proceedings*, January, pp89–90

Herbert, W. W. (1969) *Across the Top of the World*, Longmans, London

Nilsen, T. and Bøhmer, N. (1994) *Sources to Radioactive Contamination in Murmansk and Arkangel'sk Counties*, Bellona Foundation, Oslo

Sísteních, F. (2007) 'Frühlings erwachen um Nordpol', *An Bord*, vol 4, pp3–8

Splettstoesser, J. F. and Headland, R. K. (2009) 'Russian icebreakers for tourism and science in polar regions: Changes due to climate change', in *Proceedings of the 20th International Conference on Port and Ocean Engineering under Arctic Conditions*, Luleå, Sweden

Stroeve, J. (2008) 'Arctic sea-ice', in A. S. Goudie and D. J. Cuff (eds) *The Oxford Companion to Global Change*, Oxford University Press, Oxford

Todd, F. S., Headland, R. K. and Lasca, N. (1992) 'Animals at the North Pole', *Polar Record*, vol 28, no 167, pp321–322

Toomey, P. R. M. (2001) 'Explanation for the reported thinning of sea ice at the North Pole', *Polar Record*, vol 37, no 201, pp171–172

van Meurs, R. and Splettstoesser, J. F. (2003) 'Farthest north polar bear (*Ursus maritimus*)', *Arctic*, vol 56, no 3, p309

Vuilleumier, F. (1995) 'A large colony of ivory gulls *Pagophila eburnean* on Victoria Island, Russia', *Alauda*, vol 63, no 2, pp135–148

4

Selling the Adventure of a Lifetime: An Ethnographic Report on Cruising in the Antarctic

Arthur Asa Berger

*A small-ship expedition to Antarctica might be the single greatest adventure travel opportunity of your life. We're proud to say that in 1966, Lindblad became **the first to offer expedition travel to Antarctica**. That's over 40 years of experience in the most wild place on earth. So we understand fully the responsibility as well as the potential for life changing experiences that this vast landscape carries. No mere drive-by, our Antarctica expedition cruises go deeper. You'll have the opportunity to **travel with National Geographic experts and the most experienced Ice Team on earth**. With their leadership, step foot on land overflowing with life. Zodiac past soaring icebergs. Kayak in protected waters, padding around icebergs as penguins swim by. And encounter Antarctica from the safety and comfort of our new expedition ship, National Geographic Explorer.* (Lindblad, 2009, emphasis added)

On 19 February 2008, my wife and I left the apartment we had rented for a week in downtown Buenos Aires and took a cab for a short ride to the pier where the *Star Princess* was docked. Thousands of people were there and the situation was chaotic. People who had booked a cruise on the *Star Princess* were milling around, suitcases were stacked here and there on the sidewalk, porters were running back and forth. Fortunately, we had gone to a meeting at a hotel a few days earlier and secured boarding passes, and so we were able to board the ship immediately. Somehow or other, everyone who had booked passage on the ship boarded it and most of them got their suitcases.

What follows is an ethnographic analysis of our Antarctic cruise and of the Antarctica cruise industry. I will provide some context by discussing the ocean cruise industry, in general, describe the cruises with specialized vessels whose passengers actually land on Antarctica (taking advantage of what the Lindblad company calls an 'opportunity' for 'the single greatest adventure' trip available), and offer some suggestions about why landing on Antarctica is so important to people.

The ocean cruise industry:
An American form of tourism

In 2008, according to the Cruise Lines International Association (CLIA), an estimated 13.2 million people took cruises, up considerably from the 12.5 million people the year before. Some 9.57 million of these passengers were Americans – that's 76 per cent of all cruise-takers – so cruising is very much an American kind of tourism (CLIA, 2008).

Why Americans are so over-represented as passengers on ocean cruises is an interesting question. It may be that many Americans are not used to foreign travel. For many Americans, cruising is a 'safe' and easy way to visit foreign countries, and as the cruise lines keep repeating in the advertisements: 'You only have to unpack once.' It may also be that the cost of cruising is now relatively inexpensive for Americans, especially when compared to travel in Europe where the Euro and the UK pound have been very strong in recent years.

In January 2009, the Costa Cruise line was advertising seven-night cruises for US$399 – for the least expensive cabins. You have to add tips and other expenses to the basic price of a cruise; but this price for a week of cruising is relatively inexpensive and much cheaper than many other kinds of vacations. Of course, other ocean cruise lines are also offering bargain cruises now since it is worth getting passengers, at almost any price, to fill empty cabins.

Although the following tables on the number of people taking cruises are impressive, only 17 per cent of Americans have ever taken cruises, so while cruising is increasing in popularity, it still is only a relatively small part of the American tourism industry. At one time, many years ago, ocean cruising was reserved for wealthy elites who had the time and could afford the cost of booking a passage on a cruise liner; and cruise liners had different classes of passengers. This earlier notion that cruising was for wealthy elites may still linger on in the popular imagination, although the cruise industry has become a mass industry and ocean liners have eliminated different classes of cruises. Passengers who wish to take cruises now can obtain social distance by choosing luxury lines such as Seabourn and Silversea. Birds of a feather flock, and cruise, together.

Categories of ocean cruise lines

There are various categories of ocean cruise lines. The cost of a cruise is based on the kind of cruise line on which one books passage and cabin locations, as well as other services that may be provided. The classification system shown below is one commonly used to differentiate cruises (see Table 4.1).

It costs a great deal more money to book a cruise on a luxury line than on a contemporary line, such as Costa. A day on a Seabourn or Silversea liner can cost more than a week on a Costa ship or many other cruise lines. Table 4.2 provides details of prices of selected cruises.

Table 4.1 *Classification of mainstream cruise lines*

Contemporary	Premium	Luxury
Carnival	Princess	Seabourn
Royal Caribbean	Holland America	Crystal
Costa	Celebrity	Cunard
Norwegian		Regency Seven-Seas
		Silversea

Table 4.2 *Prices of selected cruises*

Line	Ship	Length	Price
Norwegian Line	*Norwegian Sun*	14 days	US$697
Seabourn Line	*Seabourn Odyssey*	14 days	US$8954

Source: Cruise (2009)

This table is for the least expensive cabin in each line. A 14-day cruise on the *Seabourn Odyssey*, in the least expensive cabin, costs almost 13 times as much as a 14-day cruise on the *Norwegian Sun*. These mainstream cruise companies, listed above, carry most of the passengers who take cruises. The ships are usually large and, in recent years, some of them have become gigantic, as they provide their passengers with entertainers, lecturers, bands for dancing, elaborate dining, pools and hot tubs, and many other facilities and services. CLIA (2008) reports that in 2008:

- The median income for passengers was US$93,000.
- Sixty-nine per cent of passengers had college degrees.
- The median age of passengers was 46 years old.

This suggests that cruising primarily appeals to middle- and upper middle-class, middle-age, and relatively affluent Americans, though the bargain rates for some cruises are now attracting a large number of less affluent passengers. Mainstream cruising is now, to a considerable extent, a mass market resort experience at sea.

Specialty cruise lines to Antarctica

In addition to the regular or mainstream ocean cruise lines, there are what we might describe as specialty lines – generally small 'expedition' cruise ships with unusual itineraries – that take passengers to small ports in various countries and to polar regions such as Antarctica. The specialty lines that go to Antarctica have ships with reinforced hulls and other structural features to protect them from the ice, but they are not the only ones that sail in Antarctic waters. A number of the mainstream lines, such as Princess and Holland America, sail through Antarctic waters; but they do not land passengers on the continent. According to Weaver (2001), the first scenic cruise to Antarctica with a 1000 passenger ship was in 2000.

The International Association of Antarctica Tour Operators (IAATO) has strict rules about the number of people who can land in Antarctica at one time, which precludes large passenger liners from doing so. In addition, it can be difficult to land on Antarctica – you have to use small zodiac boats to get to the continent – so it would be impossible for large cruise liners with thousands of passengers to land them all on Antarctica even if they were allowed to do so. Most of the specialty expedition-style cruise vessels that land their passengers on Antarctica carry between 40 and 150 passengers.

Table 4.3 shows some typical fares for cruises that land passengers on Antarctica. They sail between November and March, when it is possible to visit the area.

Table 4.3 *Fares of ships that land on Antarctica*

Ship	Days	Price (least expensive cabin)
Silversea/*Prince Albert II*	11	US$8225
GAP Adventures/*Expedition*	13	US$6695
Lindblad/*National Geographic Explorer*	15	US$10760

We can see that cruises to Antarctica can be quite expensive. If you add the cost of airfare to Buenos Aires (around US$1250 per person from many cities in the US) plus the cost onwards to the departure point of Ushuaia, to the cost of cruising on these small boats (anywhere from US$3500 to $20,000 per person), you can see that a cruise to Antarctica can easily cost a couple between US$20,000 to $40,000, and sometimes even more. However, it is possible to sail in Antarctic waters and *see* Antarctica for a moderate amount of money. I will describe our cruise through Antarctic waters on the *Star Princess*, discuss in more detail the small ships that land people on the continent, and suggest some reasons why setting foot on Antarctica is so important to people.

A mainstream cruise to Antarctica
on the *Star Princess*

When my wife and I took our 17-day cruise on the *Star Princess*, it cost US$1850 for an inside cabin, and we got US$100 to spend on the cruise, along with flowers from our agent and a free steak dinner in one of the *Star Princess* specialty restaurants. I met one woman on the cruise who only decided to take it at the very last minute, when Princess was selling cabins and airfare connections at great discounts. 'A week ago', she told me, 'I wasn't booked on this cruise. They were practically giving the tickets away.' Another person I met told me that he waited until two weeks before the cruise was to begin and paid US$4500 for airfare and a small cabin with a window for himself and his wife.

If you are willing to wait until the very last minute, and want to take a chance that a particular cruise you would like to take won't be fully booked, you can get some remarkable bargains on the mainline cruise ships. We flew into Buenos Aires a week early, rented a small apartment in the centre of the city, and spent a week recuperating from the flight and exploring Buenos Aires, a charming and very interesting city, known – justly so – for its fabulous steaks. So we did not wait until the last minute to get the best possible price; but the cruise was not expensive, as cruises go, and we were able to spend a week visiting Buenos Aires.

People who take cruises tend to spend a great deal of time talking with other passengers at their dining tables. And one of their favourite topics is the cruises that they have taken and the ones they are planning to take. Several people I met during our meals told me that this cruise in Antarctica waters was their 'cruise of a lifetime'. Our itinerary on the *Star Princess* cruise is shown in Table 4.4.

Table 4.4 *Itinerary of a Star Princess Antarctica cruise*

Tuesday, 19 February 2008	Buenos Aires
Wednesday, 20 February 2008	At sea
Thursday, 21 February 2008	At sea
Friday, 22 February 2008	**Stanley/Falklands**
Saturday, 23 February 2008	At sea
Sunday, 24 February 2008	At sea; Elephant Island
Monday, 25 February 2008	At sea; Esperanan Station
Tuesday, 26 February 2008	At sea; Intercurrance Island
Tuesday, 26 February 2008	At sea; Sigma Island
Wednesday, 27 February 2008	At sea; Deception Island
Thursday, 28 February 2008	At sea; Cape Horn
Friday, 29 February 2008	**Ushuaia**
Saturday, 1 March 2008	**Punta Arenas**
Sunday, 2 March 2008	At sea
Monday, 3 March 2008	At sea
Tuesday, 4 March 2008	At sea
Wednesday, 5 March 2008	**Montevideo**
Thursday, 6 March 2008	Buenos Aires

What this itinerary shows is that you have to do a good deal of sailing from Buenos Aires to reach Antarctica. We only landed at four ports during this cruise, but we spent a number of days cruising in Antarctic waters. These ports are shown in boldface. They were extremely interesting and provided the passengers with the chance to visit various penguin colonies, see some beautiful scenery and explore some remarkable sites. This itinerary also explains why so many small ship cruises to Antarctica leave from Ushuaia.

On our cruise, the naturalist said that only 300,000 people had ever seen Antarctica and only 50,000 people had actually set foot on Antarctica. There is reason to question these figures since the International Association of Antarctica Tour Operators (IAATO, 2009) claims that 46,000 people visited Antarctica and 30,000 people set foot on Antarctica during 2007 to 2008 alone. When we were in Antarctic waters, I wrote the following notes in my travel journal:

> *The captain said today's the cleanest that he had ever seen Antarctica. He said that we are very lucky because some cruises are fogged in. He said we might expect a day like today just a few times a year. The mountains are remarkable ... there are glaciers one after another... What is it about the scenery that is so mesmerizing? Perhaps it's the clarity of the mountains and the icebergs shimmering in the sun against a blue sky. The scenery today was incredible and adding to the experience was the realization that days like today are really rare.*

I wrote 40 pages of notes on the cruise. The passages I quoted show my response to the scenery. I'm sure that almost everyone onboard felt the same because all the passengers were snapping photographs one after another, and exclaiming in excited voices how beautiful they found Antarctica's scenery.

While the idea of doing something adventurous or different may have motivated many of the passengers on the ship, I think it was their desire to see this pristine and spectacularly beautiful continent that was the major motivator. The scenery generated high spirits and blissful, almost ecstatic, reactions in many of the passengers. I wrote in my journal that after the cruise to Antarctica, I didn't feel that I wanted to take any more ocean cruises because none of them could possibly match the Antarctic experience.

Specialty cruise ships to Antarctica

The passengers on the *Star Princess* were interested in seeing Antarctica, but also wanted a more typical cruise experience, with fancy dinners, spas and entertainers. People who take cruises on the specialty expedition-style vessels have a different kind of experience and land frequently on Antarctica – taking small zodiac boats to get ashore. There are three categories of specialty cruise ships that visit Antarctica (Quark Expeditions, 2009):

1   Icebreakers
2   Adventure ships
3   Expedition ships

All of these different kinds of ships are specifically designed to sail in Antarctic waters. Some of the ships, the icebreakers, have specially reinforced hulls that enable them to break through ice floes that they may encounter. All of these ships are built with reinforced hulls to cruise in Antarctic waters.

One of the motivations for passengers on these kinds of ships is a sense of high adventure and a desire to visit a continent on which few people have set foot. Many of the people who take these cruises do not like the kind of cruise experience that one has on large mainstream cruise liners. The adventure cruise ships may feature activities such as overnight camping, sea kayaking and mountaineering on their expeditions.

A relatively small number of people actually go ashore on Antarctica. Given the nature of the Antarctic cruise experience, the marketers for the companies that sell cruises to the area use different strategies to position these cruises from those found for mainstream cruises. Most of the passengers on the *Star Princess* had taken other cruises and were looking for a somewhat different kind of cruise experience.

To take any of the standard cruises to Antarctica, it is necessary to fly to Argentina (the exception being cruises south from New Zealand and Australia). This means that you have to spend a good deal of time and money to get to a port where you can take a cruise – whether it is Buenos Aires for a cruise on a large ocean liner or Ushuaia, on the southern tip of South America, for a cruise on a small expedition ship that features landing on Antarctica. Some of these small expedition shipping lines provide free air transportation from Buenos Aires to Ushuaia and return.

Luxury adventure cruises

As I pointed out earlier, there is a considerable difference in price between cruises on small ships that land on Antarctica and those on large passenger liners that sail in Antarctic waters. The passengers on the small ships are also different in that they are not interested in the mainstream cruise experience, but in having a learning experience, an adventure, and actually setting foot on Antarctica. This means that the marketing of these cruises focuses upon the experiential and existential aspects of being on Antarctica rather than on the luxurious nature of mainline ocean cruisers.

We can see the difference between mainstream ocean liners and small specialty ships in Table 4.5. It offers a set of oppositions that characterize the two markets for cruises in Antarctica. Mediating between these oppositions are the various luxury expedition ships such as Silversea's *Prince Albert II*.

Table 4.3 shows that it can cost more than four times as much to visit Antarctica on a small ship than to see it on a mainstream liner, generally with few of the luxuries found on large ocean liners. During recent years a new category of luxury expedition ships has entered the Antarctica cruise industry, such as the recently acquired and refitted Silversea *Prince Albert II*. We can describe these luxurious ships as cross-over expedition ships. Silversea promises all the luxury of a six-star cruise line with the same adventures available to those on small ships. The Silversea website contains descriptions of the ship:

She will carry 132 passengers in 66 ocean view accommodations, many featuring private verandas, 18 of which have more than 400 sq. ft. of luxury … 8 zodiac boats and other landing craft will allow her guests to visit even the most remote island locations. (Silversea Cruises, 2009)

With Silversea, you have a combination of the adventure elements of the small specialty ships and the luxury of mainstream ocean liners. The price for the cheapest cabin on an 11-day cruise on the *Prince Albert II*, including a flight from Buenos Aires to Ushuaia and back, is US$6798. This means that Silversea is competitive with cruises on many other Antarctic ships despite the fact that the *Prince Albert II* is a

Table 4.5 *Ships that visit Antarctic waters*

Large Ocean Liners	Luxury Explorer Ships	Small Ships
Princess	Silversea/*Prince Albert II*	Lindblad
Luxury		Simplicity
Pleasure		Adventure
See Antarctica		Land on Antarctica
Moderate cost		Expensive
Mainstream passengers		Selective passengers

Table 4.6 *Itinerary of a Prince Albert II Antarctica cruise*

Day 1	Ushuaia, Argentina
Day 2	Day at sea
Day 3	West Point Island, Falkland Islands, Carcass Islands
Day 4	Stanley, Falkland Islands
Day 5	Day at sea
Day 6	Day at sea
Day 7	South Georgia
Day 8	South Georgia
Day 9	Day at sea
Day 10	South Orkney Islands
Day 11	Elephant Island, South Shetland Islands
Day 12	Antarctic Peninsula
Day 13	Antarctic Peninsula
Day 14	Antarctic Peninsula
Day 15	Drake Passage
Day 16	Drake Passage
Day 17	Ushuaia, Argentina

Source: Silversea Cruises (2009)

very luxurious cruise ship. People who want luxury and adventure can take this ship and have, so to speak, the best of both worlds. The fact that Silversea is luxurious may deter some cruise takers who feel that being on a luxury liner is not congruent with visiting Antarctica or other polar regions. The itinerary, according to the *Silversea 2009 Voyage Atlas*, for the 'Explorer's Antarctica' 16-day cruise on the *Prince Albert II* is shown in Table 4.6.

This trip costs US$8430 for the least expensive cabin, which is 351 square feet in size. Considering the cost of many Antarctic expedition cruises, these luxury cruises are bargains, relatively speaking. There are other lines with voyages to Antarctica that are not luxurious and cost more money.

The sacred, the profane and Antarctica

Why is seeing Antarctica and landing on the Antarctic continent so important to people? The passion shown by many of the passengers on the *Star Princess* made me wonder whether there might be an unrecognized sacred or hidden religious dimension to the trip. Could it be that many of the passengers were, without fully recognizing what they were doing, on some kind of a religious pilgrimage and that Antarctica's incredible natural beauty was similar, in nature, to the sacred destinations of many religious pilgrims?

In his book *The Sacred and the Profane: The Nature of Religion*, Eliade (1961) argues that for religious people, time and space are seen differently than by non-religious people. Thus, for religious men and women, there are certain spaces that can be described as sacred – think of churches, synagogues, temples and certain areas in countries where religious ceremonies are held. These places are perceived as quite different from profane everyday places. Eliade (1961, p116) writes:

> *For religious man, nature is never only 'natural'; it is always fraught with religious value. This is easy to understand, for the cosmos is a divine creation; coming from the hands of the gods, the world is impregnated with sacredness. It is not simply a sacrality communicated by the gods, as is the case, for example, with a place or an object consecrated by the divine presence. The gods did more; they manifested the different modalities of the sacred in the very structure of the world and of cosmic phenomena [emphasis in the original].*

So, sailing to Antarctica can be interpreted, if we keep Eliade's ideas in mind, as involving a visit to sacred space and an attempt to establish a more harmonious relationship with nature and with God. There may also be an element, not recognized by the passengers, of a search for paradise and for some kind of a Shangri-La in visiting Antarctica, except that the Shangri-La the visitors to Antarctica are seeking exists not in the Himalayas but in their imaginations, hidden away somewhere in the vast wilderness of Antarctica's empty and mysterious interior. The ice and snow in Antarctica are pure and virginal, and except for the perimeter of the continent, seldom visited by human beings. Antarctica is, then, a kind of virgin land, unoccupied by humans (except for a few thousand scientists) and uncorrupted by civilization.

For some passengers, visiting Antarctica is part of a quest, and enabled them to check off one more continent in their attempt to visit all the continents. During our cruise I met a number of people who sailed to Antarctica because they wanted to be able to say that they had seen, visited or spent time in all seven continents. One woman on the cruise told me that this cruise meant that she had been to (or seen) six continents and only had to visit Australia to complete her quest.

Visiting Antarctica can also be seen as a kind of time travel, offering passengers an opportunity to experience what the world may have been like millions of years ago. Whatever else it may be, Antarctica is also a gigantic ice desert and wilderness. Most of the time Antarctica is a vast and empty continent, with an interior that very few people get to see. It is possible to fly to certain areas beyond the coast and land on Antarctica for short periods of time. A videotape I saw of a planeload of tourists to these regions on their return flight showed absolutely exhausted adventurers. They looked as if they were recovering from an ordeal, caused by the cold and wind during the limited time they had spent on Antarctica.

The myth model and Antarctic travel

Anthropologist and folklorist Raphael Patai (1972, p2) suggests in *Myth and Modern Man* that there are unsuspected mythic motivations that shape much of our behaviour. He defines a myth as follows:

> *Myth ... is a traditional religious charter, which operates by validating laws, customs, rites, institutions and beliefs, or explaining socio-cultural situations and natural phenomena, and taking the form of stories, believed to be true, about divine beings and heroes.*

Eliade (1961) talks about camouflaged myths and makes the same argument. I have taken this notion that myths shape behaviour and developed a model that enables us to see the ways in which myths impact upon various areas of our culture – what I call the myth model (see Table 4.7). I argue that we can take a myth and see how it informs historical experience, elite culture, popular culture and everyday life. I will use this myth model to offer an explanation of why tourists go to Antarctica.

Table 4.7 *The myth model*

Myth	Dangerous voyage of Odysseus
Historical experience	Amundsen, Shackleton, Byrd in Antarctica
Elite culture	*Antarctic Navigation* (a novel) by Elizabeth Arthur
Popular culture	*Justice League Antarctica* (graphic novel/comic)
Everyday life	Cruise to Antarctica and/or landing on Antarctica

This model shows how a myth, removed from its sacred origins, has an impact upon various aspects of a culture. It argues that many of the things we do are shaped by myths that we may not be conscious of, but which affect our behaviour. In other words, there may be a mythic impetus, of which we are unaware, behind our desire to see Antarctica or to land on the continent.

Landing on Antarctica

It is the experience of actually setting foot on remote locations in Antarctica and seeing the wildlife up close that is one of the prime motivators of those who sail on small ships in search of adventure and the opportunity to be among the very few people who have ever visited the continent. Bauer and Dowling (2006, p201) offer an overview, based on a survey, of the way in which some cruise-takers felt about their cruises:

> *After having visited the Antarctic, the visitors ranked the importance of various aspects of their trip… They noted that most important for them was to see the continent, its wildlife, natural beauty, historical sites and remoteness. When asked what was the 'best' part of their trip, the comments included 'being up close and personal with the wildlife and icebergs', 'the short landings by zodiacs', 'the vastness of the continent' … and 'the incredible heights of the mountains and the overall beauty left me spellbound'.*

Many of them indicated that the trip exceeded their expectations and that they felt that Antarctica was really special and that humans should not be allowed to alter it. As the statistics about cruises to Antarctica demonstrate, anyone who cruises in Antarctic waters or actually lands there is one of a very tiny minority of cruise-takers and therefore is a member of an 'elite' group of those who have either seen or landed on the continent. The term 'elite' has negative connotations, although many of the advertisements for these cruises do suggest, often in guarded language, that people who take these cruises are members of a tiny group of people (an elite) who are willing to travel long distances to remote areas for adventures, with varying degrees of comfort and luxury. There is also an element of danger in taking small ships to Antarctica. A Quark Expeditions ship, the *Ocean Nova*, with 65 passengers and 41 crew members aboard, was grounded in February 2009 and there have been other ships that experienced similar problems in recent years, notably with the sinking of the *Explorer* in November 2007 (Stewart and Draper, 2008).

A polar cruise website describes its 'Expedition Antarctic' cruises as follows: 'Expedition cruising began in 1966. This category of ship still adheres to the principles of conservation and preservation and world exploration for *the fortunate few*' (Polar Cruises, 2009, emphasis added). We see, then, a note of elitism in this advertising copy. It is not simply 'the few' who get to visit Antarctica, but the 'fortunate few'.

The advertising copy for the Lindblad Antarctic cruise, with which this analysis began, suggests that a trip to Antarctica might be, and strongly implies that it will be, 'the single greatest adventure travel opportunity of your life'. The Lindblad text adds that the trip has 'the potential for life changing experiences', so travelling to Antarctica with Lindblad, the first company to offer travel to Antarctica, promises great adventure and personal growth. It also offers security, since Lindblad has 'the most experienced Ice Team on earth' to 'the most wild place on earth'. The language here is full of superlatives as Lindblad distances its expeditions – a term which suggests adventure and some kind of a lofty goal being pursed, such as exploration – from mere 'drive-by' cruises such as those offered by Princess, Holland America and other mainstream cruise lines, and from other cruise lines that offer expeditions to Antarctica.

The fortunate few and Antarctica's good fortune

Antarctica has fewer visitors than any other continent, in part because it is so remote and because it is so cold and inhospitable most of the year. During the months when it is possible to visit the continent, more and more people go there, although the numbers of those who cruise in its waters are small and the numbers of people who land on the continent are tiny compared to those who take cruises in the Caribbean or Alaska. Antarctica's remoteness and the cost of visiting it may actually be a blessing because Antarctica has a very fragile environment and large numbers of tourists would inevitably cause considerable damage. Not only is Antarctica a destination for 'the fortunate few'; it is fortunate, ecologically speaking, that only relatively few people go there.

References

Bauer, T. G. and Dowling, R. K. (2006) 'The Antarctic cruise industry', in R. K. Dowling (ed) *Cruise Ship Tourism*, CABI Publishing, Wallingford, UK

CLIA (Cruise Lines International Association) (2008) www.cruising.org, accessed 4 July 2009

Cruise (2009) www.cruise.com, accessed 4 July 2009

Eliade, M. (1961) *The Sacred and the Profane: The Nature of Religion*, Harper & Row, New York, NY

IAATO (International Association of Antarctica Tour Operators) (2009) www.iaato.org, accessed 4 July 2009

Lindblad Expeditions (2009) www.expeditions.com, accessed 4 July 2009

Patai, R. (1972) *Myth and Modern Man*, Prentice-Hall, Englewood Cliffs, CA

Polar Cruises (2009) www.polarcruises.com, accessed 4 July 2009

Quark Expeditions (2009) www.quarkexpeditions.com/antarctic/three-ways-to-travel, accessed 4 July 2009

Silversea Cruises (2009) *Silversea 2009 Voyage Atlas*, www.silverseacruises.in/itineraries?catid=52, accessed 4 July 2009

Stewart, E. J., and Draper, D. (2008) 'The sinking of the MS Explorer: Implications for cruise tourism in Arctic Canada', *Arctic (InfoNorth)*, vol 61, no 2, pp224–231

Weaver, D. B. (ed) (2001) *The Encyclopedia of Ecotourism*, CAB International, Wallingford, UK

Part II
HUMAN DIMENSIONS

5

Cruises and Bruises: Safety, Security and Social Issues on Polar Cruises

Ross A. Klein

Introduction

Polar cruising at one time was limited to a handful of small expedition-type cruise ships – ships with capacity for 100 passengers or less. However, today it is not only these small intimate ships that visit polar regions. Increasingly, mainstream cruise lines, with ships accommodating 3000 or more passengers, are arriving. As a result, the number of visitors has increased dramatically, from a couple of hundred visiting Antarctica in 1969 to more than 45,000 tourists and 28,000 crew and staff in 2007/2008 (IAATO, 2008; Foreign and Commonwealth Office, 2009). In 2007/2008 53 ships sailed to Antarctica, accounting for more than 300 voyages (Ganesh, 2009). According to a 2007 United Nations report, the number of tourists going ashore in Antarctica increased 757 per cent in just ten years (Berglund, 2007).

Part of the recent growth is attributable to large cruise ships being deployed to the region. According to the Cruise Lines International Association (CLIA) (composed of 23 cruise lines that represent 97 per cent of the cruise capacity marketed from North America), the number of passenger days for cruises by its members to Antarctica increased almost sixfold between 2000 and 2008, from 49,000 to 285,000 (CLIA, 2009). Cruise-only passengers practically doubled between 2006/2007 and 2007/2008, from 6930 to 13,000 (Higgins, 2009), most arriving on large ships. Cruise-only tours allow passengers to view icebergs from the comfort of heated cabins and lounges, but they do not go ashore. Princess Cruises describes its Antarctica and South America trip as scenic cruising involving glaciers, penguins and a dazzling landscape. It makes no mention that Antarctica remains a thoroughly hostile environment, prone to savage storms, sub-zero temperatures even in summer, and howling winds of up to 320 kilometres per hour. Although these larger ships offer many luxury extras, most are built for cruising in warmer waters and lack ice-strengthened hulls. There is a dual question about sustainability. Is the scale of growth sustainable, and is the use of large cruise ships designed for warmer climes responsible and safe?

Large cruise ships have similarly increased their presence in the northern hemisphere. Cruise tourism in Alaska has grown to almost 1 million passengers per year. There has also been significant growth in cruise ship visits to Iceland, Greenland, the coasts of Norway, Sweden and Finland, and the coast of Labrador. For example, between 2000 and 2008, the number of cruise passengers visiting Akureyi (Iceland) increased from 16,803 to 57,508; Reykjavik (Iceland) from 25,576 to 59,308; and Bergen (Norway) from 99,630 to 232,210 (*Cruise Europe News*, 2002, 2008). At the same time, visitor numbers to Svalbard (Norway) remained stable given strict restrictions on vessel numbers and vessel size (Geitz, 2004).

Safety and security

There are two areas of concern when it comes to safety and security. One is safety of the ship, especially given the characteristics of polar cruising. The other concern is passenger safety. Some of the passenger issues are generic to cruises in all regions of the world.

Safety of the ship

Issues of ship safety are in some respects unique in polar regions given ice, cold, and quickly changing weather and sea conditions. Most expedition cruise ships are designed for these conditions. They have ice-strengthened hulls, which provide some protection against damage when confronted by icebergs or slab ice. However, there can still be problems. In November 2007, GAP Adventures' *Explorer* sank after the ship hit ice that put a 5 to 6 inch hole through both hulls. The ship took on water, listed 25° to 30°, and started sinking (having an adverse impact upon the fragile environment). All passengers and crew boarded lifeboats and, after 4 or 5 hours in active seas, were picked up by another ship in the area, Hurtigruten's *Nordnorge* (Batty and Orr, 2007; Canadian Press, 2007). Just ten months earlier (30 January 2007), Hurtigruten's *Nordnorge* also rescued passengers from *Nordkapp* after it grounded near Deception Island in Antarctica, causing an 82 foot long gash to its outer hull (Tisdall, 2007).

While it is uncommon for ships to sink, groundings are more common. This can be seen in Table 5.1, which shows reported groundings of cruise ships in Alaska, and in or near Antarctica and the Arctic. Groundings cause inconvenience to passengers, have potential for serious injuries, and often negatively affect the environment.

Table 5.1 *Ships running aground in Antarctic, near-Arctic and Alaska's waters, 1995–February 2009*

Date	Ship/incident
February 2009	*Ocean Nova*, Quark Expeditions Ran aground about 2km from the San Martin base (Antarctica), pushed by extremely high winds into craggy rocks. Non-official sources onboard report that the engines were shut off for maintenance and the ship was unable to start the engines immediately when the winds picked up because they had to put together whatever had been disassembled.
January 2009	*Richard With*, Hurtigruten Ran aground at the port of Trondheim on the west coast of Norway. It suffered propeller damage and took on water through a leak in a seal. All passengers were evacuated.
December 2008	*Ushuaia*, Fathom Expeditions Ran aground on a rock close to Wilhelmina Bay in Antarctica. The ship had been scheduled to make a landing at Danco Island, but due to strong winds cancelled and went north to Wilhelmina Bay to find a more protected landing place. It hit a rock on the way and ran aground, causing a breach of the hull and a leak of diesel fuel oil.
July 2008	*Spirit of Glacier Bay*, Cruise West Grounded in Tarr Inlet near Glacier Bay, causing a crack in the hull. Passengers were evacuated to a coast guard vessel.
July 2008	*Antarctic Dream*, Antarctic Shipping Ran aground off Svalbard, just east of Spitsbergen. The vessel suffered no damage; but it took a rescue vessel more than six hours to be freed (Berglund, 2008).
June 2008	*Sprit of Alaska*, Cruise West Touched bottom in Tracy Arm, 72km south of Juneau. It damaged its propulsion system. Passengers were transferred to the *Spirit of Endeavour*.
November 2007	*Explorer*, GAP Expeditions More than 150 passengers and crew abandoned ship near the South Shetland Islands, 120km north of the Antarctic peninsula, after the ship hit an unidentified object (probably ice), which put a 25×10cm hole through both hulls. The ship took on water, listed 25–30° and started sinking – it sank several hours later. A distress call was issued at about 5am GMT and passengers boarded lifeboats 90 minutes later in the dark. After 4 or 5 hours in open lifeboats in active seas, passengers were transferred from lifeboats to Hurtigruten's *Nordnorge*, which was in the area.
August 2007	*Spirit of Columbia*, Cruise West Ran aground in Prince William Sound near Evans Island after getting too close to shore for bear watching. It was stuck in the mud until it refloated at high tide.

Date	Ship/incident
June 2007	*Disko II*, Albatros Travel Ran aground after hitting rocks near the island of Qeqertarsuaq, Greenland, 250km north of the Arctic Circle. The 52 passengers and two tour guides were taken ashore as a precaution; the 18-member crew remained aboard.
May 2007	*Empress of the North*, Majestic America Line Ran aground off the Alaskan coast and began taking on water near Hanus Reef in Lynn Canal. It was listing 6° at the southern end of Icy Strait, about 25km south-west of Juneau, when all passengers and most crew were evacuated to a tugboat and barge.
January 2007	*Nordkapp*, Hurtigruten Touched ground near Deception Island in the Antarctic and sustained a 25m long gash to its outer hull, spilling as much as 757 litres of diesel oil. Passengers were transferred to *Nordnorge* to return to Ushuaia.
November 2006	*Lyubov Orlova*, Quark Expeditions Ran aground in Whalers' Bay while visiting Deception Island in the South Shetland Islands. Freed eight hours later at high tide with the help of a Spanish rescue vessel, returning to Ushuaia on its own power.
August 2005	*Hanseatic*, Hapag-Lloyd Ran aground near the island of Luroy off the Norwegian coast just south of the Polar Circle, causing a 5m hole in the hull. The ship remained stable and sailed to Bodo, from where passengers flew back to Germany.
July 2005	*Mona Lisa*, Holiday Kreuzfahrten Ran onto rocks near Spitsbergen, damaging both propellers and the hull.
July 2004	*Clipper Odyssey*, Clipper Cruise Line Ran hard aground on rocks in the Aleutian Islands, forcing 153 passengers and crew to transfer to other ships and spilling an undetermined amount of fuel from a ruptured tank. The ship floated free with the tide and proceeded on its own power to Unalaska.
May 2004	*Wilderness Adventurer*, Glacier Bay Cruiseline Evacuated after striking ice (puncturing a 3 inch hole into the hull) and taking on water in Tracy Arm in south-eastern Alaska. Passengers and crew were evacuated to another ship.
July 2003	*Mona Lisa*, Holiday Kreuzfahrten 670 passengers were evacuated after the ship ran onto rocks near Spitsbergen. Both propellers and the hull were damaged.
June 2003	*Spirit of Columbia*, Cruise West Hit bottom and possibly bent the port shaft and propeller in Jackpot Bay (Prince William Sound), approximately 120km south of Whittier. All passengers were safely off-loaded in Whittier.

Date	Ship/incident
May 2003	*Safari Spirit*, American Safari Cruises Hit rocks on its cruise to Alaska. All aboard were safely evacuated to lifeboats. The ship sank in about 9m of water (NTSB, 2004).
February 2003	*Marco Polo*, Orient Line Hastily returned to Ushuaia after being blown aground in shallow waters while in the South Shetland Islands. An inspection found three large cracks along the outer hull. The head of the coast guard station at Ushuaia said that the ship was never at risk, 'but it wasn't in condition to continue sailing' (Merco Press, 2003). Three inch thick plates were welded over the cracks at Ushuaia and the cruise continued.
November 2002	*Clipper Adventurer*, Clipper Cruise Line Ran aground in the vicinity of Deception Island (King George Island, Antarctica); freed by a Chilean icebreaker. There was minor damage but no pollution.
May 2001	*Wilderness Explorer*, Glacier Bay Cruiseline Ran aground on an Alaskan cruise; refloated by the coast guard.
July 1999	*Spirit of 98*, Cruise West Struck a rock in Tracy Arm and started sinking – resting aground on a small beach. All passengers and most crewmembers boarded inflatable rafts and shuttled to a nearby ship.
July 1999	*Wilderness Explorer*, Glacier Bay Cruiseline Grounded in Idaho Inlet about 129km west of Juneau; refloated about four hours later. No injuries or pollution.
June 1999	*Wilderness Adventurer*, Glacier Bay Cruiseline Ran aground in Dundas Bay, Alaska, and remained on a rock pinnacle with a 40° list to port. The ship cracked its hull, and spilled about 180 to 230 litres of fuel mixed with water. Passengers were safely evacuated.
July 1997	*Hanseatic*, Hapag-Lloyd Ran aground and was pulled free from a sandbank near Spitsbergen after passengers had been evacuated. No injuries and no damage to the ship.
August 1996	*Hanseatic*, Hapag-Lloyd Ran aground on a shingle bank in the Northwest Passage of Canada; refloated following evacuation of all passengers (TSB, 1996).
June 1995	*Star Princess*, Princess Cruises Ran aground and holed on Poundstone Rock, Lynn Canal, Alaska – 40 foot (12m) by 8 inch (20cm) wide gash and a 100 foot (30m) gash, with modest pollution. Evacuated by tender (NTSB, 1997).

Source: Cruise Junkie (2009a, 2009b)

Mechanical problems also pose a problem. For example, a number of ships were plagued by mechanical and other problems in 2008/2009 alone. *Lyuba Orlova* had to cancel four trips due to mechanical problems. Even after repairs, Argentinean port authorities did not allow the ship to sail, so the ship changed its registration to the Cook Islands and managed to sail on its first trip of the season on 20 December. Swan Hellenic's *Minerva* cancelled its first two cruises of the season because of mechanical problems. *Antarctic Dream* operated on two of its three engines much of December, cruising at as little as half its usual cruising speed. Also in December, Hurtigruten's *Fram* had an engine failure and was without power for about two hours while near Brown Bluff on the northern tip of the Antarctic Peninsula. It drifted into a towering wall of ice, bending a railing and completely crushing a lifeboat. Polar Cruises' *Corinthians 2* was delayed leaving Ushuaia in January 2009 because of problems with fuel, and in March 2009 Silversea Cruises' *Prince Albert II* had to alter its itinerary after a door was blown open at the front of the ship by the force of the seas in the early morning hours. Approximately 2 tonnes of seawater entered the ship. The door had no alarm, so it was fortunate that the fire patrol found the door open, with water spilling into the ship (Collins, 2009).

Polar cruising has other elements of unpredictability. In August 2008, Quark Expeditions' *Akademik Ioffe* was expected to end its journey in Resolute Bay, Canada, where passengers would disembark and take a flight to Ottawa. However, ice conditions did not allow for the crew's zodiac boats to take passengers from the ship to the community, so the ship continued on to Arctic Bay. A charter flight, expected to take the passengers to Ottawa from Arctic Bay, encountered mechanical problems and was grounded at the airport in Nanisivik while a mechanic and parts were flown in. Passengers were already ashore, so arrangements were made for them to overnight in Arctic Bay. The majority stayed in the gym, while others stayed in the 20-bed hotel or the 8-bed B&B. The ship had disembarked 97 passengers plus crew (Ryder, 2008). In January 2005, Semester at Sea's *Explorer* lost power in three of its four engines when a 15m wave broke bridge windows, damaged controls and injured two crew members. The ship was dead in the water in rough seas and in peril in the middle of nowhere – 1050km south of Adak in Alaska's Aleutian Islands, about 2090km south-west of Anchorage. Crew members were able to start a second engine and the ship 'limped' to Honolulu for needed repairs.

In addition to unpredictable problems, some ships appear to push their luck. *Prince Albert II* is operated by Silversea Cruises, an ultra-luxury cruise line. Keeping with the line's standards, dinner is served by white-gloved waiters and tables are adorned with lit candles. It is a classy touch, but appears to overlook the severe risk of an onboard fire, especially given the unstable sea conditions in waters near Antarctica. One crew member onboard the ship wrote to this author that it had been more than a decade since s/he had seen any cruise ship take the risk of an open flame, and management on the ship were deaf to concerns raised about the practice.

The increasing deployment of large cruise ships in polar regions is another case of pushing luck. Virtually none of these ships have ice-strengthened hulls. Although they tend to avoid shallow coastal areas, they cannot avoid severe weather or ice, and are particularly vulnerable if they suffer engine failure or other mechanical break-downs. Their thin-skinned hulls make them particularly vulnerable. As Jan Huber, the executive secretary of the Antarctic Treaty Secretariat in Buenos Aires warns: 'If they get into trouble they can't be rescued by off-loading their complement onto another ship' (Reynolds, 2009). It is unclear how passengers would be rescued if one of these giant leisure vessels, not equipped for the ice, got into trouble. *The Economist* cites officials in Chile and Argentina who worry about the risk of a fatal accident – a new *Titanic*, as they put it (*Economist*, 2009).

Safety of passengers

A separate issue from safety of the ship is the safety and security of passengers. Some concerns are common to all ships in polar regions, such as slips and falls associated with greater movement with rough sea conditions. However, other concerns appear to be a greater problem onboard larger cruise ships, which are less intimate and less like a small community than 100-passenger expedition-type cruise ships. Of particular worry are the problems of sexual assaults, passengers disappearing under mysterious circumstances and excessive alcohol consumption. As large cruise ships increase their presence in polar regions, the problems endemic to these ships also increase on polar cruises.

Sexual assaults were first acknowledged as a problem on cruise ships in the late 1990s (Frantz, 1998); but it wasn't until 2007 and US congressional hearings that the problem became widely known (Klein, 2008a, pp34–37). In June 2008, Senator John Kerry and Representative Doris Matsui introduced in both the US House and US Senate the Cruise Vessel Security and Safety Act of 2008. The legislation did not pass before the end of the year and was reintroduced in March 2009 as the Cruise Vessel Security and Safety Act of 2009.

Sadly, there is a stark contrast between industry claims that a cruise is the safest mode of transportation and the fact that a sexual assault is more likely to occur onboard a cruise ship than on land in Canada or the US – the US Federal Bureau of Investigation received 260 reports of sex-related crimes against Americans on cruise ships represented by the Cruise Lines International Association (CLIA) between 1 April 2007 and 31 April 2008 (Klein, 2009a). One problem is that sexual assaults occur. Another problem is the limited security onboard ships and often the absence of prosecution of perpetrators. The fact that cruise ships are foreign registered, mainly staffed by foreign nationals, and operate in international waters makes it difficult for crime victims to have the same legal remedies that are normally available on land. As well, incidents are often not made public, or are characterized as isolated exceptions or as statistically insignificant.

According to data received by this author in his role as an expert witness in cases involving sexual assaults on cruise ships, one cruise line alone had 451 sexual assaults between 1998 and 2005. The overwhelming majority – 77.2 per cent – were perpetrated by a crew member against a guest (13 per cent were guest against guest; 8.4 per cent were crew against crew; and 1.4 per cent were guest against crew). The victim of an assault was a minor in more than 17.5 per cent of incidents. Most frequently, the perpetrator was a service provider onboard (34.8 per cent of the cases involved a room steward, 25 per cent involved a waiter, and 13.2 per cent involved a bartender) and the most frequent location for an assault to occur was a passenger cabin (36.4 per cent); however, significant numbers of assaults occurred in crew areas, a bar or disco, the spa and public bathrooms (Klein, 2009b).

Attention to disappearances from cruise ships is also relatively recent. Although there were 47 disappearances from cruise ships reported between 1995 and 2004 (Cruise Junkie, 2009c), the issue didn't reach public interest until 2005 when George Allen Smith went missing from a Mediterranean cruise while on his honeymoon onboard Royal Caribbean's *Brilliance of the Seas*. His disappearance led to congressional hearings in December 2005 (Moewe, 2005) and the formation in early 2006 of the International Cruise Victims Association (Moewe, 2006).

Between 2005 and 2008, another 66 passengers and crew members disappeared from cruise ships – in some cases, the person was rescued alive; in others the disappearance was clearly suicide or was the result of an accident, but many remained mysterious. Alcohol was a factor in a fair number of suicides and accidents; large gambling losses were a factor in at least three cases; and an argument with a spouse or travelling companion preceded four incidents. There was a single case where one passenger was observed throwing another overboard. In September 2001, a 69-year-old woman was pushed overboard, as her husband watched, by a fellow passenger who was a former mental patient. They were on the third day of an 11-day cruise of Norway's fjords (Klein, 2008b).

It has already been noted that alcohol plays a role in a number of mysterious disappearances. Alcohol also plays a role in sexual assaults and other crimes (Lipcon, 2008, p60). In fact, following the death of Dianne Brimble from having a drink spiked with GHB (also known as fantasy, often referred to as a date rape drug) on a P&O Australia cruise in 2002 (Topham, 2006, pp68–72; Klein, 2008a, pp32–33), the cruise line came under pressure to better train crew members in the responsible serving of alcohol and to remove economic incentives to bartenders and waiters to serve more alcoholic drinks. Similar calls surfaced in North America and Europe following the death of Lynsey O'Brien, a 15-year-old girl who disappeared on 5 January 2006 from Costa Magica – she had apparently been served more than ten alcoholic drinks within a short timeframe and was so intoxicated that she fell overboard while vomiting over a balcony railing.

Sensitivity

Another issue for cruise ships visiting polar regions is sensitivity. Sensitivity has two main components: cultural sensitivity and sensitivity to wildlife and scenery. Put bluntly, cruise passengers need to be taught cultural sensitivity. They often visit far reaches of the world and expect people to have the same values and accoutrements that the passenger has at home. They are not malicious, often just naive. I recall a port call at Punta Arenas – the southernmost city in Chile – and taking a tour to a penguin rookery. Along the way, a passenger asked the tour guide whether children sold Chicklets (chewing gum) on street corners to make money. The passenger's insensitive question assumed a level of poverty and lifestyle that did not exist. On top of that, a group of other passengers complained most of the day about the tour guide's heavy accent. They failed to appreciate that he had stayed up the night before to write out his presentation in English so that it would be clear and complete. All that these passengers could concentrate on was that his English was not perfect.

Cruise passengers also frequently make assumptions based on misconceptions. A resident of Carcross, Yukon Territory, in Canada wrote to me saying that passengers he meets often assume his house has a dirt floor, no running water, an outhouse, and that children in the community are culturally and educationally deprived. He is more than happy to correct their misperceptions; but the need to do this becomes tiresome after the same questions are asked by thousands of passengers each year.

Attitudes such as these underlie the tendency for manufactured cruise destinations such as Hoonah, Icy Straits, in Alaska – a former cannery that has been rebuilt using public funds (Richtmyer, 2004) and then turned over to the local aboriginal community and leased for a nominal fee to the partnership that developed the port. In return for the several cruise ship visits a week, the port has agreed to refrain from ever implementing any tariffs, head taxes, tonnage or similar user fees or charges for the use of the dock facility (Point Sophia Development Company, 2001). The port is a money-maker for the local community (even though workers cannot be guaranteed full-time work during the cruise season, and there are reports of fighting in the community over division of jobs, with the person who is currently directing the operation accused of handing out positions to family and friends) so long as cruise ships continue to visit and local merchants are allowed to keep the money paid to them by cruise passengers. For cruise ships, it is an alternative to Alaska's other already congested ports. For cruise passengers, it is modern, clean and has most of what a passenger wants, including shopping, and it reflects the rustic and rugged north that they expect without them having to be uncomfortable. While most cruise passengers arriving at isolated areas on smaller expedition ships (with naturalists and guides) are prepared for what they find, those on large cruise ships are often unprepared.

What is required is not only sensitivity towards people, but sensitivity towards wildlife and scenery. On the trip to the penguin rookery mentioned above, passengers were told that many of the penguins were in their hovel with their young and could only be seen by looking in; passengers were explicitly told not to disturb the penguins and not to cross beyond ropes demarcating the underground tunnels. Regardless, within several minutes of arriving passengers were jumping up and down on top of hovels attempting to scare penguins out into the open. They had virtually no respect or sensitivity for nature.

Ship captains can be as bad as passengers. In late 2007, a video was posted on YouTube showing *Antarctic Dream* nosing up against a huge iceberg in order to make it calve. This involved not only risk to the ship, but also to the passengers who navigated alongside in zodiacs. They were shown in the video cheering as the ship caused large chunks to fall into the ocean. A passenger onboard wrote, when she sent me the link to the video: 'The iceberg thing was really scary for us. I feel this captain is overconfident around ice. Maybe this experience sobers him up a little bit. [But the company appears to] ... not have a clue about how the ship operates, how the forces of nature rule the cruise.'

Similar bad judgement has been reported in Disenchantment Bay, Alaska. Residents of Yakutat, Alaska, complained in 2001 about the impact of cruise ships upon Disenchantment Bay and the seal population. One local resident reported: 'I was up there when several ships were blasting their horns to try and make the glacier calf... It was quite a racket' (Sica, 2001). The noise also frightened mothers away from pups and chased seals from the safety of the bay. According to another resident: 'One time last summer I saw five or six pods of killer whales feeding on little seal pups... Without the protection of the ice floe they were prime targets' (Sica, 2001). It is obvious that cruise ships need to do a better job of educating passengers about local culture and about being respectful of both people and nature; but they also must be better at setting examples. Ramming icebergs with a ship or blasting a horn to cause icebergs to calve and thereby causing seal pups to fall into the water, unprotected, is inconsistent with viewing a natural environment.

The issue of carrying capacity

Despite the growth in cruise tourism to Antarctica, and concern expressed about environmental impacts, there appears to be little effort to limit the size and number of ships. The same is often true of the North. Some communities have recognized the problem of people pollution created by cruise ships, but these are not communities in polar regions (Baekkelund, 1999). Curson (2009) describes the problem, calling it pack behaviour:

> ... *almost as if all passengers were connected by a common behavioural umbilical cord, is the order of the day. Thousands disembark together, congregate in the terminal area, and then proceed through the city centre en masse, often producing more than a ripple of unease to run through the local population, who may well avoid the downtown area when large cruise ships are in.*

This occurs in most ports in Alaska that see 10,000 or more passengers a day in communities such as Skagway, with a population of less than 1000. The number of passengers exceeds the capacity of the town. As cruise tourism expands into the further reaches of polar regions, the problem of people pollution will no doubt surface.

The problem has already been recognized by some communities. Residents of Kodiak, Alaska, have expressed a desire to limit the number of cruise calls to between 15 and 30 per year, as well as the size of ships that visit – they do not want ships carrying 2000 or more passengers (Zint, 2009). The town of Tenakee Springs, Alaska, was more aggressive with its proclamation that cruise ship tourism is incompatible with the community's lifestyle, facilities and services. It vowed to take whatever steps necessary to prevent this type of tourism in the town. When the first cruise ship came to visit in August 1998, a small ship with only 120 passengers, the city tried to persuade the ship to cancel the visit. Failing that, cruise passengers were handed leaflets as they disembarked and were told that they were not welcome as part of a large organized tour, but to return on their own. Most businesses had closed during the visit (Zuckerman, 1999).

The Haida Nation in the Queen Charlotte Islands, British Columbia, similarly stopped cruise ship visits. For several years small cruise ships stopped at Gwaii Haanas National Park Reserve and Haida Heritage Site (a site co-managed by Parks Canada and the Council of the Haida Nation); however, given strict limits on the number of people allowed in the park at a time (i.e. carrying capacity), they realized that cruise tourists were displacing those who came to the area to camp and to stay for several days. Community leaders told this author during his participation in an Oceans Forum in January 2009 that it was, in part, a matter of treating land-based tourists fairly and, in part, recognition that economic impact is greater from those who stay for a while than from day-trippers arriving by cruise ship.

Economics of cruise tourism

There are two relevant issues regarding the economic relationship between ports and cruise ships. On the one hand, increased effort by cruise lines to generate onboard revenue has a negative impact upon the amount of money passengers have to spend ashore. On the other hand, ports are pressured to keep their fees low and local excursion providers often receive half or less of what passengers spend onboard for a land-based tour. While this has been a problem for ports in warmer climes, without attention to management and issues of sustainability it is likely to surface as well in polar regions, especially as large cruise ships increase their presence, particularly in North America with extended navigation of the Northwest Passage between the Atlantic and Pacific oceans. Larger ships pose different issues and economic dynamics than cruise ships accommodating 200 passengers or less.

Onboard revenue

A decline in onshore spending has been hastened in recent years by the cruise industry's greater emphasis on onboard spending as a core element of their profit. In 2006, the 'Big Three' cruise operators had combined net revenue of US$3.5 billion from onboard revenue. This translates into a profit of US$43 per passenger per day (more profit than generated from ticket sales) and constitutes 24 per cent of the total net revenue for all cruise companies combined; the percentage is significantly higher for the large US-based mass market cruise lines (Cramer, 2006). Cruise columnist Mary Lu Abbott wisely warned in November 2004 that extras can cost more than the cruise (Abbott, 2004).

Not only have prices increased for onboard purchases, but the number of onboard revenue centres has ballooned. Traditionally, a cruise ship made money from bars, casinos, a couple of small shops, and, beginning in the late 1990s, art auctions. Today, the number of shops has increased – the *Voyager of the Seas* has a four-storey tall shopping mall (the Royal Promenade) deep in the bowels, running a considerable length of the ship (Cochran, 2003). In addition, like others, it generates income from a range of sources, including rock climbing walls, bungee jumping platforms, golf simulators and ice-skating rinks. As well, there are virtual reality games, pay-per-view movies, in-room video games, yoga classes, fitness classes, wine-tasting events, culinary workshops, self-improvement classes, and art and craft classes. And it goes further. Most ships have ATMs, in-room mini bars and in-room gambling, and extra-tariff restaurants. The newest innovation in onboard revenue is ship tours, something that typically was provided free of charge. Princess Cruises, for example, offers visits to the galley, laundry, backstage in the theatre, the engine control room, print shop, photo lab, funnel and bridge for US$150 (Honeywell, 2009). One writer says of the *Voyager of the Seas*: 'The idea is to grab a larger slice of the vacation market by offering so many things to do and places to explore on board – so that even people who don't particularly care for sea cruises may want to go because the experience may not seem like they're on a ship' (Blake, 2003).

The prospect of hosting larger cruise ships that rely heavily on onboard revenue may appear economically attractive to ports in polar regions. However, the potential onshore income per passenger is likely to fall far short of expectations given the increasing focus of large cruise ships to extract as much onboard passenger spending as possible. There is comparatively less emphasis on onboard revenue on small expedition-type cruise ships.

Cruise ship–port economics

Ports are put under further pressure by cruise lines wanting to keep to a minimum the cost of using a port. Port fees in some places are as low as US$5 per passenger; in others, it is as high as US$60 per passenger. Given the investment needed to build and maintain a port, as well as the cost for local infrastructure to accommodate cruise passengers, it is important for ports to set per-passenger fees at a level that covers their expenses (Klein, 2009a). The State of Alaska, through its 2006 Cruise Ship Ballot Initiative, has gone so far as to charge a head tax of US$46 per passenger traversing Alaskan waters; it also taxes cruise ship profits from operating casinos while in state waters. The state is a role model for other ports that need to do better at capturing income from cruise visitors. Ports in polar regions have an opportunity, given the nascent form of cruise tourism in many towns and communities in the far North and South, to set port fees at adequate levels now rather than face opposition later when they attempt to raise them to levels that cover actual costs and need for future investment.

Another feature of the relationship between cruise ships and ports is the practice of a cruise ship retaining 50 per cent or more – in some cases as much as 90 per cent (Sandiford, 2003; CMC, 2007) – of what passengers pay onboard for a shore excursion. On most itineraries, between 50 per cent and 80 per cent of passengers buy an excursion in each port. The problem with the division of proceeds is that a passenger spending US$100 for an excursion expects a product worth US$100, but the shore excursion provider is in the uncomfortable position of being paid US$50 or less. Some tour providers find the split disconcerting, while others accept this as the price of doing business. Beth Kelly, who owns and runs Aquilla Tours in Saint John, New Brunswick, in Canada, says: 'the cruise industry brings in millions of dollars to the Canadian economy, so [I don't] mind when the cruise lines take up to half the money from each tour ticket sold on the ship' (CBC, 2003). However, disappointed passengers are likely to blame the port, not the cruise ship. Ports in polar regions, like elsewhere, need to ensure that local tour providers receive fair and equitable payment for the tours and services provided.

Port-based excursion providers are further marginalized by the terms of their contract with cruise lines. Carnival Cruise Lines' standard contract, for example, gives the cruise line the authority to refund the cost of an excursion to a passenger who complains and the ship charges the refund back to the excursion provider, even if the complaint is unfounded. Furthermore, the provider is only paid for tickets collected from passengers. This means that the cruise line keeps all monies, even when a passenger loses their ticket and is allowed on the shore excursion anyway or when a passenger is a no-show.

It is important for ports to keep in mind that cruise tourism is big business. Carnival Corporation, which controls more than 50 per cent of the industry, earned more than US$2.2 billion in net profit each year from 2006 to 2009. Ports need to ensure that they get their fair share given that most passengers, especially on polar cruises, are there for the sites and the ports. In addition, ports in polar regions need to be cautious in making investments to improve port facilities so that large cruise ships can berth. They need to be sure to accrue adequate income to cover their investment. A lesson can be learned from the aboriginal community in Campbell River, British Columbia. The community invested CA$14 million on a new cruise terminal and necessary infrastructure, only to find that no large cruise ships came (despite assurances that they would when plans for the terminal were initially discussed). The main problem is that ocean currents make it difficult for large cruise ships to enter the harbour (Klein, 2008a, p119).

The cruise ship virus

Ports must also be cognizant of health issues related to cruise tourism. Norovirus outbreaks on cruise ships have become so frequent that it is often referred to as 'the cruise ship virus'. Norovirus causes gastrointestinal illness lasting 24 to 60 hours. It is highly contagious and as few as ten viral particles may be sufficient to infect an individual. There is no known immunity to becoming ill after coming in contact with the virus. Given the genetic variability of noroviruses, individuals can be repeatedly infected. But this may not be totally random. Recent findings suggest that people with blood type O are more susceptible than others (CDC, 2007). As well, research reported in 2003 found that 29 per cent of a study population lacked the gene required for norovirus binding – they did not become infected after receiving a dose of the virus (Lindesmith, 2003).

The illness has caused some ports to refuse passengers to disembark. Spain shut its border with the British colony of Gibraltar for the first time in two decades on 3 November 2003 when *Aurora* arrived in Gibraltar's harbour with 600 sick passengers. Those who were judged to be healthy were allowed to disembark in Gibraltar, but the frontier to Spain was closed and their travel severely restricted. The same passengers were forced to stay onboard while the ship took on supplies at Piraeus, in Athens, three days earlier because local authorities there would not allow them to disembark. *Aurora*'s sister ship *Oceana*, a year earlier, was denied permission to dock at Philipsburg, St Maarten, because 269 passengers and 24 crew members had contracted a stomach illness. The incident came a day after four people working in St Lucia's tourism industry reported stomach illness after meeting visitors when the ship docked there two days before (Hokstam, 2002).

Concern about spread of illness is particularly salient for small communities in the polar regions visited by cruise ships, especially those in remote areas that are not normally exposed to illnesses commonly found in more populated areas of the world. Ports need to be attentive to the problem and to the risks posed to their population, especially given the virulent nature of norovirus. In addition, influenza outbreaks on cruise ships have been a problem in the past (Klein, 2003, p73) and raise their own concerns for small town ports in polar regions.

Cruises and bruises

While cruise tourism provides wonderful opportunities for passengers and ports alike, there are sustainability issues that need to be considered. Accidents at sea and onboard crime have impacts upon the attractiveness of a cruise vacation, and directly affect potential growth. However, a larger concern for cruising in polar regions is the huge growth in the number of large cruise ships, many of which are not constructed for ice and weather conditions found in these areas. There have been no serious accidents yet; but the risk is ever present and should one occur it will potentially have a devastating impact upon the growth of cruise tourism in the region, not to mention serious impacts upon the environment. Passengers need to be concerned about safety and security, and to be aware of the unique qualities of polar regions so that they can choose a cruise ship which is safe and one which allows them to see all that polar cruising has to offer. It may be that the best way to see and experience polar regions is on smaller cruise ships that provide naturalists and educational programmes designed to increase passenger awareness and sensitivity.

Policy-makers and port cities also need to be attuned to the problem of accidents. In addition, they need to focus on the economics of cruise tourism in order to ensure that they receive an equitable share of revenues and cover their costs for port facilities and infrastructure needed for cruise ships. This is a critical issue for the sustainability of cruise tourism in polar regions. If ports are unable to realize economic returns covering their capital costs and yielding reasonable income to local merchants, vendors and tour providers, then cruise tourism is likely to be a drain on the community and short lived. Ports need to recognize their value as a tourism product and to generate income commensurate with their value. While cruise lines have an interest in keeping their costs low, ports have an interest in keeping their income as high as possible, both to ensure the sustainability of cruise tourism and that the local economy fully benefits. A related element in ensuring sustainability is to have a realistic idea of the carrying capacity of a port such that all visitors have a high-quality and positive experience. A port should not be lured into landing more cruise passengers than can be comfortably accommodated.

Another sustainability issue is the need for port cities and health officials to protect citizens from the risk of illness spread by passengers. Cruise ships have had outbreaks of norovirus and influenza, both of which can have disastrous impacts upon a small polar community. The risk was illustrated in mid 2009 when the swine flu broke out on two cruise ships in Australia and returning passengers brought the illness ashore. At one point, a returning cruise ship was quarantined in Sydney (*Herald Sun*, 2009), and New Caledonia refused a scheduled cruise ship visit (ABC News, 2009; *Australian*, 2009). As stated earlier, similar closing of ports has occurred as a result of norovirus. While such closures have occurred outside polar regions, they should be instructive to communities and ports welcoming polar cruises.

In summary, ports in polar regions must ensure that cruise tourism is and remains sustainable. This means making certain that growth is consistent with local capacity for providing a positive visitor experience, and that income is fair, equitable and adequate for continued growth and expansion; and taking steps to guarantee the safety and health of local citizens. These are concerns over which local communities need to take full responsibility, avoiding the temptation to allow cruise lines, which have an economic interest in port calls, to make decisions that are the port's to make alone. Ports need to look out for their own best interests, both short and long term.

References

Abbott, M. L. (2004) 'Extras can cost more than the cruise', *New Orleans Times-Pacayune*, 7 November, www.nola.com/printer/printer.ssf?/base/living-0/109981480177200.xml, accessed 7 November 2004

ABC News (2009) 'Cruise ship turned away amid flu fears', *ABC News*, 2 June, www.abc.net. au/news/stories/2009/06/02/2586888.htm, accessed 2 June 2009

Australian (2009) 'Cruise ship *Pacific Dawn* quarantined near Cairns over swine flu', *The Australian*, www.theaustralian.news.com.au/story/0,25197,25546377-601,00.html, accessed 27 May 2009

Baekkelund, A. (1999) 'Solving the people pollution problem', *Seatrade Cruise Review*, December, p61

Batty, D. and Orr, J. (2007) 'Safety questions over doomed Antarctica cruise ship', *The Guardian*, 23 November, www.guardian.co.uk/world/2007/nov/23/antarctica, accessed 23 November 2007

Berglund, N. (2007) 'Limits put on Arctic cruises', *Aftenpost*, 6 June, www.aftenposten.no/ english/local/article1818931.ece?service=print, accessed 8 March 2009

Berglund, N. (2008) 'Cruiseship refloated east of Spitsbergen', *Aftenpost*, 23 July, www. aftenposten.no/english/local/article2556075.ece, accessed 24 July 2008

Blake, S. (2003) '"Megaship" set to sail', *Florida Today*, 11 November, www.floridatoday.com, accessed 11 November 2003

Canadian Press (2007) 'Canadian cruise ship sinks in Antarctica', *Toronto Star*, 23 November, www.thestar.com/News/article/279244, accessed 23 November 2007

CBC (Canadian Broadcasting Corporation) (2003) 'Cruise ship passengers leave cash onboard', *CBC.CA News* (Saint John, NB), 19 March

CDC (Centres for Disease Control) (2007) 'Norovirus: technical fact sheet', Centres for Disease Control, Atlanta, www.cdc.gov/ncidod/dvrd/revb/gastro/norovirus-factsheet. htm, accessed 12 November 2007

CLIA (Cruise Lines International Association) (2009) *2008 CLIA Cruise Market Overview: Statistical Cruise Industry Data Through 2007*, Cruise Lines International Association, Fort Lauderdale, cruising.org/Press/overview2008/#cruiseCapicity, accessed 8 March 2009

CMC (2007) 'Beache warns that islands need united approach to cruise tourism', *CBC Barbados,* 23 October, www.cbc.bb/content/view/13018/45, accessed 23 October 2007

Cochran, J. (2003) 'The ship hits the fans', *MSNBC,* 24 November, www.msnbc.com/m/pt/printthis_main.asp?storyID=995770, accessed 24 November 2003

Collins, C. (2009) *Day 8, March 4, 2009, At Sea* (Online blog from ship), www.silversea.com/silversea.aspx?id=1584&page_id=princealbertII, accessed 4 March 2009

Cramer, K. (2006) 'The art of piracy', *Broward–Palm Beach New Times,* 9 November, www.browardpalmbeach.com/2006-11-09/news/the-art-ofpiracy, accessed 9 November 2006

Cruise Europe News (2002) 'Cruise Europe's port statistics 2000, 2001, and 2002', *Cruise Europe News,* vol 9, no 4, pp 6–7

Cruise Europe News (2008) 'Cruise Europe's port statistics for 2006–2008', *Cruise Europe News,* vol 14, no 4, pp6–7

Cruise Junkie (2009a) *Reported Incidents of Ships Sinking, 1979–2007,* www.cruisejunkie.com/Overboard.html, accessed 2 March 2009

Cruise Junkie (2009b) *Reported Incidents of Passenger Ships Running Aground, 1972–2008,* www.cruisejunkie.com/Overboard.html, accessed 2 March 2009

Cruise Junkie (2009c) *Cruise and Ferry Passengers and Crew Overboard, 1995–2009,* www.cruisejunkie.com/Overboard.html, accessed 2 March 2009

Curson, P. (2009) 'When fantasy cruises run aground on reality', *New Zealand Herald,* 3 February, www.nzherald.co.nz/travel/news/article.cfm?c_id=7&objectid=10554816, accessed 3 February 2009

Economist (2009) 'Waiting for another Titanic', *The Economist,* 12 February, www.economist.com/world/americas/displaystory.cfm?story_id=13110412, accessed 12 February 2009

Foreign and Commonwealth Office (2009) *Tourism in Antarctica,* Foreign and Commonwealth Office, London, www.fco.gov.uk/en/fco-in-action/global-network/antarctica/visitors, accessed 8 March 2009

Frantz, D. (1998) 'On cruise ships, silence shrouds crimes', *New York Times,* 16 November, www.nytimes.com/library/national/111698cruise-ship-crime.html, accessed 14 July 1999

Ganesh, N. (2009) 'The lure of Antarctica', *The Times of India,* 15 March, timesofindia.indiatimes.com/Sunday-TOI/The-lure-of-Antarctica/articleshow/4265654.cms, accessed 15 March 2009

Geitz, M. (2004) *Cruise Tourism on Svalbard: A Risky Business?,* WWF International Arctic Programme, Oslo

Herald Sun (2009) 'Cruise ship quarantined amid swine flu scare', *Herald Sun,* 23 May, www.news.com.au/heraldsun/story/0,21985,25527895-5005961,00.html, accessed 23 May 2009

Higgins, M. (2009) 'Is Antartica getting too popular?', *New York Times,* 22 March, www.nytimes.com/2009/03/22/travel/22pracantarctic.html?_r=1&ref=travel, accessed 22 March 2009

Hokstam, M. (2002) 'Cruise ship with sick passengers abandons visit to St. Maarten', *Miami Herald,* 10 December, www.miami.com, accessed 15 December 2002

Honeywell, J. (2009) 'Pay up for a view from the bridge', *Daily Mirror,* 11 February, blogs.mirror.co.uk/captain-greybeard/2009/02/pay-up-for-a-view-from-the-bri.html, accessed 11 February 2009

IAATO (International Association of Antarctica Tour Operators) (2008) *2007–2008 Summary of Seabourne, Airborne, Land-Based Antarctic Tourism*, International Association of Antarctica Tour Operators, Providence, RI, www.iaato.org/tourism_stats.html, accessed 8 March 2009

Klein, R. A. (2003) *Cruise Ship Blues: The Underside of the Cruise Industry*, New Society, Gabriola Island, British Columbia

Klein, R. A. (2008a) *Paradise Lost at Sea: Rethinking Cruise Vacations*, Fernwood, Halifax, Nova Scotia

Klein, R. A. (2008b) *Testimony of Ross A. Klein Before the Subcommittee on Surface Transportation and Merchant Marine Infrastructure, Safety, and Security Senate Committee on Commerce, Science, and Transportation, Hearings on 'Cruise Ship Safety: Examining Potential Steps for Keeping Americans Safe at Sea'*, 19 June, commerce.senate.gov/public/_files/SenateTestimonyKlein.pdf, accessed 20 June 2009

Klein, R. A. (2009a) *Cruising without a Bruising: Cruise Tourism and the Maritimes*, Canadian Centre for Policy Alternatives, Halifax, Nova Scotia

Klein, R. A. (2009b) *Analysis of Reports of Sexual Harassment and Sexual Assault on Royal Caribbean International*, www.cruisejunkie.com/SA-RCI.html, accessed 2 March 2009

Lindesmith, L. (2003) 'Human susceptibility and resistance to Norwalk virus infection', *Nature Medicine*, vol 9, no 5, May, pp548–553

Lipcon, C. R. (2008) *Unsafe on the High Seas*, I. Adels Inc, Miami, FL

Merco Press (2003) 'Marco Polo in Antarctic emergency', *Merco Press*, 19 February, received via e-mail 19 February 2003

Moewe, M. C. (2005) 'Congress reviews cruises', *Jacksonville Business Journal*, 16 December, jacksonville.bizjournals.com/jacksonville/stories/2005/12/19/story1.html, accessed 17 December 2005

Moewe, M. C. (2006) 'Families of missing cruise passengers form group', *Jacksonville Business Journal*, 13 January, jacksonville.bizjournals.com/jacksonville/stories/2006/01/16/story7.html, accessed 14 January 2006

NTSB (National Transportation Safety Board) (1997) *Grounding of the Liberian Passenger Ship Star Princess on Poundstone Rock, Lynn Canal, Alaska June 23, 1995*, NTSB/MAR-97-02, National Transportation Safety Board, Washington, DC

NTSB (2004) *Grounding and Sinking of US Passenger Vessel Safari Spirit Kisameet Bay off Fisher Channel, about 20 Miles Southeast of the Towns of Bella Bella and Shearwater, Denny Island, British Columbia, Canada on May 8, 2003*, NTSB Report Number MAB-04-01, National Transportation Safety Board, Washington, DC

Point Sophia Development Company (2001) *Proposal for Planning, Development, Financing and Construction of a Large Vessel Marine Berthing Facility at Hoonah, Alaska*, Point Sophia Development Company, 10 October 2001

Reynolds, R. (2009) 'Tourists on icy voyage sail into perilous waters', *Sydney Morning Herald*, 7 March, www.smh.com.au/world/tourists-on-icy-voyage-sail-into-perilous-waters-20090306-8re0.html?page=-1, accessed 6 March 2009

Richtmyer, R. (2004) 'State development agency approves tourism grant for Hoonah, Alaska', *Miami Herald*, 8 April, www.miami.com, accessed 9 April 2004

Ryder, K. (2008) 'Cruise passengers sleep in gym', *Northern News Services*, 11 August, nnsl.com/northern-news-services/stories/papers/aug11_08cs.html, accessed 12 August 2008

Sandiford, K. (2003) 'Port authority: Carrying the wallets of thousands of fun seekers, the cruise industry receives a warm welcome from the theme park named Halifax', *The Coast*, 14–21 August, www.thecoast.ca/archives/140803/feature.html, accessed 22 August 2003

Sica, M. (2001) 'Yakutat may protest over ships, seals', *Juneau Empire*, 29 January, www.juneauempire.com, accessed 30 January 2001

Tisdall, J. (2007) 'MS Nordkapp aground', *Aftenposten*, 31 January, www.aftenposten.no/
    english/world/article1623435.ece, accessed 1 February, 2007

Topham, G. (2006) *Overboard: The Stories Cruise Lines Don't Want Told*, Random House
    Australia, Sydney

TSB (Transport Safety Board of Canada) (1996) *Grounding - Passenger vessel 'Hanseatic',
    Simpson Strait, Northwest Territories, 29 August 1996*, Report Number M96H0016,
    Transport Safety Board of Canada, Ottawa, www.bst.gc.ca/eng/rapports-reports/
    marine/1996/m96h0016/m96h0016.asp, accessed 9 March 2009

Zint, B. (2009) 'Survey shows desire for fewer cruise ships', *Kodiak Daily Mirror*, 13 February,
    www.kodiakdailymirror.com/?pid=19&id=7254, accessed 13 February 2009

Zuckerman, S. (1999) 'Come again, but leave your tour at home', *Tidepool Archives*,
    6 October, www.tidepool.org, accessed 20 October 1999

Exploring the Ethical Standards of Alaska Cruise Ship Tourists and the Role they Inadvertently Play in the Unsustainable Practices of the Cruise Ship Industry

Valerie Sheppard

Introduction

Although there has been considerable research and a literary deluge on the topic of sustainable tourism, the practical application of sustainable concepts in the tourism industry is not widely evident (Wheeler, 1993). Perhaps this is due, in part, to the fact that two key pieces of the sustainability puzzle appear to have received scant attention by researchers. One is the role that tourists currently play in the sustainability of the industry and the role that they will need to play in the future. Two is the role of ethics and ethical behaviour on the part of tourists in the implementation of a more sustainable industry.

Research conducted by Sheppard (2005), examining the ethical standards of cruise ship tourists, forms the basis of this chapter and was an attempt to begin examining these two important puzzle pieces. Alaska was chosen as a case study for a number of reasons. First, the cruise ship industry has had an ongoing tumultuous relationship with the residents of Alaska – the relationship having been tested over the years by resident protests, environmental legislation, cruise ship taxes and, in September 2009, a lawsuit filed by the Alaska Cruise Association, challenging the legality of the state's US$50 head tax. Second, Alaska, often billed as *the last frontier*, is experiencing climate change at a more rapid pace than other non-polar regions of the world due to the amplification of temperature change in polar regions (Wendler and Shulski, 2008). Consequently, the very elements of Alaska's natural environment that attract visitors are being threatened by rising temperatures, of which human activities are an acknowledged contributor. Third, the cruise ship industry has experienced astounding growth in Alaska since the first steamship of tourists arrived in Alaska in 1884 (Alaska Department of Environmental Conservation, 2004). The combination of these three elements combines to make this an interesting case study.

Overall, it was anticipated that this research would provide valuable information about the role that a segment of tourists play in the current business practices of the tourism industry and what role they will be required to play in the future. As the tourism industry moves forward with the implementation of more sustainable business practices, it is further anticipated that this research will, hopefully, assist communities, educators, governmental and non-governmental agencies, the tourism industry, and specifically the cruise ship industry understand how best to ensure tourist buy-in and participation in sustainability programmes and practices: a cornerstone in the foundation for a more sustainable industry.

Background to the study

Since 1990, the global cruise industry has experienced an impressive growth rate of 7.4 per cent per annum (CLIA, 2009). Despite the challenges that have faced other sectors of the tourism industry over the last few years, such as terrorism, health-related issues and the global financial challenge of 2008/2009, the cruise market potential remains strong, with 51 million North Americans indicating an intent to cruise in the next three years (CLIA, 2009). In Alaska, the industry's growth patterns have mimicked those of the global market. Between 2001 and 2007, cruise passenger volume increased by an incredible 49 per cent. The geographical location and accessibility challenges of Alaska make cruising a popular mode of travel to and from the state. Not surprisingly, nearly half (49 per cent) of all visitors to the state arrived by a cruise ship in 2007 (McDowell Group, 2007). The success of the cruise ship industry has, however, frequently been overshadowed by the fact that it has been fined millions of dollars for environmental offences (Klein, 2002). And while the North American cruise ship industry has slowly been making improvements to its environmental practices, commissioning the construction and the retrofitting of ships with technological advancements, most of these changes have come about because of the continued pressure of environmental groups and scientists.

Globally, the International Convention for the Prevention of Marine Pollution from Ships, or the MARPOL regulations, is the overriding international convention that regulates the operational and accidental pollution of marine environments by all ships, including cruise ships. The International Maritime Organization (IMO), which is an offshoot of the United Nations, is the governing body under which the MARPOL convention falls. Violations to the MARPOL convention are punishable by either the flag state in which the ship is registered, or by the jurisdiction in which the offence occurs (IMO, 1997).

There are currently six annexes to the MARPOL regulations which prevent the discharge of oil, noxious liquid substances in bulk, synthetic ropes and fishing nets, and plastics, while regulating where treated and untreated sewage as well as food waste and garbage (including glass, metal, crockery, paper products, rags and similar-type refuse) can be discharged at sea. In 2005, Annex VI began regulating the discharge of sulphur oxide and nitrogen oxide emissions from ship engines and made it illegal to purposefully discharge emissions known to deplete the ozone layer. And while cruise ships continue to be fined for violations (at the time of writing, 50 fines are pending in Alaska for the operating season of 2008), ongoing amendments to the annexes are strengthening the protection of the marine environment and progressively broadening the scope of the MARPOL regulations (IMO, 2009). Despite the existence of the MARPOL regulations and the environmental record of the cruise ship industry, most jurisdictions have not sought to enforce the MARPOL convention. Alaska, however, is one jurisdiction that has actually enforced and gone beyond MARPOL, developing its own regulations for marine vessels operating in Alaskan waters, including cruise ships.

Alaskan people have what can only be classified as a love–hate relationship with the cruise ship industry: loving the tourists who come to hopefully spend their tourism dollars, but hating the impact of so many ships and so many tourists converging on their small communities (Klein, 2002). In response to a number of environmental foulings in Alaskan waters in the 1990s, the Alaska Department of Environmental Conservation (ADEC) initiated a public forum in 1999. The ADEC forum brought together various stakeholders, including the US Coast Guard, the US Environmental Protection Agency, concerned citizens and industry representatives. The purpose of the forum was to examine the cruise ship industry's waste management and disposal practices while in Alaskan waters. The work of the ADEC forum, which became known as the Alaska Cruise Ship Initiative (ACSI), culminated in the passage of cruise ship legislation that prohibited the discharge of untreated sewage in Alaskan waters and eventually set in place the first regional legislation to control cruise ship waste disposal practices and cruise ship air emissions.

In 2001, further legislation was passed entitled the Commercial Passenger Vessel Environmental Compliance Programme, which mandated the monitoring and testing of wastewater and air opacity readings of cruise ships in Alaskan waters. What was most progressive about this piece of legislation was that the implementation of the legislation and monitoring of marine vessels was financed through a US$1 per passenger levy on all ships travelling to or passing through Alaskan waters. In 2006, the fee was increased to US$50 per passenger, which now includes a US$4 per passenger fee to run the state's environmental monitoring programme, and a US$46 per passenger tax to provide infrastructure and programme benefits to Alaska's residents (Bluemink, 2009).

Research methodology

As previously mentioned, this research sought to better understand the role that tourists currently play in inadvertently supporting the environmental practices of the cruise ship industry and to better understand how tourists can and should contribute to the sustainability of the industry in the future. To answer these questions, this research employed Reidenbach and Robin's (1990) Multidimensional Ethics Scale (MES) in order to measure the ethical standards of Alaskan cruise ship passengers. Additional questions concerning the MARPOL regulations were included in the survey instrument in order to provide an understanding of the respondent's level of acceptance of the environmental practices of the industry. Other questions were built into the survey to provide an understanding of whether the respondents believed that they and/or the cruise industry have an ethical responsibility to lessen their impact upon the environment, while other questions provided an understanding of who the respondents believe should pay for improved practices.

The MES was designed to measure an individual's ethical opinion, which is influenced by, amongst other factors, individual values, experiences and comprehension ability (Reidenbach et al, 1995). Although some researchers such as Hansen (1992), Skipper and Hyman (1993) and Sheppard and Fennell (2009) have taken issue with various aspects of the design of the MES, the scale has been validated and utilized in a variety of applications by researchers such as Cohen et al (1993), Fennell and Malloy (1999), Loo (2004) and Sheppard (2005). While Fennell and Malloy (1999) used the MES to measure the ethical nature of tourism, and Hudson and Miller (2005) used the scale to look at the ethical nature of tourism students, it appears that the MES had never, until this research in 2004, been employed to examine the ethical nature of tourists.

The development of the MES came about when researchers began to take an interest in investigating how marketing could be enhanced through corporate social responsibility (Maignan, 2001). Robin and Reidenbach (1987) are perhaps two of the earliest researchers to conceptualize corporate social responsibility with the development of their Multidimensional Ethics Scale. Robin and Reidenbach's (1987) approach sought to develop a methodology that would permit the combination of the concepts of social responsibility and ethics into the marketing strategies of corporations. In particular, the scale was developed in an attempt to measure the ethical nature of individuals undertaking the survey (Reidenbach and Robin, 1988).

Reidenbach and Robin (1990) developed the MES through a series of steps which involved an examination of contemporary normative moral philosophies. After several refinements, a seven-point, eight-item list of items was designed, reflecting normative moral philosophy (see Figure 6.1). The design of the MES also included three scenarios that were reflective of normal business practices, but which required the respondent to make a judgement on the behaviour reflected within the scenario. After reading each of the scenarios, respondents were required to rate the behaviour of the individual in the scenario using the bipolar scale. Based on an analysis of the respondents' answers, the researchers were then able to determine which ethical theories the respondents had utilized in their analysis of the behaviour outlined in

Fair	*1* 2 *3* 4 *5*	Unfair
Just	*1* 2 *3* 4 *5*	Unjust
Morally right	*1* 2 *3* 4 *5*	Not morally right
Acceptable to my family	*1* 2 *3* 4 *5*	Not acceptable to my family
Traditionally acceptable	*1* 2 *3* 4 *5*	Traditionally unacceptable
Culturally acceptable	*1* 2 *3* 4 *5*	Culturally unacceptable
Does not violate an unspoken promise	*1* 2 *3* 4 *5*	Violates an unspoken promise
Does not violate an unwritten contract	*1* 2 *3* 4 *5*	Violates an unwritten contract
Ethical	*1* 2 *3* 4 *5*	Unethical

Figure 6.1 *Multidimensional Ethics Scale (MES) word pairings used in this research*
Source: adapted from Reidenbach and Robin (1990)

the scenario and, consequently, the ethical nature or standards of the respondents. While this research employed the MES as designed by Reidenbach and Robin (1990), a number of design changes were made based on the results of a pre-testing of the instrument. Following in the footsteps of preceding tests of the MES, this research employed a new scenario that was reflective of cruise ship industry practices and was thought to be of relevance to the respondents:[1]

> *Although all ships can **legally** discharge garbage 12 miles out to sea, it is **against** the law for ships to discharge plastic items anywhere at sea. On a large cruise ship, there are glass and plastic recycling bins located around the pool area for passengers to use. On this same ship, employees usually discharge most of the ship's garbage 12 miles out to sea, including the items from the plastic and glass recycling bins. This is done to save time and the cost of offloading the garbage on shore.*

> *Action:*
> *The captain of the ship is aware of his employees' actions, but has done nothing to stop such practices. Your response to the **captain's** action is that it is...* (Sheppard, 2005)

The bipolar scale was modified so that all positive statements now appeared on the left-hand side of the MES scale, and the bipolar scale was reduced from a seven-point to a five-point scale. Respondents were asked to read the scenario and then, based upon the captain's action in the scenario, to rate nine pairings of words on a five-point bipolar scale (as shown in Figure 6.1). An eighth pairing was added to the bipolar scale: ethical/unethical. Respondents' answers to each of the nine pairings were then summed to provide an understanding of the ethical nature of respondents, as it related to their opinions of the captain's behaviour in the scenario.

In addition to the MES section, the questionnaire contained questions that were related to the MARPOL regulations. This section of the questionnaire contained four statements that required the respondent to choose one response from the following choices: acceptable, slightly acceptable, slightly unacceptable, or unacceptable. The intention of this section of the questionnaire was to discover the level of respondent acceptance, or non-acceptance, in relation to the environmental practices of the cruise ship industry, as defined within the boundaries of the MARPOL regulations. Specifically, the statements informed respondents that ships are within their legal rights to discharge garbage, treated and untreated sewage, and food waste at sea, as long as certain distance requirements for discharge are abided by. Each of the statements required respondents to indicate how acceptable or unacceptable the cruise ship practice of discharging garbage and sewage at sea was to the respondent.

Findings

Overall, the results of the research indicated that the respondents found the environmental practices of the cruise ship industry, as defined within the MARPOL regulations, to be unacceptable. However, the majority of respondents indicated that the environmental practices of the cruise ship industry were ethical or somewhat ethical. One of the most interesting findings of the research was the significant negative correlation between the number of cruises taken by the sample of respondents and their responses on some of the MARPOL and MES statements. Specifically, the more cruises the respondents had been on, the significantly more acceptable they found the discharge of garbage, untreated sewage and food waste at sea. Similarly, the more cruises the respondents had been on, the significantly more acceptable they found the actions of the captain in the MES scenario. In other words, the ethical standards that respondents used to rate the captain's action in the scenario appeared to lessen in relation to increasing number of cruises. However, it was encouraging to see that an overwhelming majority of respondents felt that cruise lines and tourists are ethically responsible to lower their impact upon the natural environment and that both the cruise line and passengers should bear the costs of improvements to the environmental practices of the industry. The following paragraphs will provide

Figure 6.2 *Map of Alaska*

Source: Anchorage.net, www.anchorage.net/library/akmap.gif, accessed 28 September 2009

more details on the significant and interesting findings of the research, followed by a discussion of the results.

The instrument was self-administered by respondents who self-identified themselves as being a passenger on a cruise ship in port at one of two data collection sites: Skagway or Juneau, Alaska (see Figure 6.2). The survey was administered from 19 to 30 August 2004. A total of 237 people responded to the survey, while 110 refused, resulting in a participation rate of 68.3 per cent. An analysis of the data revealed that the average respondent in the research was an employed American female, 51 years old, urban dwelling, with an education beyond the high school level.

As previously mentioned, one of the sections of the questionnaire contained four statements related to the MARPOL regulations. Each of the statements required respondents to indicate how acceptable or unacceptable they found the cruise ship practice of discharging garbage and sewage at sea. Specifically, statement number one related to the discharge of garbage at sea. As indicated by Table 6.1, the discharge of garbage at sea was unacceptable to 64.1 per cent of respondents and slightly unacceptable to a further 12.6 per cent of respondents. Statement number two related to the discharge of untreated sewage at sea. Overall, this practice was found to be unacceptable by 69.7 per cent of respondents and slightly unacceptable by a further 15.6 per cent of respondents. Statement number three related to the discharge of food waste at sea. The discharge of food waste at sea was unacceptable to 42.9 per cent of respondents and slightly unacceptable to a further 20.8 per cent of respondents. The fourth statement related to the practice of discharging treated sewage 6.4km from shore. Table 6.1 illustrates that 55.8 per cent of respondents found the practice unacceptable and a further 18.6 per cent of respondents found it to be slightly unacceptable.

Table 6.1 *Responses to MARPOL statements*

Response	*Discharging garbage 12 miles (19.3km) from land is ...*		*Discharging untreated sewage 12 miles (19.3km) from land is ...*		*Discharging food waste 12 miles (19.3km) from land is ...*		*Discharging treated sewage 4 miles (6.4km) from land is ...*	
	N	%	N	%	N	%	N	%
Acceptable	16	6.9	9	3.9	35	15.2	22	9.5
Slightly acceptable	38	16.5	25	10.8	49	21.2	37	16.0
Slightly unacceptable	29	12.6	36	15.6	48	20.8	43	18.6
Unacceptable	148	64.1	161	69.7	99	42.9	129	55.8

Notes: N = number responding.

%   = percentage of valid responses.

Source: Sheppard (2005)

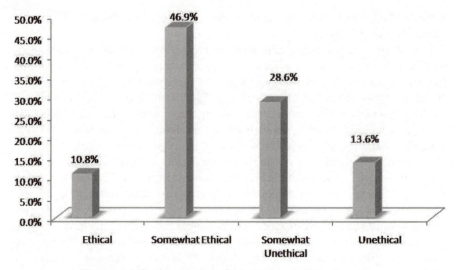

Figure 6.3 *Response to: 'Overall I find the environmental practices of the cruise ship industry to be ...' (N = 213)*

Source: Sheppard (2005)

Another question in the survey required respondents to react to the following statement: 'Overall, I find the environmental practices of the cruise ship industry to be ...' This question followed the four MARPOL statements. Respondents were indicating how ethical or unethical they found the practices of the industry based upon the information provided in the preceding section of the questionnaire. The respondents had a choice of four responses: ethical, somewhat ethical, somewhat unethical and unethical. Overall, 10.8 per cent of respondents felt that the environmental practices of the industry were ethical, 46.9 per cent felt the practices were somewhat ethical, 28.6 per cent of respondents found the practices were somewhat unethical, and 13.6 per cent of respondents felt the practices were unethical (see Figure 6.3).

As previously mentioned, there was a significant negative correlation between the number of cruises and respondents' answers on three of the MARPOL statements in the questionnaire. Specifically, there was a significant negative correlation between the number of cruises and the level of acceptance of the discharge of garbage, untreated sewage and food waste, but no significant correlation was found between the number of cruises and the level of acceptance regarding the discharge of treated sewage. In other words, the more cruises the respondent had taken, the more acceptable the respondent found the practice of discharging garbage, untreated sewage and food waste at sea. The correlation between number of cruises and how acceptable the respondent found the discharge of garbage was significant: $r\,(225) = -0.212$, $p < 0.01$. The correlation between the number of cruises and how acceptable the respondent found the discharge of untreated sewage was significant: $r\,(225) = -0.181$, $p < 0.01$. The correlation between number of cruises and how acceptable the discharge of food waste was to the respondents was significant: $r\,(225) = -0.148$, $p < 0.05$.

Table 6.2 *MES response percentages*

MES categories	Valid percentage responding (N = 98)				
	I	2	3	4	5
Fair/unfair	3.1	3.1	21.4	34.7	37.8
Just/unjust	3.1	3.1	18.4	35.7	39.8
Morally right/not morally right	2.0	3.1	12.2	28.6	54.1
Acceptable/unacceptable to my family	1.0	4.1	22.4	34.7	37.8
Traditionally acceptable/ unacceptable	7.1	10.2	39.8	32.7	10.2
Culturally acceptable/unacceptable	3.1	6.1	38.8	29.6	22.4
Violates/does not violate unspoken promise	3.1	7.1	21.4	35.7	32.7
Violates/does not violate unwritten contract	4.1	9.2	28.6	25.5	32.7
Ethical/unethical	0	7.1	14.3	31.6	46.9

Notes: responses: 1 = ethical; 2 = somewhat ethical; 3 = neither ethical/or unethical; 4 = somewhat unethical; 5 = unethical.

Source: Sheppard (2005)

As discussed in Sheppard and Fennell (2009), some of the respondents experienced difficulty in responding to the MES section of the questionnaire. In total, 19.8 per cent of respondents did not respond in part or in whole to the MES section and the data of these respondents was removed before analysis. Additionally, 36.7 per cent of respondents chose the same answer for each of the nine categories in the MES section. Alreck and Settle (1985) refer to this bias as *routine responses*, where respondents choose the same number in each available rating category. In order to eliminate this bias, the data of these respondents was removed from the analysis. Consequently, 98 surveys were analysed relating to the results of the MES section of the questionnaire.

The frequencies of fully completed MES sections are presented in Table 6.2. The majority of respondents indicated an answer of four or five in all nine categories of the bipolar scale, with the exception being the traditionally acceptable/unacceptable category. Answers closer to five indicated that the respondent found the captain's behaviour in the scenario to be unfair, unjust, not morally right, not acceptable to his or her family, traditionally unacceptable, culturally unacceptable, violating an unspoken promise, violating an unwritten contract, and unethical. Overall, none of the respondents indicated a ranking of 1 on the ethical/unethical bipolar ranking, indicating that all of the respondents found the captain's action in the scenario to be unethical to varying degrees.

There were significant negative correlations between the number of cruises a respondent had participated in and how the respondents answered on all of the MES word pairings. In other words, the more cruises the respondents had been on, the more likely they were to have found the captain's behaviour fair, just, morally right, acceptable to their family, traditionally acceptable, culturally acceptable, not in violation of an unspoken promise or an unwritten law, and ethical.

Specifically, on the fair/unfair category, the correlation between number of cruises and how fair the respondent found the captain's action in the scenario was significant: r (98) = –0.291, p < 0.01; for the just/unjust category, the correlation was significant: r (98) = –0.339, p < 0.01; on the morally right/not morally right category, the correlation was significant: r (98) = –0.347, p < 0.01; on the acceptable/not acceptable to my family category, the correlation was significant: r (98) = –0.363, p < 0.01; on the traditionally/not traditionally acceptable category, the correlation was significant: r (98) = –0.224, p < 0.05; on the culturally acceptable/ unacceptable category, the correlation was significant: r (98) = –0.308, p <0.01; on the violates/does not violate an unspoken promise, the correlation was significant: r (98) = –0.296, p <0.01; on the violates/does not violate an unwritten law, the correlation was significant: r (98) = –0.256, p <0.05; and on the ethical/unethical category, the correlation was also significant: r (98) = –0.325, p < 0.01.

A final area of the questionnaire elicited some interesting, but non-statistically significant, findings. Specifically, this section of the questionnaire contained a number of statements and questions related to ethics and responsibility. The first statement was designed to determine how important a clean ocean was to the respondents. With regard to the statement: 'A clean ocean is important to my enjoyment of a cruise', 56.6 per cent of respondents strongly agreed, 42.1 per cent of respondents agreed, 0.9 per cent disagreed, and 0.4 per cent strongly disagreed (see Table 6.3).

The second statement asked the respondents to indicate their level of agreement or disagreement with the statement that 'Cruise line operators are ethically responsible to lessen the impact of their ships on the environment'. Specifically, 58.3 per cent of respondents strongly agreed with this statement and 39 per cent of respondents agreed, while 1.3 per cent disagreed and 1.3 per cent strongly disagreed (see Table 6.3).

The last statement asked the respondents to indicate their level of agreement or disagreement to the statement that 'Tourists are ethically responsible to lessen their impact on the environment.' In particular, 55.3 per cent of respondents strongly agreed with this statement, 42.1 per cent of respondents agreed, 1.3 per cent of respondents disagreed, and 1.3 per cent strongly disagreed (see Table 6.3).

Respondents were also questioned as to whether or not they thought the industry needed to improve its environmental practices and, if so, who should pay the costs related to doing so. Question one specifically asked the respondents: 'Do you think the cruise ship industry needs to improve its environmental practices?' The respondents had a choice of answering yes or no to this question. Specifically, 87.4 per cent of respondents indicated that the industry needed to improve its environmental practices.

Table 6.3 *The importance of a clean ocean and responsibility towards the environment*

Responses	A clean ocean is important to my enjoyment of a cruise		Cruise line operators are ethically responsible to lessen the impact of their ships upon the environment		Tourists are ethically responsible to lessen their impact upon the environment	
	N	%	N	%	N	%
Strongly agree	129	56.6	133	58.3	126	55.3
Agree	96	42.1	89	39.0	96	42.1
Disagree	2	0.9	3	1.3	3	1.3
Strongly disagree	1	0.4	3	1.3	3	1.3

Source: Sheppard (2005)

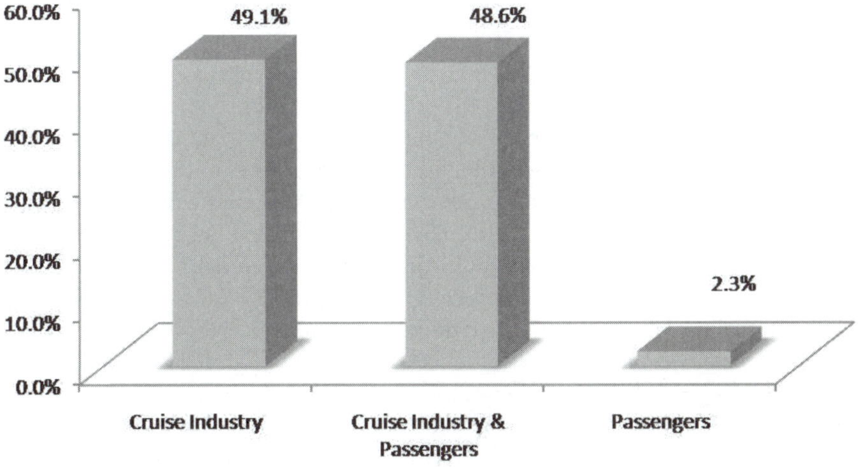

Figure 6.4 *Who should bear the costs? (N = 214)*

Source: Sheppard (2005)

The next question built upon the previous question and asked: 'If yes, who should bear the costs of improving the environmental practices of the cruise ship industry?'. Respondents were required to circle one of three answers: 'cruise industry', 'cruise industry and passengers' or 'passengers'. Overall, 49.1 per cent of respondents indicated that the cruise industry should bear the costs, 48.6 per cent of respondents felt that the cruise industry and passengers should bear the cost, and 2.3 per cent of respondents felt that passengers should bear the cost (see Figure 6.4).

Discussion of the results

The negative correlations found on both the MARPOL statements and the MES statements are both interesting and troublesome. In particular, the findings indicate that the more cruises the respondents had been on, the more likely they were to accept the environmental practices of the industry and the more likely they were to accept the captain's behaviour. This is a particularly thought-provoking finding, especially in light of the fact that 55 per cent of respondents had indicated on an earlier survey question that they were on the cruise to see the natural beauty of Alaska. However, caution should also be exhibited when examining the results related to the MES scale, as the response rate for usable surveys (98) was relatively low.

The findings of this research seem to indicate a hedonist utilitarian orientation on the part of the respondents in correlation to the number of cruises taken. Utilitarianism is an ethical theory of moral reform that seeks the main ideal of doing *the greatest good for the greatest number*. There are three main features of utilitarianism. The first feature is that an action is considered right if it leads to the greatest balance of good consequences over bad consequences for everyone involved. The second feature relates to intrinsic value – that individuals should search out experiences and conditions that are good or have value for themselves personally. The third feature relates to the ability to compare one person's pleasure to another person's pleasure in order to determine which is greater, thereby enabling individuals to decide which act will provide the greatest happiness to the greatest number of people (Beauchamp and Bowie, 1993). Specifically, an analysis of the results appears to indicate that the more cruises the respondents had taken, the more likely they were to display a hedonistic utilitarian orientation in their responses to the MARPOL and MES sections of the questionnaire. In other words, their enjoyment of cruising, as evidenced by their number of cruises taken, led these multi-time cruisers to elevate their own personal pleasure above what would be considered the accepted ethical standards of North American society, which, generally speaking, implements regulations and legislation to protect the environment.

This finding stands in stark contrast to the fact that the majority of respondents indicated that they felt cruise line operators as well as tourists have an ethical responsibility to lessen their impact upon the environment. Perhaps there was an unseen societal pressure to choose what the respondent saw as being the *right* answer in this research. Cohen (1973) warns that one of the limitations with attitude data is that the statement a person agrees or disagrees with may not reflect the actual choices an individual makes on a daily basis. The results of the correlations seem to bear out this warning. The respondents seem to be stating that they disagree with the environmental practices of the industry and that they find the captain's behaviour unethical; however, the more cruises they had participated in, the more acceptable they found these practices.

One of the more thought-provoking findings from the research was that the majority of respondents (57.7 per cent) indicted that the environmental practices of the industry were ethical or somewhat ethical, regardless of the fact that the majority of respondents had previously indicated that they found the environmental practices of the industry, as defined by the MAROL regulations, to be unacceptable. While this finding may appear to indicate a contradiction on the part of the respondents, it is more likely that the respondents did not view the actions of the industry as being unethical because the industry is acting legally, within the boundaries of the MARPOL regulations. Rather, they were disagreeing with the environmental practices of the industry from a moral perspective. Ethical standards are often reflected in the laws of society and while one may disagree with the practices of the industry from a moral standpoint, they are nonetheless legal. There may also have been reluctance on the part of some respondents to judge the actions of the cruise ship industry based upon ethical standards. Although respondents were comfortable indicating their own personal level of acceptance or non-acceptance of the actions of the cruise ship industry as it relates to the environment, they may have been uncomfortable taking that one step further to pass judgement on the actions of the captain in the scenario, from an ethical standpoint.

Despite this finding, it is interesting to note that an overwhelming majority (98.7 per cent) of respondents agreed that a clean ocean was important to their enjoyment of a cruise. Juxtaposed with this finding was the result that respondents found the discharge of garbage to be more acceptable than the discharge of untreated sewage. Of further encouragement is the fact that an overwhelming majority (97.3 per cent) agreed that cruise line operators are ethically responsible to lessen their impact upon the environment and 97.4 per cent agreed that tourists are ethically responsible to lessen their impact upon the environment. Similarly encouraging was the finding that respondents acknowledge the responsibility of both tourists and the industry to bear the costs of improvements to environmental practices.

An analysis of the data collected in this research revealed interesting findings that may begin to lay the foundational knowledge for future studies into the ethical nature of tourists. Respondents in this research demonstrated an increasing acceptance of the industry's practices in correlation to an increasing number of cruises. Certainly the hedonistic nature of tourism factors into these results. Tourism is often about getting away from everyday life, forgetting one's troubles, and 'living it up'. Therefore, it makes logical sense that the more cruises one takes, the more likely one is to develop a hedonistic utilitarian orientation; indeed, the attractions of cruising seem to be the excesses – the excesses of food and drink, the array of entertainment and amenities, such as shopping malls, rock-climbing walls and skating rinks, the glamour and the opulence, and the ever-increasing size of the ships, all of which Wilkinson (1999) refers to as the *illusion* (fantasy, romance and adventure) of cruising. The love of cruising and all it stands for would naturally create a loyal following amongst cruisers who are consequently more likely to turn a blind eye to the behaviour of the industry and the fact that by being on the ship they are indirectly complicit in the environmental practices of the industry.

Conclusions and recommendations

Without modifications to the practices and behaviour of all tourism stakeholders, the tourism industry will continue to exert increasing pressure on the natural environment. Similarly, cruise tourism will continue to exact an ever-increasing toll upon the natural environment unless the environmental practices of the tourism industry are modified. This study has contributed to the existing research on tourism sustainability, but has gone one step further by laying the foundation for future studies that seek to examine the relationship between tourists, ethics and sustainability. It is anticipated that this information will be of value to tourism educators, governments, non-governmental agencies, communities and tourism businesses as the industry begins a systemic shift to more sustainable tourism practices, products and services.

The concept of sustainable tourism development is increasingly being put forth as the means of controlling the negative aspects of tourism, while maximizing the benefits of the industry (Mastny and Paterson, 2001). However, Johnson (2002) points out that sustainable tourism is difficult to implement and evaluate. Perhaps part of the difficulty in implementing sustainable tourism lies in the fact that in the past there has been little emphasis of the application of ethics in tourism, despite the growth of the industry (Fleckenstein and Huebsch, 1999). Without a doubt, there is a need to have a more complete understanding of the role that all stakeholders in the industry must play, particularly from an ethics perspective.

Fortunately, the importance of ethics in the tourism industry is increasingly being seen as an important ingredient in the development and management of the industry (Yaman, 2002). Codes of ethics have been proposed by some academics as a means to achieve a more moral industry (Malloy and Fennell, 1998), while others such as Hultsman (1995) have set forth the concept of *just tourism* as a means of establishing an ethical framework for the provision of tourism services. On the implementation side, increasing numbers of jurisdictions around the world are putting sustainability theory into practice as they establish tourism business certification programmes, while individual businesses strive to adopt sustainability practices in their operations and within their communities.

As evidenced in this research, the more cruises a respondent had taken, the more likely they were to lower their own personal ethical standards when rating the behaviour of the captain in the scenario and the more likely they were to find the practices of the industry acceptable. If the ethical nature of the respondents in this research is indicative of the behaviour of most tourists, then implementing sustainable tourism may prove even more difficult. Consequently, it would be valuable to undertake further studies with the MES to determine whether or not the scale is practical for use with tourists. Certainly, the debate regarding the construct of the MES is not settled and needs to continue; however, this research exposed a new area of concern – the apparent difficulty of a number of respondents in understanding some of the concepts within the MES. Therefore, a recommendation is made that further studies be undertaken with the MES and cruise tourists, as well as with different types of tourists, such as eco-tourists, expedition tourists, adventure tourists or resort tourists. Of particular interest would be the replication of this study with expedition cruise tourists in order to study whether or not there are differences in the ethical nature of mass cruise tourists compared to specialized cruise tourists. As previously mentioned, cruising is a form of tourism that is often defined by its excesses, and perhaps the results would be different with tourism experiences that are defined by their minimal impact upon the natural environment, such as ecotourism, nature-based tourism or smaller specialized cruises, such as expedition cruises.

Overall, the findings of this research highlight some of the difficulties of ensuring that tourists adopt the required behaviour that will accompany more sustainable tourism practices. While the results of the research could lead one to believe that the respondents in this research care about the impact of cruise ships upon the environment, the findings appear contradictory in a number of different areas. Cruising seems to elicit a utilitarian hedonistic orientation on the part of some cruisers, and, as such, some cruisers may be more likely to lower their ethical standards with regards to the environmental practices of the industry. Indeed, the overall findings of the research do seem to indicate that tourists have different levels of ethical standards and that their level of enjoyment of a tourism experience (as evidenced by multi-time cruisers) may, in fact, influence them in turning a blind eye to practices that, while legal, are not morally acceptable by certain societal standards.

Perhaps the only hope of ushering tourists into the folds of more ethical behaviour is to begin educating tourists about the impacts of tourism and their impacts as tourists. Utilitarian theorists consider character training to be essential so that individuals are aware of appropriate moral rules (Benn, 1998). If tourists were asked to take responsibility for their actions while planning or while on their vacation – for example, searching out businesses that were undertaking sustainable practices, or participating in hotel recycling programmes – more tourists might begin realizing that their behaviour can be a part of the problem or an important part of the solution. As Roberts and Bacon (1997) state, it is important to educate consumers on environmental issues so that they may make ecologically conscious buying decisions. Considering the impact of consumer buying choices, one could state that tourists have a significant role to play in the sustainability of the industry. If more tourists were to make their travel decisions based on the sustainability of the businesses that they choose to patronize, businesses who choose not to adopt sustainable practices would be penalized and those businesses that have adopted the triple bottom line approach to business sustainability – socio-cultural, economics and environment – would be rewarded with customer patronage and loyalty. As a result, sustainable business practices would become standard operating practices and those businesses that had failed to implement sustainability practices would no longer be viable and would slowly fade into history as businesses that had failed to change with modern times.

Polar environments are becoming increasingly popular destinations for tourists and the most common mode of transportation to these locations is often cruise or expedition ships. Consequently, it is likely that there will be increasing pressure on these sensitive environments in future years. As the United Nations Environment Programme (UNEP, 2007) points out, commitment to mutually accepted goals is the first step in establishing critical management techniques in polar regions. Fortunately, Alaska has had the foresight to work with key stakeholders to set in place the legislation that is necessary to assist in the management of its natural environment. As discussed in this chapter, the next logical step, and the missing piece in the sustainability puzzle, appears to be the necessity of ensuring that tourists have greater awareness of their (and the industry's) impact upon the natural environment, particularly in ecologically sensitive areas. And while it will be an undeniable challenge, as indicated by the findings in this research, the time has come to acknowledge the role that tourists inadvertently play in the unsustainable practices of the industry so that these key stakeholders in the industry can become part of the sustainability solution.

Note

1   In March 2003, the author witnessed the discharge of garbage at sea by the cruise ship on which she was cruising. Some of the discharged items were illegal, including the discharge of whole wine bottles (which must be crushed before discharge) and Styrofoam plates. The incident was reported to the ship's captain by the author and ultimately reported to the Hawaiian branch of the Environmental Protection Agency (EPA). After a year's investigation the ship was determined to be beyond the jurisdiction of the US and beyond prosecution by the EPA.

References

Alaska Department of Environmental Conservation (2004) 'Assessment of cruise ship and ferry wastewater impacts in Alaska', www.dec.state.ak.us/water/cruise_ships/pdfs/assessmentreport2004.pdf, accessed 26 September 2009

Alreck, P. L. and Settle, R. B. (1985) *The Survey Research Handbook*, Richard D. Irwin, Inc, Homewood, IL

Beauchamp, T. L. and Bowie, N. E. (eds) (1993) *Ethical Theory and Business*, 4th edition, Prentice Hall, Englewood Cliffs, NJ

Benn, P. (1998) *Ethics*, McGill-Queen's University Press, Montreal, Canada

Bluemink, E. (2009) 'Cruise ship association sues state over passenger tax', www.adn.com/money/industries/tourism/story/939980.html, accessed 28 September 2009

CLIA (Cruise Lines International Association) (2009) *2009 CLIA Cruise Market Overview*, www.cruising.org/Press/overview2009, accessed 26 September 2009

Cohen, J., Pant, L. and Sharp, D. (1993) 'A validation and extension of a multidimensional ethics scale', *Journal of Business Ethics*, vol 12, no 1, pp13–26

Cohen, M. R. (1973) 'Environmental information versus environmental attitudes', *The Journal of Environmental Education*, vol 5, no 2, pp5–8

Fennell, D. A. and Malloy, D. C. (1999) 'Measuring the ethical nature of tourism Operators', *Annals of Tourism Research*, vol 26, no 4, pp928–943

Fleckenstein, M. P. and Huebsch, P. (1999) 'Ethics in tourism – reality or hallucination', *Journal of Business Ethics,* vol 19, no 1, pp137–142

Hansen, R. S. (1992) 'A multidimensional scale for measuring business ethics: A purification and refinement', *Journal of Business Ethics,* vol 11, no 7, pp523–535

Hudson, S. and Miller, G. (2005) 'Ethical orientation and awareness of tourism students', *Journal of Business Ethics,* vol 62, pp383-396

Hultsman, J. (1995) 'Just tourism: an ethical framework', *Annals of Tourism Research,* vol 22, no 3, pp553–567

IMO (International Maritime Organization) (1997) *MARPOL 73/78 Consolidated version,* IMO, London

IMO (2009) *International Convention for the Prevention of Pollution from Ships,* www.imo.org/Conventions/contents.asp?doc_id=678&topic_id=258, accessed 3 June 2009

Johnson, D. (2002) 'Environmentally sustainable cruise tourism: a reality check', *Marine Policy,* vol 26, no 4, pp261–270

Klein, R. A. (2002) *Cruise Ship Blues: The Underside of the Cruise Industry,* New Society Publishers, Gabriola Island, British Columbia

Loo, R. (2004) 'Support for Reidenbach and Robin's (1990) eight-item multidimensional ethics scale', *Social Science Journal,* vol 41, pp289–294

Maignan, I. (2001) 'Consumers' perceptions of corporate social responsibilities: A cross-cultural comparison', *Journal of Business Ethics,* vol 30, pp57–72

Malloy, D. C. and Fennell, D. A. (1998) 'Codes of ethics and tourism: An exploratory content analysis', *Tourism Management,* vol 19, no 5, pp453–461

Mastny, L. and Paterson, J. A. (2001) 'Toward a sustainable tourism industry', in L. Mastny and J. Paterson (eds) *Traveling Light: New Paths for International Tourism,* Worldwatch Institute, Washington, DC, pp47–56

McDowell Group, Inc (2007) *Alaska Visitor Statistics Program V Interim Visitor Volume Report,* www.dced.state.ak.us/oed/toubus/pub/AVSP_Summer_2007.pdf, accessed 26 September 2009

Reidenbach, R. E. and Robin, D. P. (1988) 'Some initial steps toward improving the measurement of ethical evaluations of marketing activities', *Journal of Business Ethics,* vol 7, no 11, pp871–879

Reidenbach, R. E. and Robin, D. P. (1990) 'Toward the development of a multidimensional scale for improving evaluations of business ethics', *Journal of Business Ethics,* vol 9, pp639–653

Reidenbach, R. E., Robin, D. P. and Donald, P. (1995) 'A response to "On measuring ethical judgments"', *Journal of Business Ethics,* vol 14, no 2, pp159–162

Roberts, J. A. and Bacon, D. R. (1997) 'Exploring the subtle relationship between environmental concern and ecologically conscious consumer behaviour', *Journal of Business Research,* vol 40, pp79–89

Robin, D. P. and Reidenbach, R. E. (1987) 'Social responsibility, ethics, and marketing strategy: Closing the gap between concept and application', *Journal of Marketing,* vol 51, pp44–58

Sheppard, V. (2005) *Ethics, Tourists and the North American Cruise Ship Industry: A Comparison Study of the Ethical Standards of Alaskan and Caribbean Cruise Ship Tourists,* MA thesis, Brock University, Ontario, Canada

Sheppard, V. and Fennell, D. A. (2009) 'The multidimensional ethics scale and cruise ship tourists: Testing the troubled waters', *Tourism in Marine Environments,* vol 4, no 5, pp259–270

Skipper, R. and Hyman, M. R. (1993) 'On measuring ethical judgments', *Journal of Business Ethics,* vol 12, no 7, pp535–546

UNEP (United Nations Environment Programme) (2007) *Tourism in Polar Regions: The Sustainability Challenge,* UNEP, Paris, France

Wendler, G. and Shulski, M. (2008) 'A century of climate change for Fairbanks, Alaska', *Arctic,* vol 62, no 3, pp295–300

Wheeler, B. (1993) 'Sustaining the ego', *Journal of Sustainable Tourism,* vol 1, no 2, pp121–129

Wilkinson, P. (1999) 'Caribbean cruise tourism: Delusion? Illusion?', *Tourism Geographies,* vol 1, no 3, pp261–282

Yaman, H. R. (2002) 'Skinner's naturalism as a paradigm for teaching business ethics: A discussion from tourism', *Teaching Business Ethics,* vol 7, pp107–122

7

Students on Ice:
Learning in the Greatest Classrooms on Earth

Geoff Green

Introduction

One day while I was standing on a beach in Antarctica with a few hundred thousand Chinstrap penguins, a simple thought emerged: imagine if we could give this experience to youth at the beginning of their lives. Imagine how this might change their perspectives, inspire their futures, help to connect them to the natural world, and so much more!

That was in 1999. I had been working as a school teacher and an expedition leader travelling to some of the most remote places on Earth from the Arctic to Antarctica, from Madagascar to Patagonia. During those expeditions I witnessed how people were becoming incredibly impassioned and inspired. The idea to start a programme that would take youth to the polar regions was born, and within the year I founded Students on Ice.

Ten years later, Students on Ice (SOI) has become an internationally recognized programme for polar and environmental education that shares knowledge, fosters respect for the planet's global ecosystem, and inspires creative ways to protect and conserve it. The programme has now taken over 1500 high school and university students, teachers, scientists, historians, artists, explorers, authors, leaders, innovators and polar experts from 40 countries on educational expeditions to both poles. Thousands more have been introduced to the polar regions through SOI outreach activities such as school presentations and speaking tours. Thanks to the generous support of governments, corporations, philanthropists and other groups around the world, the SOI Foundation helps to provide scholarships, grants and bursaries for most of the participating students.

I have had the great privilege of leading over 100 expeditions to both the Arctic and the Antarctic. The awe-inspiring polar regions have come to represent many things to me. They are natural treasures, symbols of peace and understanding, windows to our world, and cornerstones of our remarkable global ecosystem. They remind us that everything is interconnected and that Mother Nature is in control. We are also learning that the polar regions are the health barometers of Planet Earth, providing us with an early warning system for the greatest challenge of our time – climate change. I also like to think of them as the greatest classrooms on Earth … without walls.

What I love best about my job is the impact the expeditions have upon youth from diverse cultures, backgrounds and regions of the planet. These educational journeys that Students on Ice organize have the potential to transform participants and catalyse meaningful change at local, regional, national and international levels. Students on Ice provides teachers and learners with a powerful platform for hands-on learning through research activities, workshops, seminars, participatory presentations, hikes and exploration, making meaning from and understanding the environment, and so much more. Over the years, our alumni have accomplished many amazing things. Many are already leaders who are spearheading conferences, organizing campaigns and programmes, conducting cutting-edge research, writing books, giving presentations, influencing international decision-makers, earning scholarships, awards and other recognitions for their efforts, and making sustainable lifestyle choices. At the time of writing, SOI was very proud to know that 12 alumni were in Copenhagen, Denmark, working for a comprehensive global climate change agreement during the United Nations Climate Change Conference.

As SOI prepares to celebrate its tenth anniversary, one cannot help but think about how much the polar regions have changed during the last decade. The impacts of human-caused global warming that we are seeing are alarming. Sea ice is disappearing and permafrost is melting in the Arctic, glaciers are receding at unprecedented rates, wildlife is under tremendous pressure to cope with changes to their habitat, and every year Arctic temperatures keep climbing. These changes will affect all of humanity no matter where one lives.

For these reasons and many more, I want to ensure that Students on Ice continues its important work for many years to come. In this chapter I describe the programme in more detail and touch on some of our exciting plans for the future. Much of this information can be followed up on the SOI website (Students on Ice, 2010), and while this chapter is not overly academic, it showcases our unique programmatic example that inspires youth to make a difference at home and around the world.

Foundations and *raison d'être* (mandate)

Founded in 1999, Students on Ice offers unique educational expeditions to Antarctica and the Arctic. The programme's mandate is to provide students, educators and scientists from around the world with inspiring educational opportunities at the ends of the Earth and, in doing so, help them to foster a new understanding and respect for the planet.

Students on Ice aims to:

- provide life-changing experiences for youth;
- inspire and facilitate the 'passing of the torch' to the next generation of leaders, innovators, researchers, scientists, artists and authors;
- promote education and career options and opportunities;
- raise awareness and take action on environmental issues;
- provide experiences that connect youth to the natural world;
- connect thousands of youths around the world
- further scientific research and understanding of the Arctic and Antarctica;
- make the Arctic and Antarctica better known and understood by youth and the general public;
- motivate and inspire youth ambassadors;
- investigate and raise awareness about the impacts of climate change on the polar regions, and the solutions, actions and adaptations required by all of us to reduce these effects;
- use new and traditional media tools to share the expedition, experiences and messages with the international community;
- expand participants' knowledge about the circumpolar world, and gain a new global perspective of our planet, its wonders, and its present and future challenges.

Education programme

Students on Ice recognizes that we are at a critical point in the Earth's history. Accordingly, SOI is engaged in environmental education that provides experiences that connect students with nature; this is in line with the work of Gruenewald (2003, 2008), who posits that place-based learning creates attachment between citizens and the world in which they inhabit. It is the hope that connections made on SOI programmes will change the way in which students understand and act in the world. These types of experiences will make issues very real and personal, and encourage action of an engaged citizenry towards global sustainability. On SOI ship-based and land-based expeditions, students develop the knowledge, skills, perspectives and practices needed to be polar ambassadors and environmentally responsible citizens. Students learn that youth have a key role to play in shaping the world of today and the world of tomorrow. Every day it is reinforced to young participants that youth make a difference. This fosters the belief that the youth of today can be the leaders of today and tomorrow (see Maher, 2005, for further Antarctic examples of experiential education).

Students on Ice believes in providing students with unique educational experiences that will challenge the way in which they perceive the world. The aim is not to simply provide students with a trip to a unique destination, but rather to give students an opportunity to have an aesthetic experience in some of the most wild and awe-inspiring ecosystems in the world. Students should not just pass through a place with camera in hand but, rather, listen to the land, *feel* these natural places and, in turn, explore how humans feel when immersed in such places.

SOI's approach to education weaves together elements of experiential, expeditionary and problem-based learning. In starting with a very hands-on approach, active participation and critical thinking are important elements in the Students on Ice learning process. Through posing questions, experimenting and constructing meaning, the learning becomes personal, relational and exploratory in nature. SOI expeditions should become symbolic learning journeys from the initial development of ideas, to addressing problems and possible solutions, to final reflections. The journey will be unique for each student, as will the manner in which each student effects positive change in their individual lives following the expedition. This method is in keeping with the cycle of experiential learning espoused by Kolb (1984): experiencing, reflecting, generalizing and applying.

On expedition, several different learning formats are used depending on the topic being explored, the location, the weather conditions, and the skills and experiences of the education team members. These learning formats include lectures, participatory presentations, seminars, workshops and hands-on activities that will be shore-, zodiac-boat- and ship-based in setting. SOI also incorporates small group discussion and reflection opportunities within its expedition days through 'pod teams'.

Pod teams support student learning by connecting students with peers and mentors in a smaller educational circle. The purpose of the pods is to give students an opportunity to reflect, question, share and digest the overwhelming beauty, experiences and information that they are witnessing and receiving each day on their journeys. Working with skilled facilitators, team members consider different topics, themes and leading questions, and work through learning activities that guide their reflection. These types of varied debriefing sessions have been shown to be an important component of praxis for students (Mackenzie, 2002; Breunig, 2005). Pod facilitators consult with students to determine how they would most like to use their time together. They also help students to think deeply about profound experiences, explore their impact upon their individual consciousness, and translate them into positive outcomes in their respective home communities and lives. Like other aspects of the SOI education programme, pods offer students a framework through which they can create personal knowledge.

SOI expeditions' education programmes have three main goals. The first goal is to promote student learning about *polar fundamentals*. Students on Ice *polar fundamentals* include such areas of study as the geological, geopolitical and cultural history of the region in which the group is travelling; terrestrial ecology, covering flora and fauna; the history of exploration in the region; oceanography; atmospheric sciences; glaciology; marine biology; geography of place, and more. The second goal is to engage students to consider *environmental issues* and *solutions*. In addition to exploring climate change and the role that humans have played in influencing recent rates of global warming, Students on Ice is interested in developing environmentally literate citizens. Students explore environmental issues and solutions, such as conservation, biodiversity, energy, resource depletion, population growth, pollution and consumption. Students learn about the dependency of social and economic systems on natural systems. They learn to regard the planet as a global ecosystem – a system whereby all natural and human-created systems are interconnected and how they interact with each other. Students and staff examine the fundamental connections that we have with each other and the planet through our relationships to resources and other species, and our interaction with all living things. Considering the human and scientific dimensions of environmental issues, students learn about the importance of environmental factors to human well-being.

Woven into all Students on Ice expeditions is an overarching theme of *environmental leadership*. Humans are part of nature and bound by the laws of the natural world. However, in today's mechanistic consumer-oriented world, our lifestyles have led to a disconnection with nature. We are often unaware or apathetic to where our most basic needs come from – food, clothing and shelter. Over-consumptive practices have led to resource depletion, atmospheric pollution, diminishing biodiversity and, most commonly discussed in the media, climate change. As a global society, we need to move towards living more sustainably. Today's youth have the opportunity to lead the way.

SOI expedition presentations, discussions, workshops and activities are focused on current environmental issues facing the regions through which we travel. Some of the topics of workshops and hands-on activities have included:

- wildlife identification and observation;
- working with education team members on ongoing scientific research (e.g. seabird surveys, measuring pollution levels in ice-core samples, plankton tows focusing on marine diversity, ocean current calculations);
- nature interpretation through various activities (e.g. photography, art, journal writing, music);
- technology and nature (e.g. cetacean vocalization, geographic information system mapping);
- youth forums on leadership and steps towards sustainable living;
- hiking and shore walks;
- ecological footprint and expedition carbon footprint.

The third goal is to encourage students to join *Generation G* and make change! Students develop as leaders on SOI expeditions. SOI explores how youth are effective agents of change and how their efforts contribute to positive societal action. Youth have an opportunity to establish sustainable livelihoods and to make informed ecological-based choices early in their lives. The choices they make have a ripple effect and the actions youth take make a difference. In developing the leadership component of our expeditions' goals, we facilitate ongoing group discussions on ways to get involved in youth-based environmental initiatives upon returning home.

Students on Ice has developed the notion of a Generation G, a generation for the 21st century. It is not defined by age or any singular activity, but is, rather, a movement. It is a generation of global citizens who are becoming known for positive leadership, a caring approach, creative solutions and forward thinking. Generation G is an international movement of people who have already begun making choices for a sustainable future. Students on Ice encourages all expedition student participants to join Generation G: a global force that is fostering a broad-based environmentally literate and responsible mindset inspiring a movement to change the ways in which humans interact with the natural world and with each other; an approach that respects all life and brings meaningful change at a critical time.

The *Polar Ambassador Pledge* is a promise that students and staff are invited to make to one another on SOI expeditions. The promise is that we will make changes in the way that we live and act in the world. Part of this means sharing the experience of visiting a polar region. The other critical part of this commitment is to reduce our impact upon the planet by changing things at home, at school, in our communities and in our countries. This initiative is designed to be personally relevant for each of our students and to be a bridge between the expedition experience and the actions that students will take when they return home. The Polar Ambassador Programme provides goals and benchmarks for the students to meet. One of these is for all students to give presentations about their experiences and new knowledge to their schools, sponsors and other local groups. This has proven to be a great way for the students to process their thoughts, ideas and experiences. The students become ambassadors for the polar regions and for their country, city, communities, school and sponsor organizations.

Student success stories

Students on Ice prides itself on the successes of its alumni and hopes to grow the alumni to over 2200 members by 2015. These *agents of change* will help to inspire and motivate people to become environmentally conscious and to implement global strategies and programmes that can effect positive planetary change. The application of knowledge from experiential education has been documented across a wide variety of disciplines (Beckerman and Burrell, 1994; Cauley et al, 2001). Hope (2009) observes that when students 'see it for themselves' they experience both increased enjoyment of learning and increased understanding of the material. The material can suddenly become more relevant and more real with personal relationships having been developed (Bialeschki, 2007): if students see the poles they will protect them. Students also then develop a heightened perception of their own ability to effect positive change (Boyle et al, 2007),

There are countless success stories to share about the work that SOI alumni have done and are continuing to do. Here is a brief selection of alumni stories, used with the permission of the alumni.

Katrina Adams – budding whale and marine biologist (Arctic 2007)
Katrina recently left her home community of Chelsea, Quebec, to pursue a marine biology degree at McGill University in Montreal, Canada. She has since been selected as one of 12 young Canadian scientists to study as summer interns at the Mingan Island Cetacean Study for whale research on the Gulf of St Lawrence. Her experience with SOI informed her field of study and supported her Mingan internship application.

Jamal Alfalasi – United Nations environmental leader (Antarctic 2007). Noor Alfalasi – community and school group motivator (Antarctic 2007)
Immediately after the expedition upon returning to their home city of Dubai, Jamal and Noor were asked to be the masters of ceremony for the United Arab Emirates

premier showing of the film *11th Hour*. For the 2008 Earth Hour event, Jamal and Noor were involved in a march in Dubai to raise awareness about electricity consumption. During World Environment Day in 2008, the sibling pair joined with Salaam Youth Awards to increase awareness about pandas and polar bears. During autumn 2008, the United Arab Emirates hosted a large event called Mission Green Earth: Stand Up for the Environment in which the goal was to get 1 million people to stand up for the environment. Noor and Jamal were the coordinators for university outreach, gaining participation from six campuses and two municipalities. In 2008, Jamal went to Japan to meet with international youth to write a youth statement to present to the G8 leaders, a statement that focused on climate change and sustainable development. The following month he went to Kenya for the United Nations Environment Programme (UNEP) Global Youth Retreat to put together the 2015 strategy UNEP TUNZA Youth and Children Programme. Jamal currently works as an environmental awareness officer for the Knowledge and Human Development Authority's environmental education project. He has also become the host of a radio show that discusses important issues facing Dubai and the surrounding Emirates. In 2008, Noor and her friends held a programme at her university called Eco-warriors, which was also presented to schools throughout Dubai.

Alysia Garmulewicz – conference director and entrepreneur (Antarctic 2002; Arctic 2005)
A gifted home-schooled student from the small community of New Denver, British Columbia, Alysia envisioned and spearheaded a national Youth Climate Change Conference at Royal Roads University in 2005. She raised more than Cdn$120,000, personally secured nationally renowned speakers, and succeeded in having 100 Canadian youths in attendance. She founded the Changing Climates Educational Society, a website allowing her to maintain a vibrant dialogue with youth activists. Alysia was a member of the official Canadian government delegation to the 2005 United Nations Climate Change Conference. She was a student in environmental studies at Carleton University and led a second national youth conference (World Changing Careers) held in 2009 at the University of British Columbia. Alysia has been named a 2009 Rhodes Scholar and is currently studying at the University of Oxford.

Ankur Gupta – brimming energy and technology engineer (Arctic 2005; Antarctic 2007)
Ankur is currently a third-year student at Carnegie Mellon University in Pennsylvania, US, studying materials science and engineering with a focus on energy technology. He completed an internship in 2008 at General Electric Aviation, working on making the materials used in aircraft engines lighter and stronger in order to make the engines more fuel efficient. In his second year he worked on Carnegie Mellon's entry for the Google Lunar X Prize. Ankur worked on developing the battery system for the robot in order to better understand the field of batteries. He is very involved in the Students on Ice Alumni Committee and contributes regularly to the *Alumni Ice Cap* publication.

Duncan McNicholl – photographer and international development volunteer (Antarctic 2003)
After his expedition, Duncan completed an engineering degree from the University of British Columbia in Canada and worked on a project with the International Institute for Tropical Agriculture in Malawi through his involvement with Engineers without Borders. Duncan is currently trying to secure an internship with a great outfit in the United Arab Emirates, building the first green city. His Antarctic experience also served as a springboard to developing a passion for photography and photojournalism.

John Park – budding artist and lobbyist (Arctic 2007)
John, at the age of 17, has already been to the Arctic twice – once with SOI, and a second time the following year to study biology. With the help of Linda Mackey, Students on Ice art director and the founder of the Polar Artists Group, he learned to work the Arctic into his landscape oil paintings; as a result, his pieces were displayed under the same roof as the Group of Seven in Kleinburg's McMichael Gallery. His Arctic experiences inspired him to organize a youth group, Environmentally Concerned Students, to volunteer for the World Wide Fund for Nature (WWF) and to petition the Canadian government with over 2000 signatures from eight Canadian provinces and two territories, causing the Canadian government's selling of oil and gas rights in the Beaufort Sea to be put on hold until proper protection against oil spills is secured. John also wrote a published article for WWF International's *Arctic Bulletin* regarding the Beaufort Sea Campaign.

Megan Pizzo Lyall – nationally recognized aboriginal role model (Arctic 2005)
From Taloyoak, Nunavut, Megan was 18 years old when she received the National Aboriginal Role Model Award from Canadian Governor General Michaëlle Jean at Rideau Hall in 2006, an award given to only 12 Canadians aged 13 to 30 from First Nations, Inuit and Métis communities for their achievements, leadership and innovation. Megan had previously been selected as a youth delegate to attend the 2005 United Nations Climate Change Conference and was one of 100 international youths to write and formally table a youth declaration on climate change. Megan greatly influenced the late Dr Roy 'Fritz' Koerner, internationally renowned glaciologist, polar explorer and grandfather to Students on Ice.

Irene Shivaei – building peace projects across borders (Antarctic 2007)
After returning home to Tehran, Iran, following the SOI expedition, Irene began writing weekly columns about climate change in the national newspaper *JameJam Daily*, as well as writing a monthly environmental page in an Iranian student magazine for ages 10 to 11. She is currently studying physics at the University of Tehran and recently started a radio programme with friends about science and environmental issues. She has played a major role in developing the StarPeace programme, launched in 2009 – an official International Astronomy Year project aimed at bringing together people from nations with shared borders to the actual borderlines of their respective countries for public events to observe and learn about the stars above. It is hoped that such effort to bring together people from different, and even conflicted, countries may foster peace.

Bali Symenuk – speaking out on climate change (Arctic 2007)
From her home in Edmonton, Alberta, in Canada, Bali began giving dozens of lectures on her Arctic experience following the expedition. At the age of 17, she was selected as one of seven Canadian youths to be a National Climate Champion by the British Council, a two-year programme to help her further her environmental work. Bali was also selected as one of 200 Canadians to be trained as a climate project presenter by former US Vice-President Al Gore. In 2008, Bali led a student campaign – Bodies for Bowheads – to save bowhead whales in Isabella Bay; partial protection of the bay was announced by the Canadian federal government in 2008. That same year Bali received the Grant MacEwen United World Scholarship from the Alberta government to study at the United World College of South-East Asia in Singapore, valued at over Cdn$75,000.

Sun Ye – author of Arctic book for Chinese youth (Arctic 2007)
While on expedition, Sun Ye shared with the SOI team that she wanted to write a book for Chinese youth on climate change upon returning to her home in Shanghai. Fourteen months later, a beautiful, professionally published 84-page book arrived in the mail at the SOI office. The book is being distributed to thousands of youths across China.

Awe and wonder

In many ways, nature does most of the work as the key educator. The feelings of awe and wonder cannot be quantified in terms of educational value, but they are very powerful and profound. The emotions of being overwhelmed and humbled by the beauty and power of the natural world are what touch people in their hearts and remain with them forever.

One example of this kind of experience occurred on one of SOI's Antarctic expeditions. We came across a pod of orca whales that began hunting seals on ice floes. The whales disappeared and out of nowhere a giant wave came up from the ocean and flipped the seals off the ice into the ocean. The whales were making their own waves. They made about five or six waves and they caught three seals; but then the whales left and all three seals jumped back up onto the ice totally unharmed. The whales were teaching their young how to hunt. It was an exercise in sustainable fishing by whales. Then one of the little orca calves became bored, swam around and put its nose on the back of our zodiac and looked up at everybody in the boat. It gives me goose bumps just remembering that moment. To look into the eyes of a whale – what a direct connection that was. It changed everybody's life in the boat that day.

Comments from students and staff

With an incredible sense of pride and humility, SOI can think of no better way to convey the impact, gratitude and sense of what these students have come away with than to share their thoughts, in their own words:

Truly the most amazing place on Earth. (AH)

This experience will change my life! There are so many paths that opened with this journey to the Arctic. (JR)

I am alive! Thanks Arctic! (SC)

I hope that the beauty and peace of the Arctic stays with me forever. (MF)

I feel like this is only the beginning. (JW)

This has been an inspiration and positivity rejuvenator and forever it will remain. (DD)

Civilization is a different place, a different world ... it is clear that the world that we return to is one quite different from the one that we are leaving. (RY)

It was life changing. (LV)

The programme is a recipe for transformation. (NM)

This expedition has opened up windows in my mind that I never knew existed! (RB)

I will forever be changed and touched by Antarctica and I know why people are so passionate and protective of such a place. I hope to do the same! (IJ)

We've been passed the torch; let's keep it going. (CN)

Other recognized individuals can also see the benefits:

With programmes like SOI, we have a chance at helping the world understand that the Arctic is, indeed, an early warning beacon and health barometer for the planet. As students and adults witness for themselves the dramatic changes during an SOI trip, they get a better appreciation of what it is we are all working hard to protect. We are counting on you to keep up the great work SOI! (Sheila Watt-Cloutier, Nobel Prize nominee)

I believe the Students on Ice expedition is a unique and extraordinary adventure for students. I only wish I could have had such an opportunity when I was in high school! (Dr Mario Molina, Nobel Prize winner, MIT)

Future plans

SOI's tenth anniversary in 2010 is a great time to pause, reflect and look forward to the future. There have been several staff retreats and strategic planning sessions over the past year in order to create a five-year plan that takes us to 2015. SOI will continue with core expedition programmes to the Arctic and Antarctica each year, and the following are a few other projects that are being worked on.

University expeditions
In 2009, SOI piloted a first University Antarctic Expedition, which was a huge success. The expedition programme was in partnership with the University of Ottawa, the University of Alberta, the University of Northern British Columbia and the Canadian Circumpolar Institute. There were 65 students and 24 faculty and expedition staff on the expedition, which took place in February 2009. The programme offered three different university credit courses, including one on tourism impacts. The plan is to expand the programme and build on its successes with a second University Antarctic Expedition in February 2011. An SOI Arctic University Expedition programme is also being considered for 2012.

Carbon neutral continent
Students on Ice and alumni have initiated a campaign to advocate for a carbon neutral Antarctica. By engaging with and lobbying relevant stakeholders, SOI hopes that Antarctica will be the world's first carbon neutral continent by 2015. In June 2009, a first step was undertaken where Students on Ice representatives, including alumni, met with the International Association of Antarctica Tour Operators (IAATO) members at their annual meeting. The SOI delegation delivered a convincing presentation to the membership and meeting observers (which included governmental and non-governmental organization representatives involved with Antarctic Treaty consultative meetings). IAATO members unanimously approved the motion to recognize modern climate change as a significant threat to the Antarctic environment. This acknowledgement is a significant step for the 100+ member-driven private-sector organization. IAATO members supported Students on Ice's motion to establish a working group led by Students on Ice to explore ways of mitigating its contributions to climate change.

Arctic ice park
Students on Ice is supporting a few initiatives focused on Arctic governance and conservation for the future. One such initiative is the concept of an ice park, which would be the largest park in the world and would help to protect and manage the last remaining year-round ice habitat in the Arctic.

Arctic Tern 1
Acquired by the Students on Ice Foundation in June 2009 to serve as a platform for small group polar education and research, the *Arctic Tern 1* is a 50 foot steel expedition sailing yacht made by the French yard Caroff Duflos. With a stainless steel hull and retractable keel to meet the risks of sailing in ice-bound areas, she

can sail right onto a beach. *Arctic Tern 1* is a stepping-stone towards a larger dream of building the world's most technologically and environmentally advanced polar expedition vessel, which would be used for all future SOI expeditions.

Funding and partnerships
A major goal is to make Students on Ice a sustainably funded project for the long term. SOI is striving to reach the point where all students are fully funded and supported, and even mentored on an ongoing basis by staff. SOI will achieve this through new and continued partnerships with governments, corporations, foundations, individuals and other groups around the world.

Conclusions

My life experience since standing on that beach in Antarctica ten years ago has taught me that if you can follow your dreams, passions and visions, then good things will inevitably happen. Today, I spend a lot of time talking and writing about environmental issues and actions. I speak at international conferences and leadership forums, and to corporations, schools and universities around the world. More than anything, the birth of my son last year has strengthened my desire to continue trying to make a difference in the world.

My journeys to the ends of this incredible Earth have reinforced in me how lucky we are to share this planet and call it our home. We do not own the planet, we do not steer it; but we do have an impact upon it and it has never needed help from our species more than it does right now. If we can protect the poles, we can protect the planet. By inspiring today's youth to become agents of change and by connecting them to the natural world, we will have a better and more sustainable tomorrow.

References

Beckerman, A. and Burrell, L. (1994) 'A rock and a hard place: Trying to provide culturally-sensitive field experiences in rural, homogeneous communities', *Journal of Multicultural Social Work*, vol 3, no 1, pp91–99
Bialeschki, M. D. (2007) 'The three rs for experiential education researchers', *Journal of Experiential Education*, vol 29, no 3, pp366–368
Boyle, A., Maguire, S., Martin, A., Milsom, C., Nash, R., Rawlinson, S. et al (2007) 'Fieldwork is good: The student perception and the affective domain', *Journal of Geography in Higher Education*, vol 31, no 2, pp299–317
Breunig, M. (2005) 'Turning experiential education and critical pedagogy theory into praxis', *Journal of Experiential Education*, vol 28, no 2, pp106–122
Cauley, K., Canfield, A., Clasen, C., Dobbins, J., Hemphill, S., Jaballas, E. et al (2001) 'Service learning: Integrating student learning and community service', *Education for Health: Change in Learning & Practice*, vol 14, no 2, pp173–181
Gruenewald, D. A. (2003) 'The best of both worlds: A critical pedagogy of place', *Educational Researcher*, vol 32, no 4, pp3–12

Gruenewald, D. A. (2008) 'Place based education: Grounding culturally responsive teaching in geographical diversity', in D. Grunewald and G. Smith (eds) *Place-Based Education in the Global Age: Local Diversity*, Taylor & Francis, New York, NY, pp137–153

Hope, M. (2009) 'The importance of direct experience: A philosophical defence of fieldwork in human geography', *Journal of Geography in Higher Education*, vol 33, no 2, pp169–182

Kolb, D. (1984). *Experiential Learning: Experience as the Source of Learning and Development*, Prentice-Hall, Englewood Cliffs, NJ

Mackenzie, L. (2002) 'Briefing and debriefing of student fieldwork experiences: Exploring concerns and reflecting on practice', *Australian Occupational Therapy Journal*, vol 49, no 2, pp82–92

Maher, P. (2005) 'Lessons from the Great White South: Experiential education and Antarctica', *Pathways – The Ontario Journal of Outdoor Education*, vol 17, no 3, pp23–28

Students on Ice (2010) *Students on Ice*, www.studentsonice.com, accessed 31 January 2010

Part III
ENVIRONMENTAL DIMENSIONS

8

Environmental Impacts of Polar Cruises

Michael Lück

Introduction

When thinking of a cruise in the polar regions, blue skies, stunning scenery, crystal clear waters and the vastness of the wild ocean, untouched by human pollution, spring to mind. Cartwright and Baird (1999, p163) reflect the glossy image portrayed by the cruise lines themselves:

> *Not so long ago the traditional method for removing rubbish from ships was to dump it overboard. Such practices are now, quite rightly, outlawed and cruise ship companies have become very environmentally aware. There are large fines applied to any shipping company found guilty of pollution.*

Douglas and Douglas (2001, p336) note that 'the days when cruise ships routinely dumped waste overboard are over, although isolated instances are still reported'. Unfortunately, these 'isolated instances' are more frequent than desirable, with a variety of cruise companies and ships being charged for the breach of regulations. Indeed, the rapid increase in cruise activities in the polar regions created concern about the potential environmental impacts that this boom brings with it. Hall (1992), for example, notes that the most serious concerns about tourism in the Antarctic are potentially lasting impacts upon the environment. There are boat-based and land-based impacts; but since the vast majority of tourists in the polar regions are boat-based (Snyder, 2007), these two types of impacts are closely related. Bauer (2001, p124) notes that the principal causes for impacts in Antarctica are:

- general pollution by sewage, waste, oil, fuels and noise;
- introduction of non-native unsterilized soils, microbes, plants and animals;
- travel on foot or by vehicle and aircraft, both by scientists and non-scientists;
- disturbance of local bird- or seal-breeding colonies;

- changes in the chemical balance of natural waters, including the intentional or accidental introduction of radioisotopes;
- uncontrolled dumping of solid and liquid waste in inshore waters;
- the use of explosives;
- scientific sampling and experiments;
- non-scientific collecting;
- animals and eggs taken for food.

However, in line with the overall content of this volume, this chapter will focus on the ship-based impacts of polar cruises.

Cruise lines around the globe have a long history of environmental misconduct, including the dumping of liquid and solid wastes, the discharge of oily bilge waters and air pollution. Polar cruises are not much different, although the majority of cruise ships plying polar waters are still smaller than the ultra-modern mega-liners in other regions. However, there is a clear trend to more regular cruise ships, in addition to ice-strengthened expedition ships and ice breakers, visiting the polar and sub-polar regions. Alaska, for example, is the third largest cruise market for the member lines of the Cruise Lines International Association (CLIA), whose members almost exclusively operate 'regular' cruise vessels (i.e. no ice-going ships) (O'Grady, 2006; CLIA, 2009). Bertram (2007, p157) also notes that '[a] further trend ... is the ageing and withdrawal from Antarctic service of some of the earlier small ships and

Table 8.1 *Cruise ship incidents in polar waters, 2007–2009*

Date	Vessel	Incident	Location
February 2009	Ocean Nova	Grounding	Antarctica
January 2009	Richard With	Grounding	Norway
December 2008	Ushuaia	Grounding	Antarctica
July 2008	Antarctic Dream	Grounding	Spitsbergen
July 2008	Spirit of Glacier Bay	Grounding	Alaska
April 2008	Spirit of Alaska	Grounding	Alaska
December 2007	Fram	Collision with iceberg	Antarctica
November 2007	Explorer	Sinking	Antarctica
August 2007	Spirit of Columbia	Grounding	Alaska
June 2007	Disko II	Grounding	Greenland
May 2007	Empress of the North	Grounding	Alaska
January 2007	Nordkapp	Grounding	Antarctica

Source: CruiseBruise (2007a, 2007b); Berglund (2008); Drouin (2008); Golden (2008, 2009); Jainchill (2008); Patagonia Times (2008); Revkin (2008); Silverstein and Kazell (2008); Baldwin Paloti (2009); CNN (2009); Cruise Junkie (2009b, 2009c)

their gradual replacement by ships of larger passenger capacity'. In addition to the challenges regarding search and rescue missions in the case of groundings or sinkings in such remote locations, the potential environmental damage caused by leaking oil, fuels and other poisonous substances in the fragile polar environments can be devastating (CNN, 2003; O'Grady, 2006). Table 8.1 illustrates that such incidents are not uncommon.

Environmental impacts of cruises in polar regions

There are a number of environmental challenges related to cruise ships in the Arctic, Antarctic and the sub-polar regions, including wastewater, hazardous waste, solid waste, oily bilge water, ballast water and air emissions (Herz and Davis, 2002; Sweeting and Wayne, 2006; Cerveny, 2008; Klein, 2008). Many of these potential impacts become even more of a concern with the increasing number and sizes of vessels.

Wastewater

Cruise ships produce large amounts of two types of wastewater: greywater and blackwater. Greywater is wastewater coming from sinks, showers, galleys and similar activities onboard (Chesworth, 2007; Sweeting and Wayne, 2006; Lumma and Gross, 2009). Average cruise ships produce up to 350 litres of greywater per person per day, which amounts to up to 800,000 litres of greywater daily for an average cruise ship (2000 to 3000 passengers plus crew) (Klein, 2008; Oceana, 2008). Greywater represents the largest category of liquid waste from cruise ships (Herz and Davis, 2002) and can contain a number of pollutants, such as detergents, faecal coliform bacteria, oil and grease, food wastes, metals, organics, nutrients, medical and dental waste, and petroleum hydrocarbons (Herz and Davis, 2002; Klein, 2008). With the exception of Alaska and the Great Lakes, greywater can be legally discharged beyond the 12 mile (19km) zone (see Figure 8.1). Despite the regulations in Alaska, tests conducted on cruise ships in Alaskan waters revealed results of great concern: only one in 80 blackwater samples met federal standards, and some greywater samples contained 50,000 times more faecal coliform than the accepted standard (*Economist*, 2001).

Blackwater is untreated wastewater from toilets, urinals and medical facilities/ infirmaries (Sweeting and Wayne, 2006; Klein, 2008; Lumma and Gross, 2009). Oceana (2008) estimates that the average cruise ship produces up to 30,000 gallons (114,000 litres) of sewage daily. Untreated, these waters can contain harmful substances, such as bacteria, pathogens, intestinal parasites, viruses and harmful nutrients (Coghlan, 2007; Klein, 2008). The discharge of untreated blackwater can cause significant damage to the environment – for example, through the release of nutrients – and the resulting lower water quality through eutrophication. This, in turn, through various biological processes, can lead to the mass mortality of fish and benthic organisms (Coghlan, 2007).

TONNES OF GREYWATER PER SHIP PER	DAY	WEEK
Minimum	350	2500
Maximum	1000	7000
Average	825	5800

- Cabin Sinks & Showers
- Laundry
- Galley
- A/C Condensate
- Salon

Holding Tank → Discharge to Sea Beyond 12 miles (or) Approved Shoreside Treatment Facility

The average 825 tonnes of greywater generated every day would fill 12 residential swimming pools.

Figure 8.1 *Royal Caribbean Cruise Line's illustration of the proper disposal/retaining techniques for managing greywater under the Save the Waves Program*

Source: Spracklin (2005)

Hazardous waste

Cruise ships generate a variety of hazardous wastes, such as photo-processing chemicals, dry-cleaning waste, paint, print shop wastes, solvents (e.g. turpentine, benzene, xylene, etc.), light bulbs, expired pharmaceuticals, X-ray development fluids, and batteries (Herz and Davis, 2002; Sweeting and Wayne, 2006; Klein, 2008; Lumma and Gross, 2009). Royal Caribbean International maintains that during a normal seven-day cruise, a typical ship generates 141 gallons (534 litres) of photo chemicals, 7 gallons (26 litres) of dry-cleaning waste, 13 gallons (49 litres) of used paints, 5 pounds (2.3kg) of batteries, 10 pounds (4.5kg) of fluorescent light bulbs, 3 pounds (1.3kg) of medical waste, and 108 pounds (49kg) of expired chemicals (Klein, 2002). These wastes are toxic and can have significant negative impacts upon the marine environment, such as death or failure in the reproductive success of fish, shellfish, marine mammals and other marine organisms (Sweeting and Wayne, 2006).

Although not discharged as waste, anti-fouling paints on the ships' hulls are a major concern for the environment. These anti-fouling paints are designed to leak toxins in order to deter algae, barnacles and other organisms from attaching themselves to the vessel's hull. These paints contain tributyltin (TBT) and are extremely toxic, especially to lobsters and molluscs (Herz and Davis, 2002; Sweeting and Wayne, 2006).

Solid waste

A cruise ship produces large amounts of non-toxic solid wastes, including glass, plastics, wood, cardboard, food waste, Styrofoam, cans and other materials (Herz and Davis, 2002; Sweeting and Wayne, 2006; Klein, 2008; Lumma and Gross, 2009). Reports on the amount of waste generated vary and range from 50 tonnes of solid waste per week for an average cruise ship (Herz and Davis, 2002) to 1kg per passenger per day (Sweeting and Wayne, 2006). Much of the solid waste is being discharged at sea, which has the potential to affect the marine environment in various ways: mammals and birds can swallow the waste, which results in damage to the animal's digestive tract and, subsequently, death through starvation (Herz and Davis,

2002). Entanglement in fishing gear and garbage is another major problem with solid waste from cruise ships. According to Herz and Davis (2002, p18): 'ingestion and entanglement in marine plastic debris is responsible for the deaths of more than 1 million birds and 100,000 marine mammals each year'.

Oily bilge water

As part of the normal operation, a cruise ship produces approximately 25,000 gallons (95,000 litres) of water that collects in the bilge (the lowest part of the ship's hull) during a one-week voyage (Klein, 2008). Also part of normal operation is the leaking of oil from machinery and engine into the bilge water (Sweeting and Wayne, 2006). The bilge needs to be flushed and pumped dry in regular intervals, and any oily bilge water pumped into the sea constitutes a significant risk for the environment, as even small quantities of oil can be lethal for fish, birds and mammals, and can severely damage coral reefs, invertebrates, seaweeds and other organisms (Sweeting and Wayne, 2006; Herz and Davis, 2002; Klein, 2008).

Ballast water

Cruise ships take in ballast water to stabilize the vessel during the voyage. Close to the port of arrival, they pump out this ballast water, which allows them to get into ports with lower water depth. This way, ballast water travels over large distances, even across oceans, before it is dumped again. Along with the ballast water, ships take in organisms and animals of various sizes, and these too are being pumped out close to the next port. Thus, invasive species, often totally unknown in the area, are being introduced to the local environment (CNN, 2003), which can have devastating consequences for the balance of ecosystems. While not a polar destination, Lake Ontario in Canada, for example, experienced the introduction of European zebra mussels through ballast water. The mussels spread rapidly all over the lake and destroyed large parts of the biotopes there (Jentes, 2001; Ministry of Natural Resources (Ontario), 2006). In addition to invasive species, the exchange of ballast water can aid in the distribution of illnesses, such as cholera, and foster algal bloom (Lumma and Gross, 2009).

Air pollution

In addition to solid and liquid waste discharges, the cruise industry affects air quality through engine emissions. Commonly, the diesel engines of (cruise) ships use bunker fuels, which are residual fuels with higher concentrations of contaminants (such as sulphur) than, for example, the standard petrol for car engines (Davies and Cahill, 2000). In fact, it is estimated that the sulphur emissions of one cruise ship equal those of 350,000 cars (Waymer, 2007). Other contaminants generated by the diesel engines include nitrogen oxide, carbon monoxide and hydrocarbons (Herz and Davis, 2002). In addition, cruise ships have large incinerators onboard, producing dioxins, furans and other toxins, adding to the air pollution (Herz and Davis, 2002; Klein, 2002, 2008). Despite the large amount of carbon dioxide (CO_2) emissions, shipping has not yet been integrated in the Kyoto Protocol, and thus the Kyoto regulations do not apply to shipping, including cruise ships. Air pollution extends beyond the greenhouse effect. In fact, some substances emitted through ships' smokestacks, in combination with humidity, eventually create 'acid rain', contaminating coastal regions (Lumma and Gross, 2009).

Counteracting the problems through cruise ship pollution is not an easy task. There are a number of international, regional and local regulations in place; but ships in international waters are difficult to police.

Regulations

International shipping is regulated by a variety of international, regional and local laws, regulations and policies. This section outlines the most important regulations for cruise ships, in general, and for the polar regions, in particular.

International Convention for the Prevention of Marine Pollution from Ships (MARPOL)

The International Convention for the Prevention of Pollution from Ships (MARPOL) is a set of international regulations of what ships may and may not legally discharge at sea. Governed by the International Maritime Organization (IMO), a United Nations organization, MARPOL came into effect in 1973 and was modified in 1978; since then, the MARPOL regulations have been amended several times (Rothwell, 2000; Dowling, 2006; Sweeting and Wayne, 2006; Sheppard, 2008b). MARPOL regulates the disposal of various substances in six annexes (Rothwell, 2000, p60):

1 'The prevention of pollution by oil' (Annex I);
2 'The control of pollution by noxious liquid substances in bulk' (Annex II);
3 'The prevention of pollution by harmful substances carried in packaged forms' (Annex III);
4 'The prevention of pollution by sewage from ships' (Annex IV);
5 'The prevention of pollution by garbage from ships' (Annex V);
6 'The prevention of air pollution from ships' (Annex VI).

Greywater is not regulated under MARPOL. Sewage may be discharged at only 4 miles (6.4km) from the coast and beyond when treated, but may be released untreated at 12 miles (19.3km) and beyond. Bilge water can only be discharged outside the 12 mile zone provided that after filtration it has less than 15 parts per million (ppm) (Lumma and Gross, 2009). The discharge of garbage under MARPOL is more complicated. For example, MARPOL identifies the Mediterranean Sea, Baltic Sea, Black Sea, Red Sea, Persian Gulf, the North Sea, the Antarctic area and the Caribbean as Special Areas (Herz and Davis, 2002). The only waste that is allowed to be disposed of in these Special Areas is food waste, and only beyond the 12 mile zone (with the exception of the Caribbean, where ground food waste may be discharged at 3 miles, or 4.8km, from land and beyond). Outside these Special Areas, MARPOL's regulations are relatively lax: ships may discharge to within 12 miles of the nearest coast all garbage (except plastics), including paper, rags, glass, metal, bottles, crockery and similar refuse. The same types of garbage can even be dumped up to three miles from shore if the materials are ground (Davies and Cahill, 2000; Klein, 2002).

International Convention on the Control of Harmful Anti-Fouling Systems on Ships

In 2001, the International Maritime Organization adopted the International Convention on the Control of Harmful Anti-Fouling Systems on Ships (AFS Convention 2001), which prohibits the use of harmful anti-fouling paints on ships (Wang, 2008). Anti-fouling paints contain organotin compounds, slowly leaching into the sea, killing barnacles, algae, molluscs and other sealife that have attached themselves to the hull and prevent sealife such as algae and molluscs from clinging to the hull. Such attached organisms would slow down the ship and increase fuel consumption (IMO, 2009). While the reduction of fuel consumption is a positive environmental effect, the organotin compounds persist in water, killing non-targeted sealife, and can even enter the food chain. The AFS Convention 2001 states that by 1 January 2008, ships either:

- shall not bear such compounds on their hulls or external parts or surfaces; or
- shall bear a coating that forms a barrier to such compounds leaching from the underlying non-compliant anti-fouling systems.

This applies to all ships (except fixed and floating platforms, floating storage units (FSUs), and floating production storage and off-loading units (FPSOs) that have been constructed prior to 1 January 2003 and that have not been in dry-dock on or after 1 January 2003 (IMO, 2009).

Alaska Cruise Ship Initiative and the Commercial Passenger Vessel Environmental Compliance Program

After illegal dumping of waste in Alaskan waters by various cruise lines, the Alaska Department of Environmental Conservation (ADEC) took action in 1999 and initiated a comprehensive public consultation process, including the US Coast Guard, cruise industry representatives, citizens, and the US Environmental Protection Agency. The goal of this initiative was to document waste management (or lack thereof) by the cruise industry while in Alaskan waters. The work of this forum became known as the Alaska Cruise Ship Initiative (ACSI), and resulted in a comprehensive report on sampling and monitoring programmes (Sheppard, 2008a). Subsequently, the Alaskan state government passed House Bill 260 (Commercial Passenger Vessel Regulation and Fees) in 2001, which enforces state clean air and water standards through a strengthened monitoring programme. In addition, a passenger fee of $US1 per passenger was introduced in order to pay for this programme (Klein, 2002). While the new legislation is not more stringent than federal law, it now provides the state of Alaska with the means to carefully monitor and control the cruise industry through its Commercial Passenger Vessel Environmental Compliance Program – a world's first. The programme sets forward the following regulations (Klein, 2002, p107):

- *Wastewater Discharge Standards*:
    - *Untreated sewage:* passenger vessels are prohibited from discharging untreated sewage (i.e. sewage that has not met all applicable federal processing standards). This means that sewage must be processed through a properly operated and maintained marine sanitation device and meet the applicable effluent standards.
    - *Treated sewage:* sewage cannot be discharged if it has suspended solids greater than 150 milligrams per litre or a faecal coliform count greater than 200 colonies per 100 millilitres. Small vessels can delay compliance upon submission of a plan that provides interim protective measures.
    - *Greywater:* greywater cannot be discharged if it has suspended solids greater than 150 milligrams per litre or a faecal coliform count greater than 200 colonies per 100 millilitres. Vessels can delay compliance upon submission of an interim plan.

The Department of Environmental Conservation (DEC) can establish numeric and narrative standards by regulation for any other parameters for treated sewage and greywater, including chlorine, chemical oxygen demand and biological oxygen demand.

- *Restrictions and Discharges:*
    - Large vessels may not discharge treated sewage or greywater unless the vessel is proceeding at a speed of not less than six knots and more than one nautical mile from shore, complies with effluent standards, and is not in a no-discharge zone. Small vessels are not subject to this provision. Large passenger vessels are excused from compliance if the discharges are proven to meet strict secondary treatment standards.

Marine pollution law in the 1991 Environmental Protocol

The 1991 Environmental Protocol, implemented as a supplement to the Antarctic Treaty (1959), protects the Antarctic as 'natural reserve devoted to peace and science', and obliges parties to comprehensively protect the Antarctic environment from marine pollution (Joyner, 2000; Higham, 2008). In essence, the protocol advocates for the prevention from pollution through 'proper planning and prudent conduct' (Joyner, 2000, p107) in order to limit the negative impacts upon the environment of Antarctica. Five annexes deal with the following issues (Joyner, 2000, pp112–120):

1 'Environmental impact assessment' (Annex I);
2 'Conservation of Antarctic fauna and flora' (Annex II);
3 'Waste disposal and waste management' (Annex III);
4 'Prevention of marine pollution' (Annex IV);
5 'Area protection and management' (Annex V).

Critics argue that there is a need for additional legal measure to regulate tourism activities in Antarctica because the protocol relies on self-regulation through the International Association of Antarctica Tour Operators (IAATO) (Bastmeijer, in press).

Violations of laws and regulations by cruise ships in polar/ sub-polar waters

Despite a variety of regulatory measures in place, many cruise lines violate these, bypass systems on board, discharge solid and liquid wastes, and even falsify log entries (Klein, 2002). Some cruise lines seem to have implemented stricter regulations for the operation of their vessels and have installed wastewater treatment systems; but it appears that not all have done so. In some cases, cruise lines seem to only take such measures where they see a direct financial incentive. A case in point is the Inside Passage, where rules are tighter. Cruise lines installed such wastewater treatment systems only on the part of the fleet that operates cruises to Alaska because rules for the Inside Passage allow the discharge of treated water anywhere, while untreated water can only be discharged outside the 12 mile (19.3km) zone (Klein, 2002). There have been numerous incidents and violations recorded over the first decade of the new millennium involving a variety of cruise lines (*Economist*, 2001; Sheppard, 2003; Cruise Junkie, 2009a). Table 8.2 shows the known incidents as of October 2009. The list includes 'northern areas', such as Washington and British Columbia, because these are the departure points for most Alaska cruises.

Table 8.2 *Known pollution and environmental violations and fines in polar and sub-polar waters, 2000–2009*

Year, Ship, Cruise Line, Explanation of Offence(s)	Fine
July 2009, *Volendam*, Holland America Line Ship violated Alaska Wastewater Quality Standards in May. There were three violations. The ship's effluent on 18 May had 4800 faecal coliforms per 100 millilitres, while the limit is 43 in any one day. It had a monthly average for faecal coliform of 4800/100ml (effluent limit is 14/100ml) and was also cited for exceeding the allowable level of biological oxygen demand (44.1mg/litre; effluent limit is 30mg/litre).	Pending
July 2009, *Golden Princess*, Princess Cruises Ship twice violated Alaska Wastewater Quality Standards for zinc in May 2009. On 11 May the concentration of zinc was 0.25mg/litre (effluent limit is 0.23mg/litre); on 18 May the concentration of zinc was 0.29mg/litre.	Pending

Year, Ship, Cruise Line, Explanation of Offence(s)	Fine
July 2009, *Sea Princess*, Princess Cruises Ship violated Alaska Wastewater Quality Standards for ammonia in May 2009. On 27 May the concentration of ammonia was 99mg/litre (effluent limit is 80.4mg/litre).	Pending
July 2009, *Sapphire Princess*, Princess Cruises Ship twice violated Alaska Wastewater Quality Standards for ammonia in May 2009. On 19 May the concentration of ammonia was 99mg/litre (effluent limit is 80.4mg/litre); on 27 May it was 120mg/litre. In addition, on 19 May as a result of a hose leak that resulted in 50 gallons of untreated greywater being released at dock, the ship was cited for one violation of pH, one violation of biological oxygen demand, one violation of allowable total suspended solids, and one violation of allowable faecal coliform.	Pending
July 2009, *Island Princess*, Princess Cruises Ship violated Alaska Wastewater Quality Standards for ammonia three times in May 2009. On 14 May the concentration of ammonia was 130mg/litre (effluent limit is 80.4mg/litre), on 27 May it was 120mg/litre, and on 28 May it was 160mg/litre.	Pending
July 2009, *Coral Princess*, Princess Cruises Ship violated Alaska Wastewater Quality Standards for ammonia in May 2009. On 21 May the concentration of ammonia was 91mg/litre (effluent limit is 80.4mg/litre).	Pending
July 2009, *Spirit of Adventure*, Saga Holidays Ship was leaking oil in the UNESCO World Heritage-listed Geirangerfjorden on the western coast of Norway. According to the media, the leak was caused by an overflow, causing oil to spill into the fjord. Officials are quoted as saying that the spill was of 'significant amounts'.	Pending
February 2009, *Serenade of the Seas*, Royal Caribbean International Ship was cited for one air quality violation in Alaska during the 2008 cruise season. On 28 August the ship's smoke emissions exceeded 20% opacity.	Pending

Year, Ship, Cruise Line, Explanation of Offence(s)	Fine
February 2009, *Rhapsody of the Seas*, Royal Caribbean International Ship was cited for one air quality violation in Alaska during the 2008 cruise season. On 27 May the ship's smoke emissions exceeded 20% opacity.	Pending
February 2009, *Norwegian Star*, Norwegian Cruise line Ship was cited for two air quality violations in Alaska during the 2008 cruise season. On 27 May and 2 September the ship's smoke emissions exceeded 20% opacity.	Pending
February 2009, *Oosterdam*, Holland America Line Ship was cited for one air quality violation in Alaska during the 2008 cruise season. On 24 July the ship's smoke emissions exceeded 20% opacity. It also had an air opacity incident on 2 July, but a notice of violation was not issued.	Pending
February 2009, *Island Princess*, Princess Cruises Ship was cited for one air quality violation in Alaska during the 2008 cruise season. On 11 July the ship's smoke emissions exceeded 20% opacity. It also had air opacity incidents on 3 and 17 July, but a notice of violation was not issued.	Pending
February 2009, *Clipper Pacific*, International Shipping Partners Ship was cited for one air quality violation in Alaska during the 2008 cruise season. On 20 August the ship's smoke emissions exceeded 20% opacity.	US$32,500
February 2009, *Mercury*, Celebrity Cruises Ship was cited for an air quality violation in Alaska during the 2008 cruise season. On 28 August the ship's smoke emissions exceeded 20% opacity.	Pending
February 2009, *Millennium*, Celebrity Cruises Ship was twice cited for air quality violations in Alaska during the 2008 cruise season. On 23 July and 11 August the ship's smoke emissions exceeded 20% opacity.	Pending

Year, Ship, Cruise Line, Explanation of Offence(s)	Fine
November 2008, *Island, Sapphire*, and *Diamond Princess*, Princess Cruises Each ship reportedly violated its wastewater discharge permit in September (2008). Wastewater samples from the ships had higher than permitted ammonia.	Pending
November 2008, *Westerdam*, Holland America Line Ship reportedly violated its wastewater discharge permit in September (2008). Wastewater samples from the ship had higher than permitted levels on two parameters.	Pending
November 2008, *Silver Shadow*, Silverseas Cruise Ship reportedly violated its wastewater discharge permit in September (2008). Wastewater samples from the ship twice had higher than permitted copper.	Pending
October 2008, *Island Princess, Sapphire Princess* and *Sun Princess*, Princess Cruises Each ship reportedly violated its wastewater discharge permit in August (2008). Wastewater samples from the ship had higher than permitted ammonia (twice on *Island Princess*, once on *Sapphire Princess* and *Sun Princess*).	Pending
October 2008, *Star Princess*, Princess Cruises Ship reportedly violated its wastewater discharge permit in August (2008). Wastewater samples from the ship twice had higher than permitted copper.	Pending
October 2008, *Golden Princess*, Princess Cruises Ship reportedly violated its wastewater discharge permit in August (2008). Wastewater samples from the ship had higher than permitted zinc.	Pending
September 2008, *Seven Seas Mariner*, Regent Seven Seas Ship violated its wastewater discharge permit in May, June and July (2008). Wastewater samples from the ship had higher than permitted zinc.	Pending
September 2008, *Island Princess* and *Golden Princess*, Princess Cruises Ship violated its wastewater discharge permit in May, June and July (2008). Wastewater samples from the ship had higher than permitted zinc.	Pending

Year, Ship, Cruise Line, Explanation of Offence(s)	Fine
September 2008, *Sapphire Princess, Star Princess, Coral Princess* and *Diamond Princess*, Princess Cruises Each ship violated its wastewater discharge permit in May, June and July (2008). Wastewater samples from the ships had higher than permitted effluent limits on several parameters.	Pending
September 2008, *Norwegian Pearl*, Norwegian Cruise Line Ship violated its wastewater discharge permit in May, June and July (2008). Wastewater samples from the ship had higher than permitted pH.	Pending
September 2008, *Westerdam*, Holland America Line Ship violated its wastewater discharge permit in May, June and July (2008). Wastewater samples had higher than permitted ammonia, zinc and biological oxygen demand. The latter indicates the amount of organic waste in the water.	Pending
September 2008, *Vision of the Seas* and *Serenade of the Seas*, Royal Caribbean International Ships violated visible air emissions standards on 1 July and 9 August, respectively. Royal Caribbean may be liable for criminal or civil penalties. Past enforcement cases have cost cruise lines US$27,500 per violation.	Pending
August 2008, *Fram*, Hurtigruten An enormous oil spill in Sisimiut Harbour (Greenland) resulted in 21 firemen working to clean up 3000 litres of diesel. When the passenger ship *Fram* attempted to refuel, 10,000 litres of oil escaped into the harbour waters.	None
July 2008, *Sea Lion*, Lindblad Expeditions Ship (apparently on charter to National Geographic) was tied to the fuel dock in Sitka. It was probably discharging just greywater (not illegal), but still not consistent with a company that claims to be environmentally sensitive and responsible.	None

Year, Ship, Cruise Line, Explanation of Offence(s)	Fine
June 2008, *Rhapsody of the Seas*, Royal Caribbean International Royal Caribbean Cruises says it mistakenly broke state law in discharging about 20,000 gallons of wastewater into Chatham Strait in south-east Alaska. Crew members mistakenly discharged greywater (wastewater from cabin showers and sinks) on 10 June. The error was not discovered until a week later. The ship's captain and environmental officer were apparently suspended while a full investigation was conducted.	None
January 2008, *Lyubov Orlova*, Quark Expeditions From a passenger: 'We took a trip to Antarctica for a study abroad programme with the University of XYZ. Aboard the Lyubov Orlova through Quark Expeditions, we travelled with 25 students and 2 advisers on a ten-day Antarctic cruise on 6 to 16 January. While aboard, we witnessed dumping of trash, including plastic garbage bags, overboard. Luckily, we were able to catch the act on video and are extremely unhappy with current dumping regulations.'	None
November 2007, *Explorer*, GAP Adventures More than 150 passengers and crew (91 passengers, 9 expedition staff, 54 crew) on an Antarctica cruise abandoned ship near the South Shetland Islands, 120km north of the Antarctica Peninsula, after the ship hit an unidentified object (probably ice) which put a 5 to 6 inch hole through both hulls, took on water and listed 25° to 30° and started sinking. The ship sank overnight with 185,000 litres of fuel oil on board in addition to 1000 litres of gasoline and 24,000 litres of lubricants. It left an oil stain 5km wide by 8km long.	None
February 2007, *Safari Quest*, American Safari Cruises The ship was fined US$7178 for a diesel fuel spill that oiled boats and the shoreline near Richland Tacht Marina (Washington State). The ship spilled 16 gallons of fuel while docked on 8 October 2006.	US$7,178

Year, Ship, Cruise Line, Explanation of Offence(s)	Fine
January 2007, *Nordkapp*, Hurtigruten The ship touched ground near Deception Island in the Antarctic. No one was injured and the ship sustained an 82 foot long gash to its outer hull. Passengers were transferred to the *Nordnorge* (a sister ship), which returned to Ushuaia. *Nordkapp* sustained temporary repairs. The spill was estimated to be between 227 and 757 litres of diesel oil.	None
January 2007, *Dawn Princess*, Princess Cruises The cruise line agreed to a plea bargain under which it paid a fine of US$200,000 and restitution of US$550,000 after criminal charges were filed. The company was charged with failing to operate at a slow, safe speed while near humpback whales, and in 2001 hit and killed a humpback in Glacier Bay, Alaska.	US$750,000
November 2006, *Mercury*, Celebrity Cruises Celebrity Cruises was fined for the *Mercury* dumping 500,000 gallons of untreated wastewater into Puget Sound. Though it initially claimed it had not dumped, shipboard documents contradicted the company's claim. The dumping happened ten times over nine days in September and October 2005.	US$100,000
July 2006, *Zuiderdam*, Holland America Line (HAL) A generator malfunction caused the ship to spew black smoke and soot on Skagway, Alaska. According to HAL, 'there was a technical malfunction of one of the ship's five diesel generators which resulted in an extraordinarily abnormal emission of heavy black smoke and some soot from its stacks. The emission was exclusively from the ship's stacks and lasted approximately five minutes.'	None
May 2006, *QE 2*, Cunard Line Transport Canada confirmed that the ship had discharged 3000 litres of what crew described as 'paper pulp' in Canadian waters off Cape Breton on 9 September 2005. Investigators say it is unclear what was dumped, but there was some speculation it was primarily toilet paper.	None

Year, Ship, Cruise Line, Explanation of Offence(s)	Fine
June 2005, *Norwegian Star*, Norwegian Cruise Line While docked in Victoria, British Columbia, local residents near the port complained of a noxious odour pervading their homes following release of a billow of black smoke from the ship's smokestack. It was determined that while fixing a diesel-powered electricity generator, the engine had to be restarted several times. On two of those restarts the engine emitted heavy black smoke which triggered the ship's own onboard smoke emission alarms. On each of those two occasions the smoke was emitted for less than 30 seconds. It was the source of the noxious odour. There was no fine because the emission was due to equipment breakdown.	None
January 2005, *Zaandam*, Holland America Line, and *Sapphire Princess*, Princess Cruises The Washington State Department of Ecology issued a press release indicating three violations of its MOU with the cruise industry. One violation occurred on 13 May in Port Angeles, when Holland America Line's *Zaandam* discharged treated effluent through an advanced wastewater treatment system that the Department of Ecology had not approved. The *Zaandam* made only one port call in Washington in 2004. Princess Cruises' *Sapphire Princess* discharged treated effluent throughout the 2004 season through an advanced treatment system that had not received Department of Ecology approval. The ship also released untreated wastewater from its galleys and laundry during one voyage between Seattle and Victoria in June. The Department of Ecology is investigating the June discharge.	None
November 2004, *Volendam* and *Statendam*, Holland America Line (Carnival Corporation) In August 2004, Holland America Line was notified by the National Park Service (NPS) that the *Volendam* and *Statendam* may have violated opacity standards while operating in Glacier Bay. On 10 November 2004, NPS notified Holland America Line in separate letters that a violation of record would be entered in the permanent park files for each ship.	None

Year, Ship, Cruise Line, Explanation of Offence(s)	Fine
August 2003 At the new cruise ship terminal at the Port of Seattle, cruise ships fail to abide by requirement to use low-sulphur diesel while docked – a violation of the state environmental mandates for the project.	
May 2003, *Norwegian Sun,* Norwegian Cruise Line The ship is cited by the State of Washington for an illegal discharge of 16,000 gallons (40 tonnes) of raw sewage into the Strait of Juan de Fuca.	
August 2002, *Ryndam,* Holland America Line (HAL) Approximately 40,000 gallons (250 according to HAL) of sewage sludge discharged into Juneau Harbour.	US$2 million in December 2004
Summer 2001: Carnival Cruise Line, Celebrity Cruises, Crystal Cruises, Holland America Line, Norwegian Cruise Line, Princess Cruises 11 ships (six companies) cited for violations of air opacity regulations – Alaska	Carnival Cruise Line (US$27,500, suspended) Celebrity Cruises (US$55,000, half suspended) Crystal Cruises (US$55,000, half suspended) Holland America (US$27,500, suspended) Norwegian Cruise Line (US$27,500) Princess Cruises (US$55,000, suspended) Royal Caribbean International (US$27,5000, suspended)
June 2001, *Rhapsody of the Seas,* Royal Caribbean International Discharged 200 gallons of greywater into Juneau Harbour	Unknown (up to US$25,000 is allowed)
June 2001, *Mercury,* Celebrity Cruises Discharged treated wastewater at Juneau Harbour without required permits. Tests of the wastewater indicated that it was more acidic than permitted for discharging within 1 mile of shore.	Unknown (up to US$25,000 is allowed)

Year, Ship, Cruise Line, Explanation of Offence(s)	Fine
May 2001, *Westerdam*, Holland America Line Discharged greywater while docked in Juneau Harbour; estimated by Holland America Line at 30 to 100 gallons.	Unknown (up to US$25,000 is allowed)
May 2001, *Norwegian Sky*, Norwegian Cruise Line Discharged blackwater (sewage) for 20 to 30 minutes (meaning a waste stream of up to 0.75 mile) while the vessel was en route from Juneau to Ketchikan and within 3 miles of the Alexander Archipelago. Faecal coliform counts were 3500 times the allowable federal standard and total suspended solids 180 times the standard.	Unknown (up to US$25,000 is allowed)
Summer 2000: Carnival Cruise Line, Celebrity Cruises, Crystal Cruises, Holland America Line, Norwegian Cruise Line, Princess Cruises, World Explorer Cruises 15 ships (7 companies) cited for violating Alaska's state smoke-opacity standards when they were docked in Juneau Harbour between mid July and mid August.	Carnival Cruise Line (US$27,500) Celebrity Cruises (US$55,000) Crystal Cruises (US$55,000) Holland America Line (US$165,000–$55,000, suspended) Norwegian Cruise Line (US$27,500) Princess Cruises (US$55,000) World Explorer Cruises (US$27,500–$10,000 suspended)
January 2000, Royal Caribbean Cruises Ltd (RCCL) State of Alaska charged RCCL in August 1999 for seven counts of violating state laws governing oil and hazardous waste disposal. In January 2000, RCCL pleaded guilty to dumping toxic chemicals (including dry-cleaning fluid) and oil-contaminated water into the state's waters.	US$3.5 million

Source: adapted from Cruise Junkie (2009a)

The holistic approach

The environmental impacts of the cruise industry are not only related to the impacts caused by the cruise ships alone. Often neglected in impact assessments are the contributions of the transport to get to and from the ports of call. This has particular relevance in the case of Antarctic cruises since these depart and return from/to ports that are usually far away from the place of the passengers' place of residence. Thus, the energy consumption and environmental impacts of the transport to and from the gateway ports are important as well. Amelung and Lamers (2007) undertook a study for Antarctic tourism for the 2004/2005 season, which included the transport to and from the gateway ports, the time onboard the cruise and expedition ships, Antarctic over-flights from Australia and Chile, and land-based activities. Table 8.3 summarizes the carbon dioxide equivalent (CO_2-e) emissions and highlights that the emissions from non-direct cruise activities (i.e. return travel from place of residence to the destination (OD travel) and land-based activities) are the cause of much higher CO_2-e emissions than direct cruise activities.

Amelung and Lamers's (2007) study clearly illustrates that the environmental impacts of polar cruising are to be assessed in a much more holistic way than measuring the impacts of the cruise activities alone. Stewart and Draper (2006) also warn

Table 8.3 *Overview of total estimated carbon dioxide equivalent (CO2-e) emissions resulting from Antarctic tourism in the 2004/2005 season*

Activity	*CO_2-e (tonnes)*	*CO_2-e per passenger (tonnes)*
OD transport: South America	234,906	8.58
OD transport: New Zealand/Australia	4690	8.48
Expedition cruises	142,559	6.33
Cruise only	27,105	5.40
Land-based: Antarctic Logistics Expeditions (ALE)	9182	46.32
Land-based: Aerovias DAP (DAP)	375	0.57
Over-flights: Qantas	5102	3.25
Over-flights: LAN Chile	710	1.54
Total	424,629	
Total (excluding over-flights and DAP)	418,442	14.97

Note: OD transport = return travel from place of residence to the destination.
Source: Amelung and Lamers (2007, p130)

that there is an urgent need for a holistic integrated planning approach for Arctic Canada. They refer to the Lisbon Principles, which comprise a series of management approaches, embedded in Canada's integrated ocean management framework, and include the responsibility principle, the subsidiarity principle, the adaptive management principle, the precautionary principle and the participation principle.

Conclusions

This chapter has reviewed a variety of environmental impacts associated with the cruise industry in polar regions. With rapidly increasing numbers of cruise vessel visits, concern for potential damage to fragile environments in polar regions is of primary concern (Hall, 1992). Even if the cruise industry implements more sustainable practices (e.g. advanced wastewater treatment systems, a total ban on the discharge of liquid and solid wastes), the risk of vessels colliding with icebergs or running aground remains. This is a particular challenge due to the increase of 'regular' cruise ships visiting the regions (i.e. ships without strengthened hulls). The potential spill of large quantities of oil, fuel and other hazardous substances from a cruise vessel could potentially have devastating consequences for both marine and coastal environments. Regulations of the Antarctic Treaty or the International Association of Antarctica Tour Operators (IAATO) are of limited power since ships operating under flags of convenience are not bound to these rules (O'Grady, 2006). John Shears of the British Antarctic Survey (BAS) calls for recognition of these threats beyond the scientific community: 'The global nature of these threats and the severity of possible impacts means the international community, not just scientists, need to start thinking of Antarctica not in isolation as something at the bottom of the world but as an integral part of the earth system' (CNN, 2003). Antarctic Treaty experts met in Wellington, New Zealand, in December 2009; not surprisingly, cruise lines attempted to 'water down proposals for greater environmental protection in the Southern Ocean' (*Inside Tourism*, 2009, p8). Overall, the same issues are applicable for the Arctic and sub-polar regions.

References

Amelung, B. and Lamers, M. (2007) 'Estimating the greenhouse gas emissions from Antarctic tourism', *Tourism in Marine Environments*, vol 4, no 2–3, pp121–134

Baldwin Paloti, M. (2009) 'Damaged Hurtigruten ship *Richard With* pulled from service', *CruiseCritic.com*, 15 January, www.cruisecritic.com/news/news.cfm?ID=3016, accessed 14 October 2009

Bastmeijer, K. (in press) 'A long term strategy for Antarctic tourism: The key decision making within the Antarctic Treaty system?', in P. T. Maher, E. Stewart and M. Lück (eds) *Polar Tourism: Human, Environmental and Governance Dimensions*, Cognizant Communication, Elmsford, NY

Bauer, T. G. (2001) *Tourism in the Antarctic: Opportunities, Constraints, and Future Prospects*, The Haworth Hospitality Press, New York, NY

Berglund, N. (2008) 'Cruiseship refloated east of Spitsbergen', *Aftenpostet*, 24 July, www.aftenposten.no/english/local/article2556075.ece, accessed 14 October 2009

Bertram, E. (2007) 'Antarctic ship-borne tourism: An expanding industry', in J. M. Snyder and B. Stonehouse (eds) *Prospects for Polar Tourism*, CABI, Wallingford, pp149–169

Cartwright, R. and Baird, C. (1999) *The Development and Growth of the Cruise Industry*, Butterworth-Heinemann, Oxford

Cerveny, L. (2008) *Nature and Tourists in the Last Frontier: Local Encounters with Global Tourism in Coastal Alaska*, Cognizant Communication Corp, Elmsford, NY

Chesworth, N. (2007) 'Greywater', in M. Lück (ed) *The Encyclopedia of Tourism and Recreation in Marine Environments*, CABI, Wallingford, pp202–203

CLIA (Cruise Lines International Association) (2009) *2009 CLIA Cruise Market Overview: Statistical Cruise Industry Data through 2008*, CLIA, Fort Lauderdale, FL

CNN (2003) 'Tourists warned of polar dangers', *CNN.com Travel*, edition.cnn.com/2003/TRAVEL/09/10/antarctica.reut/index.html, accessed 11 September 2009

CNN (2009) 'Cruise ship grounded off Antarctica coast', *CNN.com*, 18 February, http://edition.cnn.com/2009/WORLD/americas/02/18/antarctica.cruise.ship/index.html, accessed 14 October 2009

Coghlan, A. (2007) 'Blackwater', in M. Lück (ed) *The Encyclopedia of Tourism and Recreation in Marine Environments*, CABI, Wallingford, p65.

CruiseBruise (2007a) '*Albatros Travel Disko II*: Cruise ship grounded off Greenland coast', *CruiseBruise*, 27 June, www.cruisebruise.com/Disko_II_Grounding_Greenland_June_27_2007.html, accessed 14 October 2009

CruiseBruise (2007b) '*Spirit of Columbia* grounding: Cruise west vessel grounds near Whittier, Alaska', *CruiseBruise*, 19 August, www.cruisebruise.com/Spirit_of_Columbia_Grounding_August_19_2007.html, accessed 14 October 2009

Cruise Junkie (2009a) *Pollution and Environmental Violations and Fines, 1992–2005*, www.cruisejunkie.com/envirofines.html, accessed 6 October 2009

Cruise Junkie (2009b) *Reported Incidents of Passenger Ships Running Aground, 1972– 2008*, www.cruisejunkie.com/Aground.html, accessed 14 October 2009

Cruise Junkie (2009c) *Reported Incidents of Ships Sinking, 1979–2007*, www.cruisejunkie.com/Sunk.html, accessed 14 October 2009

Davies, T. and Cahill, S. (2000) *Environmental Implications of the Tourism Industry*, Discussion Paper 00-14, Resources for the Future, Washington, DC

Douglas, N. and Douglas, N. (2001) 'The cruise experience', in N. Douglas, N. Douglas and R. Derret (eds), *Special Interest Tourism* (pp. 330-351) Brisbane: John Wiley and Sons.

Dowling, R. K. (2006) 'The cruising industry', in R. K. Dowling (ed) *Cruise Ship Tourism*, CABI, Wallingford, pp3–17.

Drouin, M. (2008) 'Alaska cruise ship comes to rest on sandbar; second incident for the company in 6 months', *Professional Mariner: Journal of the Maritime Industry*, October/November, www.professionalmariner.com/ME2/dirmod.asp?sid=420C4D38DC9C4E3A903315CDDC65AD72andnm=Archivesandtype=Publishingandmod=Publications%3A%3AArticleandmid=8F3A7027421841978F18BE895F87F791andtier=4andid=4111B35601DA451E934C311E439DEB8B, accessed 14 October 2009

Economist (2001) 'The things they leave behind: Black water, did you say?', *The Economist*, 19 May, p31

Golden, K. (2008) 'Cruise ship grounds near Glacier Bay', *JuneauEmpire.com*, 8 July, www.juneauempire.com/stories/070808/loc_301334527.shtml, accessed 14 October 2009

Golden, K. (2009) 'Empress of the North owner fined for grounding', *JuneauEmpire.com*, 28 April, www.juneauempire.com/stories/042809/loc_434335752.shtml, accessed 14 October 2009

Hall, C. M. (1992) 'Tourism in Antarctica: Activities, impacts, and management', *Journal of Travel Research*, vol 30, no 4, pp2–9

Herz, M. and Davis, J. (2002) *Cruise Control*, The Ocean Conservancy, Anchorage, AK

Higham, J. (2008) 'Antarctica', in M. Lück (ed) *The Encyclopedia of Tourism and Recreation in Marine Environments*, CABI, Wallingford, pp21–22

IMO (International Maritime Organization) (2009) *International Convention on the Control of Harmful Anti-Fouling Systems on Ships*, www.imo.org/conventions/mainframe. asp?topic_id–529, accessed 7 October 2009

Inside Tourism (2009) 'Operators to meet Antarctic experts', *Inside Tourism*, 3 December, p8

Jainchill, J. (2008) 'Cruise West ship runs aground in Glacier Bay', *USA Today*, www.usatoday. com/travel/cruises/item.aspx?type=blogandak=52390188.blog, accessed 14 October 2009

Jentes, J. E. (2001) *The Origin of the Great Lakes Zebra Mussels*, www.oar.noaa.gov/spotlite/ archive/spot_zebramussels.html, accessed 17 October 2006

Joyner, C. C. (2000) 'Protection of the Antarctic environment against marine pollution under the 1991 Protocol', in D. Vidas (ed) *Protecting the Polar Marine Environment: Law and Policy for Pollution Prevention* Cambridge University Press, Cambridge, pp104–123

Klein, R. A. (2002) *Cruise Ship Blues: The Underside of the Cruise Industry*, New Society Publishers, Gabriola Island, British Columbia

Klein, R. A. (2008) *Paradise Lost At Sea: Rethinking Cruise Vacations*, Fernwood, Halifax, Nova Scotia

Lumma, K. and Gross, S. (2009) 'Ökologische Auswirkungen von Hochseekreuzfahrten', in H. Bastian, A. Dreyer and S. Gross (eds) *Tourismus 3.0: Fakten und Perspektiven* ITD Verlag, Hamburg, pp197–226

Ministry of Natural Resources (Ontario) (2006) *Stop the Invasion!* www.mnr.gov.on.ca/ fishing/threat.html, accessed 17 October 2006

Oceana (2008) *Contamination by Cruise Ships*, Oceana Europe, Madrid

O'Grady, R. (2006) 'Cruise ships threaten disaster in Antarctic', *The New Zealand Herald*, 13 September, pA21

Patagonia Times (2008) 'Grounded ship set loose in Chilean Antarctica', *Patagonia Times*, 8 December, www.patagoniatimes.cl/index.php/20081208704/News/Tourism/ TOURIST-SHIP-GROUNDED-IN-CHILEAN-ANTARCTICA.html, accessed 14 October 2009

Revkin, A. C. (2008) 'Another Antarctic tourist ship in trouble', *The New York Times*, 4 December, *Dot Earth*, www.dotearth.blogs.nytimes.com/2008/12/04/another-antarctic-tourist-ship-in-trouble, accessed 14 October 2009

Rothwell, D. R. (2000) 'Global environmental protection instruments and the polar marine environment', in D. Vidas (ed) *Protecting the Polar Marine Environment: Law and Policy for Pollution Prevention* Cambridge University Press, Cambridge, pp57–77

Sheppard, V. (2003) *A Shocking Truth*, www.stopcruisepollution.com/index.cfm?fuseaction=f eaturedStoryandyourstoryID=113, accessed 3 May 2003

Sheppard, V. (2008a) 'Alaska Cruise Ship Initiative (ACSI)', in M. Lück (ed) *The Encyclopedia of Tourism and Recreation in Marine Environments*, CABI, Wallingford, p11

Sheppard, V. (2008b) 'International Convention for the Prevention of Marine Pollution from Ships (MARPOL)', in M. Lück (ed) *The Encyclopedia of Tourism and Recreation in Marine Environments*, CABI, Wallingford, pp236–237

Silverstein, E. and Kazell, K. (2008) 'Update: Ship grounded in Antarctica, 122 rescued', *CruiseCritic.com*, 5 December, www.cruisecritic.com/news/news.cfm?ID=2967, accessed 14 October 2009

Snyder, J. M. (2007) 'The polar tourism markets', in J. M. Snyder and B. Stonehouse (eds) *Prospects for Polar Tourism*, CABI, Wallingford, pp51–70.

Spracklin, B. (2005) 'Environmentally friendly cruise ships an oxymoron?', *Richmond on Campus*, 13 September, http://oncampus.richmond.edu/academics/journalism/outlook/cruise.html

Stewart, E. and Draper, D. (2006) 'Sustainable cruise tourism in Arctic Canada: An integrated coastal management approach', *Tourism in Marine Environments*, vol 3, no 2, pp77–88

Sweeting, J. E. N. and Wayne, S. L. (2006) 'A shifting tide: Environmental challenges and cruise industry responses', in R. K. Dowling (ed) *Cruise Ship Tourism*, CABI, Wallingford, pp327–337

Wang, C. (2008) 'International Convention on the Control of Harmful Anti-Fouling Systems on Ships (Anti-Fouling Convention)', in M. Lück (ed) *The Encyclopedia of Tourism and Recreation in Marine Environments*, CABI, Wallingford, p238

Waymer, K. (2007) 'Ships' soot deadly, study says', *Florida Today.com*, http://pqasb.pqarchiver.com/floridatoday/access/1719620611.html?FMT=ABSandamp;date=Nov+17,+2007, accessed 13 October 2009

9

Monitoring Patterns of Cruise Tourism across Arctic Canada

Emma J. Stewart, Dianne Draper and Jackie Dawson

Introduction

Almost a quarter century after the inaugural cruise by the *Explorer*, the number of cruises to the Canadian Arctic peaked at 26, making the 2008 summer season the busiest ever for cruise vessels in this region. Despite growth in this niche polar expedition cruising market, little is known about the scale and scope of cruise activity in Arctic Canada. In this chapter, data from the 2006, 2008 and 2009 cruise seasons is presented and routes taken by cruise vessels, as well as communities and other locations visited, are identified (data was not collected in 2007). It is argued that a basic lack of information on cruise tourism activities, alongside limited monitoring, lack of formal regulations and poor surveillance capability of cruise ship activities in the region, hinders social and environmental sustainability of both the cruise tourism industry and local communities of Arctic Canada. The chapter begins with a brief history of cruise activities in the Canadian Arctic and provides an overview of the current monitoring of cruise ship activities conducted by northern agencies. In an effort to remedy some of the problems of data collection, a dataset on cruise tourism in Arctic Canada is presented which highlights geographic patterns of cruise activity focusing on the High Arctic, Northwest Passage, Baffin Bay and Hudson Bay regions.

Cruise tourism across Arctic Canada

In 1984, with 98 tourists on board, the *Explorer* cruise ship traversed the Northwest Passage in 23 days, only the 33rd full passage ever (Marsh and Staple, 1995; Jones, 1999). This maritime 'first' signalled the start of the cruise industry in Arctic Canada (Stewart et al, 2007). Expedition cruising, a phrase used to describe the Arctic cruise concept, is styled on early cruises to Antarctica where, during the 1960s, cruising first combined brief shore visits by zodiacs (small inflatable craft) with environmental and historical education (Mason and Legg, 1999; Splettstoesser, 2000). Development of the expedition cruise industry in this region between 1984 and 1991 was sporadic and unpredictable. However, from 1992, with the increased availability of relatively inexpensive icebreakers after the collapse of the Soviet Union's economy, a more regular pattern of cruise activity emerged (Grenier, 2004). Between 1992 and 2005 there were between one and three successful expedition cruises through the Northwest Passage completed each year, as well as cruise ship visits to Baffin Island, Hudson Bay and Ellesmere Island (Stewart et al, 2007). A turning point came in 2006 when the number of cruise ships visiting the Canadian Arctic doubled to 22 cruises, up from 11 separate cruises in the previous season (Buhasz, 2006). During the 2007 season, growth stabilized with 23 separate cruises planned by six different companies, who together brought approximately 2110 visitors to the Canadian Arctic (Maher and Meade, 2008). During the 2008 cruise season, six vessels operated in the Canadian Arctic (*Kapitan Khlebnikov, Akademik Ioffe, Polar Star, Lyubov Orlova, Bremen* and *Hanseatic*) carrying passengers on 26 separate cruises. Despite deepening concerns about the global economic climate, seven vessels planned to carry passengers on 25 separate cruises that will make ports of call in the Canadian Arctic in 2009 with the *Clipper Adventurer* joining the six vessels listed for the 2008 season (see Table 9.1). However, in early 2009, anecdotal evidence suggested that at least four of these 25 cruises may be cancelled due to low bookings (we have been unable to verify whether this was the case).

Table 9.1 *Ship data for cruise vessels sailing in Arctic Canada in 2009*

Vessel	*Operator(s)*	*Tonnage*	*Passengers*	*Ice rating*
Kapitan Khlebnikov	Quark Expeditions	12,228	112	Ice breaker LL3
Akademik Ioffe	Quark Expeditions	6450	109	1A2
Polar Star	Polarstar Expeditions	4998	105	1A
Lyubov Orlova	Cruise North/ Quark Expeditions	4251	112	1A2
Bremen	Hapag-Lloyd Cruises	6752	164	E4
Hanseatic	Hapag-Lloyd Cruises	8378	184	E4
Clipper Adventurer	Quark Expeditions	4364	122	1A

Source: Cruise North (2009); Hapag-Lloyd (2009); Polar Star Expeditions (2009); Quark Expeditions (2009)

Monitoring cruise ship activity in Arctic Canada

A variety of stakeholders have been trying to determine the actual number of cruise ships entering Canadian Arctic waters, although no one agency is taking the lead in monitoring or collecting this data. The Canadian Department of National Defence and Customs Canada (for vessels entering Canadian waters from other countries, such as Greenland) collect some data regarding the cruise industry and this information is shared with Nunavut Tourism and the Government of Nunavut, and then disseminated to the hamlets where cruise visits are expected. The Northern Canada Traffic Regulation System (NORDREG) keeps track of all marine traffic north of 60° and receives some data from cruise ships; but registration with NORDREG is not mandatory. In some instances tour operators contact hamlet offices or visitor service representatives directly to make arrangements regarding cruise visits. Additionally, Parks Canada collects a limited amount of information on visitors to the four national parks of Nunavut.

Unfortunately, none of these data sources are comprehensive, providing only a partial evidence base from which to evaluate cruise visitation to Arctic Canada. Despite stakeholder efforts to track cruise activity, the inconsistency of data is problematic. Determining the scale and scope of the industry is impossible without adequate data, as are regulation and effective planning. To address this data collection problem since 2006, we have been reviewing websites that advertise cruises to Arctic Canada and building a database of planned cruises. We make note of communities that ships propose to visit, as well as other landing places, such as locations of historic, cultural or environmental interest (which we refer to as shore visits). Although this is a crude data collection methodology, to our knowledge it provides the only consistent dataset on recent cruise activity in Arctic Canada. It should be noted, however, that the dataset reviews intended cruises and locations visited, rather than actual cruises, meaning that in reality locations visited and routes taken could well be different than those reported here. This is because the dynamic variability of the Arctic environment makes actual ship routing unpredictable. The locations visited by these cruise vessels are plotted in Figure 9.1, where a distinction is made between visits to actual communities and visits to shore locations. The Canadian Arctic is divided into four main sub-regions: High Arctic, Northwest Passage, Baffin Bay and Hudson Bay (see Figure 9.1). Each of these sub-regions is discussed in the following sections in an effort to describe the scale and scope of cruise tourism throughout the Canadian Arctic.

Cruise tourism in the High Arctic

The ice-congested waterways of the High Arctic are the domain of ice-breaking cruise ships, such as the retro-fitted former Russian ice breaker *Kapitan Khlebnikov*. These most northerly Canadian Arctic waters are the least visited in the region (see Table 9.2). During the three seasons under examination, the *Kapitan Khlebnikov* ventured as far north as the Tanquary Fjord on Ellesmere Island via Eureka station, and made shore landings on Axel Heiberg Island. In 2008, the ice breaker also ventured

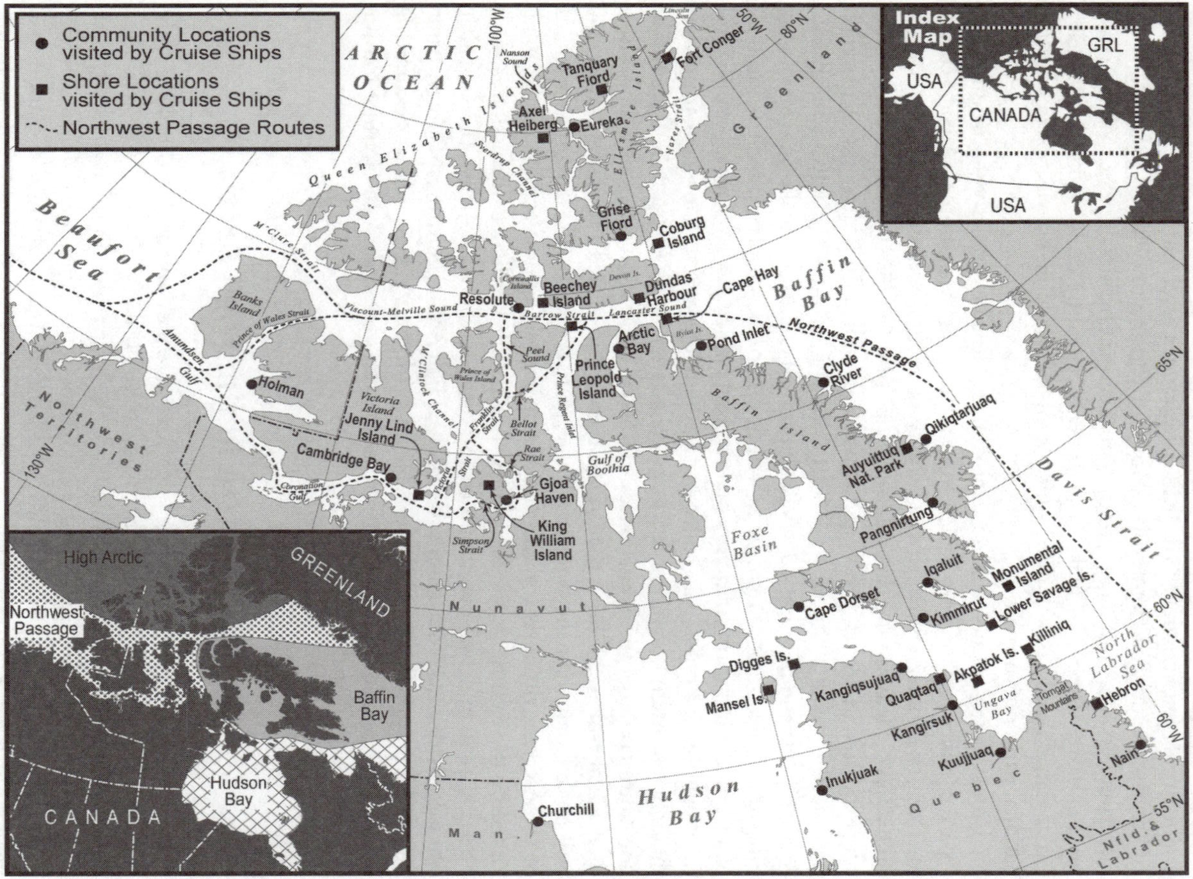

Figure 9.1 *Cruise destinations in Canada's Arctic (2006, 2008 and 2009)*
Source: Robin Poitras, Cartographer, University of Calgary

through the Nares Strait with the intention of making it as far north as the Lincoln Sea, as well as making shore visits to locations such as Fort Conger. In the southern reaches of Ellesmere Island, the small community of Grise Fjord saw three cruises in both 2006 and 2008; but this number fell to just one cruise in 2009. To the east of Grise Fjord is Coburg Island, a National Wildlife Area well regarded for bird-viewing opportunities, which has seen increased activity with five cruises expected in 2009.

Table 9.2 *Community and shore visits to the High Arctic for seasons 2006, 2008 and 2009*

Community visits	2006	2008	2009
Grise Fjord	3	3	1
Shore visits	**2006**	**2008**	**2009**
Axel Heiberg	1	1	1
Eureka	0	1	1
Fort Conger	0	1	1
Coburg Island	3	7	5

Source: Quark Expeditions (2009)

Cruise tourism in the Northwest Passage

From as early as the end of the 15th century, the commercial advantage of the Northwest Passage prompted many explorers to navigate the intricate islands and waterways of the Canadian Arctic. But this was not achieved successfully until 1906 when the Norwegian explorer Roald Amundsen finally sailed the passage from east to west. Given these unrivalled opportunities to witness the relics associated with historical exploration of the passage, as well as good wildlife viewing, this region is the most popular expedition cruise area in the Canadian Arctic. Communities along the passage such as Resolute and Cambridge Bay expect to be hosting more cruises in 2009 than in previous years. Resolute anticipates hosting 21 cruise ships in 2009, which is a higher number even than the bumper season of 2008, when 17 cruises either started or ended their journey there. Similarly, Cambridge Bay received six cruise ships in 2009, double the number of cruises this community typically has hosted. The small communities of Holman (Ulukhaktok) and Gjoa Haven also have seen a gradual increase in cruise vessels (see Table 9.3).

The most visited site along the Northwest Passage is Beechey Island, where relics associated with Franklin's 1845 Northwest Passage expedition can be found. From 2 August 2009 until 9 September 2009, Beechey Island was visited by 16 different cruises including multiple visits on the same day. Prince Leopold and Jenny Lind Islands, other landing sites along the passage, hosted more cruise visits in 2009 than in previous years due to the increase in volume of Northwest Passage tours (see Table 9.3).

Table 9.3 *Community and shore visits to the Northwest Passage for seasons 2006, 2008 and 2009*

Community visits	2006	2008	2009
Cambridge Bay	3	2	6
Gjoa Haven	0	2	3
Holman (Ulukhaktok)	1	2	4
Resolute	16	17	21
Shore visits	*2006*	*2008*	*2009*
Beechey Island	11	15	16
Dundas Harbour, Devon Island	5	8	8
Jenny Lind Island	1	1	3
King William Island	1	2	2
Prince Leopold Island	3	3	7

Source: Cruise North (2009); Hapag-Lloyd Cruises (2009); Quark Expeditions (2009)

Cruise tourism in the Baffin Bay region

For many years, Cape Dorset (located on Dorset Island in the Hudson Narrows off the south coast of Baffin Island) has marketed itself as the 'Capital of Inuit Art'. Since the 1950s, local printmaking and carving have attracted global attention; so it is not surprising that the community has been a regular port of call for cruise ships, evidenced by six visits in 2006. Strangely, in subsequent years the number of visits has diminished to only one in 2008, and two in 2009. The apparent demise may be due to the general shift northward of cruise itineraries, notably to the Northwest Passage, rather than a lack of interest in visiting this community *per se*. Similar to the situation in Cape Dorset, the community of Kimmirut appears to have seen a decrease in the number of visiting cruise vessels.

Farther north into Baffin Bay, Davis Strait has, in the past, been a focus of cruise activity in Arctic Canada. This status is evidenced by cruise visits to Nunavut's capital, Iqaluit. With 14 scheduled cruises to Iqaluit in 2008, the territorial capital was the second most visited community in Nunavut, marginally behind Resolute in the High Arctic. However, this study reveals that for 2009 Iqaluit will host only four cruise ships, again echoing the apparent shift of cruise itineraries away from southern and eastern Baffin Island. Polar cruise tourists have a tendency to be repeat clients (Grenier, 2004), so the apparent shifts in cruise itineraries identified in this study may reflect visitor demand for new destinations.

The community of Pangnirtung, nestled along the shore of Pangnirtung Fjord, is a gateway community for adventure and land-based tourism activities in the

Table 9.4 *Community and shore visits to Baffin Bay for seasons 2006, 2008 and 2009*

Community visits	2006	2008	2009
Arctic Bay	3	1	0
Cape Dorset	6	1	2
Clyde River	1	2	0
Iqaluit	8	14	4
Kimmirut	5	1	1
Pangnirtung	4	6	3
Pond Inlet	13	9	8
Qikiqtarjuaq	2	3	2
Shore visits	**2006**	**2008**	**2009**
Auyuittuaq	4	2	0
Cape Hay	1	3	3
Monumental Island	0	6	2

Source: Cruise North (2009); Hapag-Lloyd Cruises (2009); Quark Expeditions (2009)

Figure 9.2 Hanseatic *cruise vessel visiting Pond Inlet*
Source: Emma J. Stewart

neighbouring Auyuittuaq National Park. Four vessels visited in 2006, six in 2008, and three in 2009. To the south of Pangnirtung in Cumberland Sound, Kekerten Territorial Historic Park attracted the *Lyubov Orlova* twice in 2008 and the park received two visits in 2009. At the entrance to Cumberland Sound, Monumental Island (a popular place to view walrus) witnessed six cruises in 2008 and two visits in 2009.

Located on the northern shores of Baffin Island, Pond Inlet (across from the glaciated coastline of Bylot Island) has been visited by cruise ships for many years. Discussions with local stakeholders in Pond Inlet indicate that 2008 was the busiest year ever for cruise ships, with 14 vessels disembarking passengers (from the cruise itineraries we were able to identify only nine visits). Surprise visits from cruise ships and adverse weather and ice conditions may have caused adjustments to scheduled community visits. At the start of the 2008 cruise season, a one-man protest regarding the European Union ban on seal skin imports (aimed at European passengers from the *Hanseatic*) may have had unintended consequences for the cruise industry in Pond Inlet (CBC News, 2008). The protest, which took place as passengers disembarked onto the beach at Pond Inlet and caused offence to the arriving passengers, may be a contributing factor as to why only eight cruise vessels are expected in 2009. From the dataset it appears that the *Hanseatic* (see Figure 9.2) will not be disembarking passengers in Pond Inlet in 2009.

Cruise tourism in the Hudson Bay region

Churchill, the only community visited by cruise ships in western Hudson Bay, has seen a consistent two visits by the Inuit-operated *Lyubov Orlova* during each of the three cruise seasons under investigation. Cruise tourism in Churchill has had a rather uneventful history, with other land-based activities being developed in preference. To the east, the small Nunavik community of Inukjuak welcomed four separate cruises in 2006; but no cruise ships have visited since, likely reflecting a lack of demand for cruises on the eastern shores of Hudson Bay (see Table 9.5). To the north, however, passengers on board the *Lyubov Orlova* make regular shore visits to Digges and Mansel Islands where polar bear and walrus viewing is possible. Digges Island was also visited by the ill-fated *Explorer* on one of her last tours of the Canadian Arctic in 2006.

The Nunavik community of Kuujjuaq is the home base of Cruise North, the Inuit-operated cruise tour company (through Makivik Corporation). As a regional centre and transportation hub (the community sees daily flights using Nunavik's longest airstrip), Kuujjuaq is an obvious and convenient location for Cruise North's operations. With the exception of the Northwest Passage tours, all cruises offered by Cruise North either start or finish in this community, making Kuujjuaq the most consistently visited community in the Hudson Bay region during 2006 (11 visits), 2008 and 2009 (seven visits for both years). In 2009, the community hosted the *Lyubov Orlova* from mid July to late September. Similar to Resolute and, to a certain extent, Iqaluit, Kuujjuaq is likely a convenient entry-exit point for tourists to the

Table 9.5 *Community and shore visits to Hudson Bay for seasons 2006, 2008 and 2009*

Community visits	2006	2008	2009
Churchill	2	2	2
Inukjuak	4	0	0
Kangiqsujuaq	4	3	3
Kangirsuk	4	0	1
Kuujjuaq	11	7	7
Nain	0	2	1
Shore visits	**2006**	**2008**	**2009**
Akpatok Island	9	7	7
Digges and Mansel Islands	5	3	2
Hebron	2	2	1
Killiniq	3	5	3
Lower Savage Islands	2	2	1
Torngat Mountains	1	4	1
Quaqtaq	2	2	2

Source: Cruise North (2009); Polar Star Expeditions (2009); Quark Expeditions (2009)

Canadian Arctic, rather than a destination that tourists perceive as important in its own right.

Several islands and island groups in the Hudson Strait sub-region have become popular for shore visits. The most visited of these is Akpatok Island, in the entrance of Ungava Bay, where passengers are promised good wildlife viewing, particularly of polar bears, walrus, thick-billed murres, and other Arctic bird species. The majority of Cruise North's tours visit the island on their way to or from Kuujjuaq. In addition to the *Lyubov Orlova*, during each of the three cruise seasons investigated, the *Polar Star* has made the last call of the season to Akpatok Island (usually in late September) while on her way out of the Canadian Arctic. Other island groups in the vicinity are also valued by cruise operators. At the entrance of the Hudson Strait, for example, Killiniq and the Button Islands environments provide aquatic habitat for marine mammals, including several species of whales. The presence of such wildlife have made the Button Island group consistently popular with the *Lyubov Orlova* – three cruise visits were made in both 2006 and 2009, and five occurred in 2008. The *Lyubov Orlova* has made two visits to Quaqtaq and the neighbouring Diana Islands (where musk oxen roam) in each of the three cruise seasons under review. The Lower Savage Islands, just off the south-east tip of Baffin Island, have been frequented to a slightly lesser extent by the *Polar Star*, *Explorer* and *Akademik Ioffe*.

Locations such as Nain and Hebron in the North Labrador Sea have hosted a small number of cruise vessels in recent years (two each in 2008 and one each planned for 2009). These places are often visited at the start or the end of the cruise season (June and September) as vessels position or reposition themselves either in or out of the Canadian North via Newfoundland and Labrador.

Discussion

Our analysis of cruise activity indicates that cruise tourism is highly variable across Arctic Canada. Of the four regions reviewed, the Northwest Passage is the only region that is witnessing growth in the cruise sector, while communities along southern and eastern Baffin Island and some locations in the Hudson Bay area appear to be experiencing a decline in cruise visits. The High Arctic region appears reasonably stable, with two tours each year. The emerging pattern of cruise activity is most evident in the marked increase in Northwest Passage tours planned for the 2009. Concerns for both communities and tour operators should be raised if this trend and concentration of cruise activity in the Northwest Passage continues.

As the Northwest Passage transitions to an ice-free summer (some of the routes through the passage were ice free during the summers of 2007, 2008 and 2009), the ice regimes may present navigational problems due to higher levels of multiyear ice from the polar cap. Ice is an ever-present danger; for instance, the *Hanseatic* grounded in the Simpson Strait after a visit to Gjoa Haven in 1996. The incident was relatively benign, with no reports of environmental incidents or injury to passengers or crew (Transportation Safety Board of Canada, 1996). More serious incidents have also occurred internationally across the Arctic. For example, in 2007, 17 cruise passengers onboard the *Aleksei Maryshev* were injured by a wave from a calving glacier in the vicinity of the Svalbard Islands (Knight, 2007). In a similar accident later in the same year, two Danish tourists were killed while photographing a glacier in Greenland (Sermitsiaq, 2007). Incidents involving cruise vessels in Antarctica have also occurred, such as the *Lyubov Orlova* and *Nordkapp* groundings in 2006, the *Ushuaia* grounding in 2008, and the *Ocean Nova* grounding in 2009; however, the most dramatic and disastrous incident was the sinking of the *Explorer* in 2007. Incidents such as these may accelerate as polar environments are subjected to climatic changes which result in greater unpredictability of ice conditions. Such changes highlight the increased urgency to monitor, assess and regulate cruise tourism activities.

Cruise tourism growth in Arctic Canada means that certain communities and shore locations may become even more crowded than they are already, and impacts may become more concentrated. For example, Resolute and Beechey Island continue to receive the highest numbers of cruise ship visits each year, and numbers of vessels appear to be increasing (disembarking, on average, 100 passengers per ship). This acceleration and concentration of tourist activity over relatively short periods of time raises additional concerns about the socio-cultural and environmental effects of tourism in Arctic Canada. Apart from some monitoring conducted by Parks Canada during cruise ship visits to particular areas encompassed by park boundaries, there has been limited research conducted on the possible environmental concerns stemming from cruise tourism in the Canadian Arctic. Obvious concerns include repeated trampling of tundra by passengers disembarking at remote sites of interest (such as archaeological sites), wave erosion created by ships and zodiacs, and disturbance of land, marine mammals and historic relics. The socio-cultural effects of cruise tourism on small hamlets in Arctic Canada are wide ranging, including issues of intrusion and the potential for tourist's lack of appreciation for, or misunderstanding of, traditional subsistence activities. However, socio-cultural effects of cruise tourism are not always negative. Positive effects include the opportunity for Inuit to dispel some of the myths about living in the Arctic, and in some communities a regular audience of cruise visitors has revitalized traditional throat singing, Arctic sports and drum dancing (Stewart, 2009; Stewart et al, in press). Regular cruise visits to communities can be economically valuable; however, because of the absence of regulation (and the ease with which cruise operators can alter visits to destinations), communities should be mindful that cruise tourism is not a stable source of income.

No comprehensive monitoring and surveillance system exists to scrutinize actual cruise activity through Canadian Arctic waters. NORDREG is the Canadian Coast Guard's Arctic marine traffic system, which aims to keep track of all maritime traffic north of 60°, as well as within Ungava Bay and the southern part of Hudson Bay (Canadian Coast Guard, 2009). When within 100 nautical miles of the nearest Canadian land, in waters where the Arctic Waters Pollution Prevention Act (AWPPA) applies, ships of 300 tonnes or more are required to report their presence 24 hours prior to entering. The NORDREG zone corresponds closely to the regulatory zone of the AWPPA (Canadian Coast Guard, 2009). Currently, cruise ships do not have to register with NORDREG; however, efforts are under way to make registration mandatory for all ships entering Canadian waters (Office of the Prime Minister, 2009). Decisive government action is critical to establish a legally binding monitoring and surveillance system which will record, with more accuracy, which vessels are entering Canadian Arctic waters. Without such action we are left with an incomplete picture of cruise activity in Arctic Canada, making it impossible to precisely monitor patterns of cruise activity over time. This situation does not bode well for the management of cruise tourism in Arctic Canada in a sustainable manner (Stewart et al, 2010).

Furthermore, without a Canadian Arctic equivalent of the International Association of Antarctica Tour Operators (IAATO) or Association of Arctic Expedition Cruise Operators (AECO), there is no regulatory body on the industry side of the system overseeing the development of cruise tourism across Arctic Canada since AECO's remit does not extend outside of the European Arctic. Additionally, none of Canada's three Arctic territories (Yukon, Northwest Territories and Nunavut) have a cruise ship tourism policy. Despite increasing numbers of cruise vessels to Nunavut, in particular, there is no overarching Nunavut-wide policy on cruise tourism, although this has been a topic of concern for Parks Canada for some years. Similarly, there is no pan-Arctic policy on cruise tourism. Given that many of the cruise itineraries reviewed in this chapter cross international boundaries (particularly those with the US, Greenland and Iceland), there is a pressing need to address issues that will ensure polar expedition cruising is managed in a sustainable manner. As it stands at the moment, cruise ship operators are leading the industry's development, and now with a growing catalogue of accidents involving cruise vessels in polar waters, the time has come to change the status quo.

Conclusions

Current mechanisms to monitor, assess and manage cruise ship activity in Arctic Canada are woefully lacking, which, in turn, hinders the social and environmental sustainability of cruise tourism in the region. Without improved monitoring and surveillance of Arctic cruise tourism it is difficult to manage the industry in a sustainable manner. Having presented the most comprehensive dataset known to exist on cruise tourism in Arctic Canada, this research reveals that all regions in Canada's Arctic (apart from the ice-infested Queen Elizabeth Islands) experience cruise activity, although cruise activity is highly variable across the region. The Northwest Passage is currently experiencing the highest volume of cruise traffic in the industry's history in the Canadian Arctic, while places such as southern and eastern Baffin Island are witnessing declines. It is important to monitor these annual fluctuations in cruise activity, not only to help prepare communities and residents for decreases or influxes of visitors, but also to be equipped to manage adverse economic and environmental consequences arising from cruise tourism.

Acknowledgements

Emma Stewart would like to thank the Pierre Elliot Trudeau Foundation for generous funding during her doctoral studies, upon which some of the material presented in this chapter is drawn. We would like to express our thanks to Robin Poitras in the Department of Geography at the University of Calgary for creating the map used in Figure 9.1.

References

Buhasz, L. (2006) 'Northern underexposure', *Globe & Mail*, 1 July
Canadian Coast Guard (2009) 'Vessel traffic reporting Arctic Canada traffic zone (NORDREG)' www.ccg-gcc.gc.ca/eng/MCTS/Vtr_Arctic_Canada, accessed 31 March 2010
CBC News (2008) 'Nunavut officials in damage control over cruise ship incident', www.cbc.ca/canada/north/story/2008/08/14/pond-cruise.html, accessed 1 February 2009
Cruise North (2009) www.cruisenorthexpeditions.com, accessed 14 June 2009
Grenier, A. A. (2004) *The Nature of Nature Tourism*, University of Lapland, Rovaniemi
Hapag-Lloyd Cruises (2009) 'Discover the indescribable world of the Arctic aboard the Hanseatic and the Bremen'[Q91], www.cruises-arctic.com/redwork/do.php?layoutid=880&language=2, accessed 31 March 2010

Jones, C. S. (1999) 'Arctic ship tourism: An industry in adolescence', *The Northern Raven*, vol 13, no 1, pp28–31

Knight, S. (2007) *They Were Looking for Adventure*, www.timesonline.co.uk/tol/news/world/europe/article2231571.ece, accessed 2 February 2009

Maher, P. T. and Meade, D. (2008) *Cruise Tourism in Auyuittuq, Sirmilik and Quttinirpaaq National Parks*, Technical Report, ORTM Publication Series 2008-02, UNBC ORTM Program, Prince George

Marsh, J., and Staple, S. (1995) 'Cruise tourism in the Canadian Arctic and its implications', in C. M. Hall and M. E. Johnston (eds) *Polar Tourism: Tourism and the Arctic and Antarctic regions*, John Wiley and Sons Ltd, Chichester, UK

Mason, P. A., and Legg, S. J. (1999) 'Antarctic tourism: Activities, impacts, management issues and a proposed research agenda', *Pacific Tourism Review*, vol 3, pp71–84

Office of the Prime Minister (2009) 'Backgrounder – extending the jurisdiction of Canadian environment and shipping laws in the Arctic', http://pm.gc.ca/eng/media.asp?id=2246, accessed 10 February 2009

Polar Star Expeditions (2009) 'Atlantic Arctic', www.polarstarexpeditions.com/arctic/arctic_home.htm, accessed 31 March 2010

Quark Expeditions (2009) 'Arctic expeditions', www.quarkexpeditions.com, accessed 14 June 2009

Sermitsiaq (2007) 'Two Danish tourists killed: Two elderly Danes were killed by a glacial wave while visiting the Kangerluarsuk fjord in western Greenland', Sermitsiaq AG news agency website, http://sermitsiaq.gl/indland/article47379.ece?lang=EN, accessed 22 April 2010

Splettstoesser, J. (2000) 'IAATO's stewardship of the Antarctic environment: A history of tour operator's concern for a vulnerable part of the world', *International Journal of Tourism Research*, vol 2, pp47–55

Stewart, E. J. (2009) *Resident Attitudes Toward Tourism: Community-Based Cases from Arctic Canada*, PhD thesis, University of Calgary, Alberta, Canada

Stewart, E. J., Draper, D. L. and Dawson, J. D. (in press) 'Coping with change and vulnerability: A case study of resident attitudes toward tourism in Cambridge Bay and Pond Inlet, Nunavut, Canada', in P. T. Maher, E. J. Stewart and M. Lück (eds) *Polar Tourism: Environmental, Political and Social Dimensions*, Cognizant Communications, New York, NY

Stewart, E. J., Howell, S. E. L., Draper, D., Yackel, J. and Tivy, A. (2007) 'Sea ice in Canada's Arctic: Implications for cruise tourism', *Arctic*, vol 60, issue 4, pp370–380

Stewart, E. J., Howell, S. E. L., Draper, D., Yackel, J. and Tivy, A. (2010) 'Cruise tourism and sea ice in Canada's Hudson Bay region', *Arctic*, vol 63, issue 1, pp57–66

Transportation Safety Board of Canada (1996) *Marine Reports – 1996 – M96H0016*, www.tsb.gc.ca/eng/rapports-reports/marine/1996/m96h0016/m96h0016.asp, accessed 1 February 2009

10

Climate Change and its Implications for Cruise Tourism in the Polar Regions

Machiel Lamers and Bas Amelung

Introduction

Since the Industrial Revolution some 250 years ago, the Earth's climate has unmistakably changed. Global mean temperature has risen by around 0.76°C since the end of the 19th century. The Intergovernmental Panel on Climate Change (IPCC, 2007) recently stated that the 'warming of the climate system is unequivocal'. The IPCC also claims that the effects of climate change are most heavily felt at high latitudes, where there is relatively little human activity. The polar regions are particularly affected by climate warming, especially the Arctic region and the Antarctic Peninsula (ACIA, 2005; Johnston, 2006). Changes predicted include decreased sea ice, warmer and shorter winters, thawing permafrost and changes in wildlife populations. Average winter temperatures in the Arctic have already increased by 3° over the past 60 years and the sea ice extent has reduced by 10 per cent over the last 30 years (ACIA, 2005). In the Antarctic Peninsula annual mean temperatures have risen by about 2° in the past 50 years, resulting in the loss of seven ice shelves (Clarke and Harris, 2003).

At the same time, tourism – and cruise ship tourism, in particular – has grown rapidly in both polar regions. In the Antarctic, cruise tourism has increased rapidly from a few hundred passengers annually in the 1980s to over 45,000 recently (Enzenbacher, 1993; IAATO, 2008). Tourist numbers in the Arctic are considered more difficult to calculate due to unclear delineation of the Arctic region and the multitude of nations involved. Nevertheless, around Svalbard the number of cruise tourists increased from almost 15,500 on 24 ships in 1997 to 34,900 passengers on 49 vessels in 2006 (Sysselmannen på Svalbard, 2006). It has been estimated that for the European Arctic region only (consisting of Northern Scandinavia, Iceland, Greenland and Svalbard), tourist numbers already exceeded 100,000 visitors per year in 2002 (Nordic Council, 2003). Recently this figure has grown significantly, as the Norwegian North Cape alone attracts close to 200,000 visitors annually.[1] Tourism activities in the Canadian Arctic (approximately 225,000 tourists) and Alaska (more than 1 million per year) (AHDR, 2004, Dawson et al, 2007) illustrate the considerable interest in Arctic tourism. The type and scale of tourism activity in the vast Russian Arctic is largely unknown. The total number of tourists travelling to the Arctic region aboard cruise vessels has been estimated at 1.2 million in 2004; by 2007, this number had more than doubled (AMSA, 2009). The effects of climate change and the growing role of tourism in the polar regions raises questions on the relation and the combined impacts of the two sources of change (Stonehouse and Snyder, 2007).

Most of the temperature change observed globally since the middle of the 20th century can very likely be attributed to human activities that are increasing greenhouse gas concentrations in the atmosphere. One of these activities is tourism, which accounts for an estimated 5 per cent of total emissions. A large share of tourism-induced emissions is produced by aviation (40 per cent) and other modes of transport (35 per cent). Tourism's prominence as a source of emissions is growing rapidly as a result of increasing numbers of tourists, a disproportional growth of long-haul trips, and a shift towards the aircraft as the preferred mode of transport (Gössling, 2002).

Tourism as a sector is highly climate sensitive. Enjoyable weather, an interesting natural landscape, sufficient levels of biodiversity, and an adequate supply of water are only a few of the climate-related factors that are of great importance for tourist attraction and satisfaction. Climate change is therefore a very relevant issue for the tourism industry. Indeed, the impacts of a changing climate are already becoming evident at destinations around the world. Winter sport destinations have been among the first to experience the effects of climate change, as snow lines move up and snow reliability goes down (e.g. Breiling and Charamza, 1999). Major changes are also expected for other types of destinations, including the Mediterranean (Amelung and Viner, 2006; Perry, 2006), mountain regions (Scott, 2006) and small island states (Becken and Hay, 2007), and, indeed, for the global distribution of tourism activities.

After a hesitant start, the tourism industry is now quickly acknowledging climate change as a key strategic factor. The United Nations World Tourism Organization (UNWTO) has played a crucial role in this process of awareness-raising by organizing two major international conferences on climate change: the first one in Djerba (2003) and the second one in Davos (2007). Scientific information about the impacts of climate change on tourism is still scarce. Some material on impacts is available for winter sports and a few other tourism activities, and for some regions; but large gaps in our knowledge remain. Few if any empirical studies have been performed on Africa, Asia, Latin America and the polar regions (Hall, 2008). It has been argued that the relation between global (environmental) change factors and polar tourism are under researched (Stewart et al, 2005).

Specifically for the polar regions, Johnston (2006), Dawson et al (2007), Stewart et al (2007) and Snyder (2007) have identified a number of possible mechanisms through which climate change may affect tourism. The purpose of this chapter is to systematically review and critically discuss the implications of climate change for tourism in the polar regions. The aim is to identify ways to improve the knowledge base of climate change and cruise tourism in the polar regions. The assessment is limited to cruise tourism, currently the dominant type of tourism in the Antarctic and rapidly growing in both the Arctic and the Antarctic region.

The chapter is organized as follows. The latest relevant knowledge on climate change in the polar areas is summarized in the next section. A typology of climate change impacts upon tourism is introduced afterwards. Using this typology, the potential impacts for cruise tourism in the Arctic and Antarctic, respectively, are presented. This section also contains reference to the greenhouse gas emissions of cruise tourism in the polar regions. The final two sections compare the findings for the two polar regions and proposes a research agenda.

Climate change in the polar regions: An overview

Climate change typically leads to rapid warming across the polar regions. Mean temperatures in the Arctic region have risen twice as fast as in the rest of the world. Glacial melting, reduction in sea ice thickness and extent, snow and ice cover on land, and shorter and warmer winters are among the changes that are expected (Snyder, 2007). However, in the Arctic as well as in the Antarctic region change is not uniform. For instance, some areas have been reported to be cooling rather than warming. Climate in the Arctic is undergoing dynamic change – for example, in the case of variability in precipitation (Johnston, 2006).

In the European and Canadian Arctic, some endemic marine species will relocate to the north. Permafrost in Siberia and Canada will retreat northwards, and thawing will increase infrastructure damage. On a positive note, an open Northeast Sea Route is expected to generate economic activity in Siberia and facilitate access to natural resources. Sea ice retreat in the Canadian Arctic may also likely open up this sub-region for shipping (Stewart et al, 2007). In the recent Arctic Marine Shipping Assessment (AMSA), the opportunities for future cruise tourism in the Arctic receive considerable attention. The potential future physical effects caused by climate change in the Arctic are given in Figure 10.1.[2] In the Antarctic, regional differences in climate change are more profound. Climate warming is very rapid in the Antarctic Peninsula region, while average temperatures on continental Antarctica remain stable. Recent cooling has been reported at the South Pole (Clarke and Harris, 2003). Due to the limited number and length of available data series, climatic changes in the Antarctic are more difficult to establish.

Climate change is expected to have profound impacts upon the biodiversity of the polar regions. In fact, according to Sala et al (2000), climate change is the single largest threat to biodiversity in the polar regions, whereas land-use change has the greatest impact upon biodiversity on a global scale (Sala et al, 2000). Biologists have already noticed that algae and other species from the warmer waters of the Atlantic Ocean are moving into polar waters. As the endemic Arctic species have nowhere to go, this 'Atlantification' of the Arctic leads to reduced biodiversity (Schiermeier, 2007).

In general, species are migrating polewards to previously cooler climates (McCarty, 2001). Some species, such as flying birds and rapidly reproducing species, may be able to move quickly enough to keep up with climate change. The ability of other species to adapt, such as Macaroni penguins (Cresswell et al, 2008), may

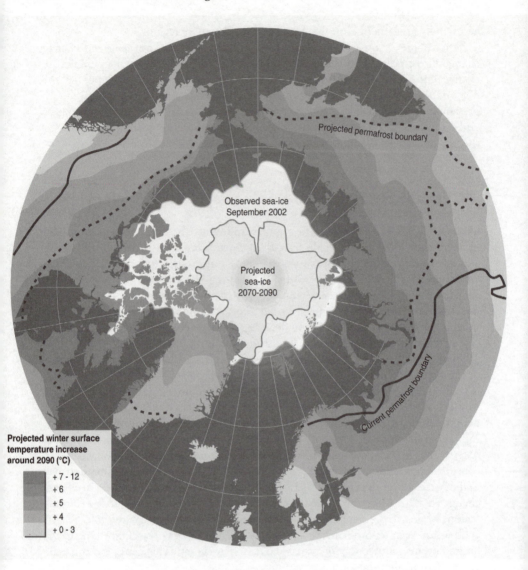

Figure 10.1 *Projected changes in the Arctic climate, 2090*

Source: ACIA (2005)

be insufficient to avoid a major decline of their populations. Species such as the collared lemming in Canada (Kerr and Packer, 1998) and the polar bear (Stirling and Derocher, 1993; ACIA, 2005) that depend on habitats which disappear altogether, run the risk of becoming locally extirpated or, at worst, extinct. An overview of the main polar climate changes is provided in Box 10.1.

Box 10.1 *Overview of polar climate changes reported in several studies*

- The Arctic and Antarctic Peninsula are warming rapidly and accelerated changes are projected.
- Arctic and Antarctic Peninsula warming have worldwide implications with regard to sea-level rise.
- Arctic vegetation zones are very likely to shift, causing wide-ranging implications.
- Animal species' diversity, ranges and distribution will change in both polar regions.
- Increased precipitation is projected.
- Many coastal communities and facilities face increasing exposure to storms.
- Reduced sea ice is very likely to increase marine transport and access to resources.
- Thawing ground will disrupt transportation, buildings and other infrastructure.
- Indigenous communities will face major economic and cultural impacts.
- Elevated ultraviolet radiation will affect people, plants and animals.
- Multiple influences interact to cause impacts upon people and ecosystems.

Source: ACIA (2005); Johnston (2006); Stonehouse and Snyder (2007); AMSA (2009)

A typology of impacts of climate change on tourism

A comprehensive overview of current knowledge about the relationships between climate change and tourism is provided by Scott et al (2008). In discussing the impacts of climate change, they distinguish four broad categories: direct climatic impacts, indirect environmental change impacts, impacts of mitigation policies, and indirect societal change impacts.

The category of direct climatic impacts encompasses the changes in climatic conditions that tourists experience in their holiday destinations. Climatic conditions may become more or less suitable for certain tourist activities and the distribution of suitable conditions throughout the year may change. On the supply side, direct climatic impacts may result in changing heating and cooling requirements. It is expected that the direct climate effects on cruise ship tourism in the polar regions will be minimal.

Indirect impacts are the effects that climate change has on the environment in which tourists spend their holidays, impacts of mitigation polices, and wider societal change mechanisms. Indirect environmental impacts consist of a broad category of impacts, including changes in landscape, coastal erosion, water shortages, biodiversity, and lack of snow. Such changes are crucial for tourism as most tourist activities are related to specific places. One needs snow for skiing, a beach for 'sea, sun and sand' fun, an attractive landscape for trekking, and water-demanding greens for playing golf. Damage to infrastructure also belongs to this category. In earlier review papers on climate change and tourism in the polar regions a distinction is made between different types of impacts that climate change might pose, such as impacts upon infrastructures, effects on access and attractions (Johnston, 2006). Dawson et al (2007) adopt this typology and add stakeholder capacity as a category of impact.

Besides these two 'traditional' impact categories, there are two other groups of impacts that are much less location specific. One of these is the impact of mitigation policies on tourist mobility. Transport is a pivotal element of tourism, and any change in its cost or accessibility can have repercussions for tourism. Further indirect societal changes may affect polar cruise tourism. Since images of the polar regions are often featured in media reports on climate change, public awareness of the polar regions is growing. Tour operators claim that tourists wish to see the beauty of the polar regions 'before it all melts'. Calving glaciers and suffering polar bears are among the main icons of the climate change public imagery that people may wish to see for themselves (Stonehouse and Snyder, 2007). At the same time, these images may result in increased public support for environmental protection of these regions.

The generic framework proposed by Scott et al (2008) lends structure to the overall assessment, but provides little guidance in identifying and discussing the climate change impacts that are most relevant to the polar regions. This holds particular truth for the direct impacts and the indirect environmental impacts that are most location

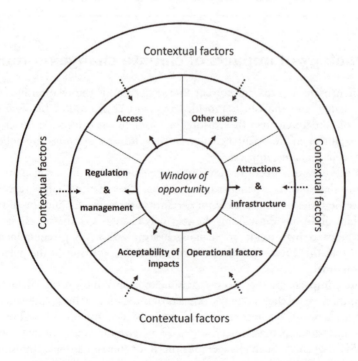

Figure 10.2 *The Antarctic Tourism Opportunity Spectrum (ATOS)*

Source: Lamers (2009)

specific. In order to structure the analysis in these two areas, the Antarctic Tourism Opportunity Spectrum (ATOS) framework complements Scott's framework. Derived from the Recreational Opportunity Spectrum (Clark and Stankey, 1979), ATOS was developed by Lamers et al (2008) to analyse opportunities and trends in Antarctic tourism, including climate change. Whereas the ATOS framework was originally developed for Antarctica, it is easily extended to include the Arctic region, as the key features of tourism in both areas are highly similar (see Figure 10.2).

In the ATOS framework, the 'window of opportunity' for tourism in polar destinations is made up of six elements: access (ease of visitation), non-tourism uses of the area (existence of rival or complementary activities), attractions and facilities (things for tourists to see and do), operational factors (know-how and equipment required to organize polar holidays), acceptability of impacts (sensitivity of the relevant stakeholders to visitor impacts), and regulation and management (institutions to control or foster tourism). Climate change may affect polar cruise tourism through each of these six factors. The ATOS framework also discusses a wide range of 'contextual' factors that affect polar tourism 'from the outside world'. In the context of climate change, the most important of these are the indirect societal impacts and the impacts of mitigation policies that feature in Scott's framework.

Impacts on polar cruise tourism

Historically, Arctic economies were almost exclusively based on the exploitation of natural resources: hunting and fishing, oil and gas exploitation, and mineral extraction. The Antarctic knows no indigenous population and the economy has emerged relatively recently with the development of science and tourism (White, 1994). Major constraining factors, such as access, extreme climatic conditions and the lack of technology to deal with these constraints are undergoing rapid change in both polar regions (ACIA, 2005; Snyder, 2007). Technically, it becomes possible to work under extreme weather conditions, while climate change leads to different, and often less extreme, weather types. Although the effects for fisheries, mineral exploitation, forestry and other economic sectors have been explored in the Arctic Climate Impact Assessment (ACIA), tourism has received little attention. Nevertheless, tourism is generally recognized as one of the important growth sectors in the Arctic, capable of diversifying and increasing the opportunity of income for local communities (AHDR, 2004; Snyder, 2007). For the Antarctic, so far, no equivalent study to the ACIA has been undertaken. Increased media attention, due to the International Polar Year as well as the visible effects of climate change, such as iceberg calving and the images of melting glaciers and wildlife at risk, is feeding the desire of people to experience the polar regions. It is generally expected that tourism in the polar regions will continue to grow and diversify in the future (Snyder and Stonehouse, 2007). Moreover, cruise tourism is among the most rapidly growing tourism sectors in the world (WTO, 2001). In this section, we discuss those effects of climate change that will probably affect polar cruise tourism (for an overview see Box 10.2).

A generally made observation is that reduction of sea ice extent will increase tourism access to the polar regions, particularly by cruise vessels (Snyder, 2007). Sea ice reduction has made it possible to circumnavigate Svalbard during the summer months.[3] Also in the Antarctic, new channels and islands have emerged from receding sea ice and glaciers, such as James Ross Island in the Antarctic Peninsula (Crosbie and Splettstoesser, 1997; Stonehouse and Snyder, 2007). However, these new sites and areas are often not attractive for tourists to see as there is no wildlife.[4] The scenic Lemaire Channel cannot be sailed at the start of the tourist season, and may open up earlier in the season in the coming decades.[5] The Antarctic summer season is also believed to become longer (Stonehouse and Snyder, 2007). Stewart et al (2007) argue that although the Canadian Arctic will become more accessible by cruise ships, the perils of hull penetration by icebergs and multiyear sea ice also grow. During recent years several incidents occurred both in the Arctic and Antarctic involving expedition cruise ships, such as the sinking of the *Explorer*. It has been suggested that incidents such as these might occur more often in the future as cruise tourism grows in both polar regions, without a solid understanding of the changing physical conditions (Stewart and Draper, 2008; AMSA, 2009). Indirect societal impacts include the awareness that climate change generates of the polar regions among the public, and the perceived accessibility.

Figure 10.3 *Kangiqsujuaq (bottom right) in Nunavik (northern Quebec):*
A place frequently visited by cruise ships in recent years

Source: Machiel Lamers, 2008

Another indirect effect of growing accessibility due to climate change is the emergence of other resource users, such as fisheries, mining and hydrocarbon extraction. Tourism may have conflicting interests with these extractive forms of resources use. It remains to be seen to what extent the local communities, particularly in the Arctic, jump on the tourism bandwagon in the coming decades to capitalize on their attractions. In recent years, Greenland has made tourism development a priority in their economic policy (AMSA, 2009). In Nunavik (northern Quebec), the Inuit have founded a cruise company called Cruise North (Dawson et al, 2007). A lot depends on the capacity of the communities to really benefit from tourism in terms of education and capital (see Figure 10.3).

Effects on key attractions of the polar cruise industry pose an obvious impact. The polar bear is a major attraction of the Arctic region that might be on the edge of extinction due to its dependence on sea ice for hunting seals. In both the Arctic and Antarctic, variations and fluctuations in sea ice may affect the growth of krill and copepods, which is the foundation of the food chain and affects attractive species, such as seals and whales. In addition, warmer temperatures have already resulted in a southward shift of species in the Antarctic. For example, populations of various penguin species have shifted considerably in the Antarctic Peninsula (Lynch et al, 2008) – shifts that have been related to climate change (Forcada et al, 2006). For example, Gentoo penguins have become more dominant on Petermann Island in recent years, whereas Adélie penguin colonies have started to abandon the island and move further south (see Figure 10.4).[6] Invasive species, pests and pathogens might also be successfully introduced in vulnerable polar ecosystems (Frenot et al, 2005). Warmer summers may lead to more insects in the Arctic region and a nuisance for shore visits. Thawing permafrost and increased exposure to storm surges may lead to coastal erosion – for example, as in the striking case of the Alaskan village of Shishmaref that is disappearing.[7] Next to impacts upon the physical landscape, the built environment and infrastructure upon which cruise tourism is dependent might also be affected. These changes may seriously affect the scenic qualities of the polar landscape as well as key tourism infrastructures. It is even reported that tourists have become disappointed with not seeing ice in the Arctic (Pagnan, 2003). Finally, climate change is reported to affect cultural heritage sites in both polar regions – for example, it has been argued that surface resources that are anchored in the permafrost may destabilize. In addition, permanently frozen materials will be subjected to freeze-thaw cycles, which may accelerate decomposition (Barr, 2008).

Changing environmental conditions, changing customer demands and growing numbers and types of tour operators may require additional or adapted operational standards and guidelines. The potential increase in operational risks for cruise tourism in certain parts of the polar regions (Stewart et al, 2007) and the increased vulnerability of ecosystems present compelling reasons for adapted operational guideline regulations. Both individual tour operators, as well as industry associations, may need to come up with adaptive strategies. It remains to be seen whether different segments of the polar cruise industry (e.g. smaller- and larger-scale cruise companies or land-based businesses) have the same interests in the face of global environmental change.

Figure 10.4 *Increasing numbers of Gentoo penguins and declining numbers of Adélie penguins on Petermann Island in the Antarctic Peninsula: How important is it to the tourist?*
Source: Machiel Lamers, 2009

As climate change and its direct and indirect effects occur, it is becoming increasingly difficult to separate impacts caused by tourism from other impacts. The acceptability of impacts in the polar regions will subsequently be greater. Since both of the polar regions are to a large degree dependent on long-haul flights, large amounts of the greenhouse gases are emitted to make polar tourism possible (Amelung and Lamers, 2007; Dawson et al, 2008). Tourism development therefore depends on the acceptability of impacts upon the local and regional scale, but also on the acceptability of the global impacts of tourism activity. At this point in time, it is not clear what the net effect will be of images of suffering polar bears, changing traditional cultures and calving glaciers: more visitation or more support for protective measures? Research has already shown that the European consumer associates Arctic destinations with climate change (Huebner, 2009). A number of polar cruise operators also suggest that the attention of climate change in the media is beneficial for their business.[8]

Finally, climate change may affect cruise tourism through climate change policies on both the national and international level. It is likely that national and international carbon mitigation policies will at some point affect the price of long-haul travel (Amelung and Lamers, 2007; Gossling et al, 2008). It has also been suggested that the management of protected areas, particularly in the North, may need to be reconsidered, as the original objective of preserving ecological and natural qualities of these parks cannot be guaranteed due to global changes (Stonehouse and Snyder, 2007). Another indirect effect of climate change and the increasing opportunities for economic development in the Arctic is the growing role of self-governance of Arctic indigenous peoples (AHDR, 2004). The degree to which they are willing to accommodate or develop cruise tourism is an important potential future factor. Furthermore, increasing geopolitical tensions in the Arctic may entail that certain areas will be militarized, or that tourism development may be used as a policy strategy to expand influence (Heininen, 2005).

Discussion

The objective of this chapter was to provide an outlook on the implications of climate change for cruise tourism in the polar regions based on the available literature and empirical evidence. It became apparent that the empirical basis for such an assessment is hardly available. Conceptualizing the impacts of climate change upon polar tourism requires a comprehensive understanding of the major historical and current climate–environment–tourism relationships. Today, this understanding is still very limited.

The available literature on the topic of climate change and polar tourism has struggled with the same problem. Studies such as those by Johnston (2006) and Snyder (2007) present a range of assumptions regarding possible or likely impacts; but empirical work is needed to test their accuracy. After all, climate change can have consequences that are different from those envisaged in conjectural exercises. For example, whereas a reduction in the amount of sea ice is commonly interpreted as facilitating access, Stewart et al (2007), in a study on the Canadian polar waters, suggest that the breaking-up of sea ice is increasing safety risks to the extent that accessibility is reduced. Climate change may increase operational risks more than previously assumed.

Perhaps even more difficult than establishing whether the projections are likely or true is gauging the relevance of the various impacts suggested and establishing priority lists of the most pressing issues. Is the dominant impact of climate change the disappearance of landmark species or landscapes, changes in access, increases in transport prices or yet another factor? To have a list of priority issues is important for adaptation by tour operators, destinations, polar managers and other stakeholders; but with the current level of understanding, such a list cannot be drawn up. This chapter adds a number of issues to the discussion that were not included in previous assessments; but it also reiterates many of the ideas from earlier overview papers. Producing lists of possible impacts is important; but what this field of research needs most is empirical work to establish some basic facts.

Thus far, climate change research and polar research have been dominated by the natural sciences. Many effects that climate and climate change may have on physical, ecological and biological systems have been identified, and their likelihood and implications assessed. The social sciences are nowhere near this level of understanding with respect to the links between climate (change) and human communities in the polar regions. As the livelihoods of millions of people – in the Arctic, Antarctic gateway

Box 10.2 *Implications of climate change for polar cruise ship tourism*

Indirect environmental impacts

Access:
- Decline in sea ice extent leads to extending shipping season.
- Glacier melting leads to increased iceberg hazards.
- Increased open water leads to increased storm surges.

Other users:
- Increasing presence of other resource users with potential conflict.
- Increased tourist ship numbers leads to local employment opportunities that may be difficult to meet due to lack of training in hospitality management.

Attractions:
- Ecosystem changes lead to changes in the distribution and abundance of species.
- Ecosystem changes lead to the appearance of new species.
- Storm surges lead to shoreline erosion.
- Scenic values are altered through physical and ecological changes.
- Impacts upon cultural heritage sites may occur.
- Changing cultures, identities and ways of life of Arctic peoples as a result of climate change are taking place.

Infrastructure and facilities:
- Sea-level rise and storm surges cause structural damage and mobility challenges.
- Permafrost melting leads to construction problems and structural damage.

Indirect societal impacts

Operational factors:
- Adaption strategies are necessary for both cruise companies and land-based service providers.
- Increased perils: safety, environment, nuclear.
- Marketing must anticipate consumers who wish to see climate change in action.

Acceptability of impacts
- Higher acceptability of impact due to difficulty to extract tourism impact from global environmental impacts.

Impacts of mitigation and adaptation policies
- Potential implementation of a carbon tax could increase transportation prices.
- Geopolitical tensions and conflicts in the Arctic region may lead to tourism development becoming a policy instrument.
- Transformation of protected areas: re-evaluation of management objectives and regulations.

Source: Pagnan (2003); Johnston (2006); Amelung and Lamers (2007); Dawson et al (2007); Snyder (2007); Stewart et al (2007); Stonehouse and Snyder (2007); Barr (2008)

cities and those employed by polar cruise operators – will be affected by climate change, and as many see tourism as a potential source of income in the polar regions, knowledge of societal impacts and options for adaptation are essential. Implications for the Arctic, with its indigenous population, may be even more profound and significant than for the Antarctic. The baseline of social scientific knowledge must be significantly expanded.

A first avenue for further work is the collection of better tourism statistics, particularly in the Arctic region. Climate change impacts and adaptation strategies vary greatly between regions and seasons, so that tourism data must be of high enough spatial and geographical resolution. A relatively detailed, consistent and reliable dataset is available for the Antarctic, and it seems worth the effort to develop a similar database for the Arctic region.

A second field of follow-up research is related to using 'analogue years' to assess the potential implications of climate change. Climate change implies a shift in the probability distributions of temperature, precipitation and other weather variables. Most regions will become warmer, and so far the polar regions have heated up much more rapidly than average. Applying the technique of 'analogue years' to polar tourism means analysing the observed response of tourism stakeholders to the weather conditions in extremely hot years or seasons (such as the summer of 2003 in Western Europe). The idea is that the 'extreme' conditions may become 'average' conditions as a result of climate change, and thus that people's response to these conditions may tell us something about adaptation to climate change.

A third possible field for further research concerns the integration of available insights from the natural sciences with relevance for tourism. It may be possible, for example, to overlay current and future maps of sea ice (i.e. accessibility), the distribution of polar bears, penguins and other interesting fauna, heritage sites worth visiting, and other crucial factors in order to create tentative maps with vulnerability and opportunity hot spots. For one thing, such maps could help to identify interesting case studies for more in-depth research. For example, comparisons of perspectives of onsite stakeholders on perceived climatic changes, risks and adaptive strategies are an important way of learning to cope with changes ahead.

Conclusions

The aim of this chapter was to provide an overview of the possible implications of climate change for cruise tourism in the polar regions. Following Scott's (2008) generic framework of climate change impacts upon tourism, four categories of impacts were discerned. Direct effects (i.e. changes in tourists' physical comfort as a result of changing weather conditions) are deemed unimportant as pleasant weather conditions are generally not among the key reasons for visiting the polar regions.

Indirect environmental effects may be much more relevant, and past review papers have focused on this category of impacts and identified a number of potential results. Reduction in sea ice extent may broaden the shipping season and open up previously inaccessible areas, but it may also increase iceberg hazards. Landscapes and the distributions of species will be altered by climate change. The shrinking habitat of the polar bear is a well-known example of a species that is endangered by climate change, but some other species will thrive. In the Antarctic area, penguin species move south in search of better conditions, with some of their former colonies being taken over by other penguin species. It is highly uncertain if tourists will notice the changes and how they will evaluate them. Visiting the sights for just a few hours, tourists will not be able to perceive any change firsthand. And with no context with which to compare the scenes, little experience may be gained. Even if changes are perceived as negative, this may have a positive (perverse) effect on tourist demand. Cruises to the polar regions are already advertised with slogans such as 'Visit the Arctic/Antarctic before it is too late.'

Apart from tourism, climate change will also affect other economic activities in the polar regions, such as the extraction of oil and other minerals. Under the current Antarctic Treaty, this is prohibited; but in the Arctic, tensions are building up over the control of the Arctic seas and their resources. In a direct sense, increased economic activity may reduce the attractiveness of the Arctic region for tourism as it affects its image as an unspoilt wilderness. In a more indirect sense, the increasing accessibility of mineral resources may lead to a more uncertain geopolitical situation, which is not conducive to a flourishing tourism industry. The same holds for a potentially considerable slow-down of economic growth, resulting from climate change, that the Stern report (Stern, 2006) warned of. The implications of the Stern report for (polar) tourism have yet to be explored.

Another issue that has so far escaped research attention is the possible effect of mitigation measures on tourism, particularly tourism to long-haul destinations (Gossling et al, 2008) such as the polar regions. Being among the most energy-intensive segments of the tourism industry (Amelung and Lamers, 2007; Dawson et al, 2008), polar tourism can potentially be hard hit by policy measures such as fuel taxes and emissions trading schemes. Transport prices will undoubtedly rise significantly, and so will holiday prices, especially for vacations with a large transport component in its price structure, such as cruise trips to the polar regions. Strange as it may seem, the first major challenge that climate change poses to polar cruise tourism may not come from climate change impacts, but from mitigation policies.

Perhaps the main conclusion of this chapter is that there is very little known about the relationships between the polar climate and polar (cruise) tourism, let alone about the possible implications of climate change. For the Arctic, part of this knowledge gap can be attributed to a lack of reliable tourism data of sufficient temporal and geographical resolution. Coordinated data collection is urgently needed. Other areas for social scientific contributions include the analysis of 'analogue years' in which human behaviour is studied in periods of extreme weather that resemble future climate conditions, and the integration of available geographical knowledge of physical, ecological and biological effects of climate change that are relevant to polar cruise tourism in order to identify vulnerability as well as opportunity hotspots.

Research into the implications of climate change for polar cruise tourism has a large societal relevance. Hundreds of thousands of livelihoods in the polar regions and beyond depend on it. It is therefore of utmost importance that a long-term approach towards monitoring and management is taken to strive for sustainable cruise tourism development.

Notes

1   Estimate made on the website of the fishing village Skarsvag, which is located close to the North Cape: www.skarsvag.no/index.php?option=com_content&view=article&id=85:north-cape&catid=45:sights&Itemid=223, accessed 25 September 2009.

2   Map produced by Hugo Ahlenius, 2005; available from the *UNEP/GRID-Arendal Maps and Graphics Library*, http://maps.grida.no/go/graphic/projected-changes-in-the-arctic-climate-2090, accessed 30 September 2009.

3   Pers comm with Dr K. de Korte, founder of (and working as itinerary planner for) Oceanwide Expeditions, November 2006.

4   Pers comm with Dr B. Stonehouse, Antarctic tourism researcher and lecturer aboard tourist ships, June 2007.

5   Pers comm with Dr K. de Korte, 2006.

6   Pers comm with Dr J. Watts, naturalist of Waterproof Expeditions, during an expedition cruise in March 2009.

7   See the trailer for the documentary *The Last Days of Shishmaref*: www.youtube.com/watch?v=TS1KRvojupA&feature=player_embedded#t=46.

8   Pers comm with P. Shaw, director of Quark Expeditions, in June 2007; and Dr K. de Korte, itinerary planner for Oceanwide Expeditions, in November 2006.

References

ACIA (Arctic Climate Impact Assessment) (2005) *Arctic Climate Impact Assessment*, Cambridge University Press, Cambridge

AHDR (Arctic Human Development Report) (2004) *Arctic Human Development Report*, Stefanson Arctic Institute, Akureyri

Amelung, B. and Lamers, M. (2007) 'Estimating the CO_2 emissions from Antarctic tourism', *Tourism in Marine Environments*, vol 4, pp121–134

Amelung, B. and Viner, D. (2006) 'Mediterranean tourism: exploring the future with the Tourism Climatic Index', *Journal of Sustainable Tourism*, vol 14, pp349–366

AMSA (Arctic Marine Shipping Assessment) (2009) *Arctic Marine Shipping Assessment*, Arctic Council, Tromso

Barr, S. (2008) 'The effects of climate change on cultural heritage in the polar regions', in M. Petzet and J. Ziesemeier (eds) *Heritage at Risk: ICOMOS World Report 2006/2007 on Monuments and Sites in Danger*, ICOMOS, Paris

Becken, S. and Hay, J. (2007) *Tourism and Climate Change, Risks and Opportunities*, Multilingual Matters Ltd./Channel View Publications, Clevedon

Breiling, M. and Charamza, P. (1999) 'The impact of global warming in winter tourism and skiing: A regionalized model for Austrian snow conditions', *Regional Environmental Change*, vol 1, pp4–14

Clark, R. N. and Stankey, G. H. (1979) *The Recreation Opportunity Spectrum: A Framework for Planning, Management, and Research*, General Technical Report PNW-98, Pacific Northwest Forest and Range Experiment Station, US Department of Agriculture and Forest Service, Portland, OR

Clarke, A. and Harris, C. (2003) 'Polar marine ecosystems: major threats and future change', *Environmental Conservation*, vol 30, pp1–25

Cresswell, K. A., Wiedemann, J. and Mangel, M. (2008) 'Can macaroni penguins keep up with climate- and fishing-induced changes in krill?', *Polar biology*, 31, pp641–649

Crosbie, K. and Splettstoesser, J. (1997) 'Circumnavigation of James Ross Island, Antarctica', *Polar Record*, vol 33, p341

Dawson, J., Maher, P. and Slocombe, S. (2007) 'Climate change, marine tourism, and sustainability in the Canadian Arctic: Contributions from systems and complexity approaches', *Tourism in Marine Environments*, vol 4, pp69–83

Dawson, J., Scott, D. and Stewart, E. (2008) 'Climate change vulnerability of the polar bear viewing industry in Churchill Manitoba, Canada', in J. Saarinen and K. Tervo (eds) *Tourism and Global Change in Polar Regions: An International Conference, 29 November – 2 December 2007*, Thule Institute, Oulu, Finland

Enzenbacher, D. (1993) 'Tourists in Antarctica: Numbers and trends', *Tourism Management*, vol 14, pp142–146

Forcada, J., Trathan, P., Reid, K., Murphy, E. J. and Croxall, J. P. (2006) 'Contrasting population changes in sympatric penguin species in association with climate warming', *Global Change Biology*, vol 12, pp411–423

Frenot, Y., Chown, S., Whinam, J., Selkirk, P., Convey, P., Skonicki, M. and Bergstrom, D. (2005) 'Biological invasions in the Antarctic: Extent, impacts and implications', *Biological Review*, vol 80, pp45–72

Gössling, S. (2002) 'Global environmental consequences of tourism', *Global Environmental Change*, vol 12, pp283–302

Gössling, S., Peeters, P. and Scott, D. (2008) 'Consequences of climate policy for international tourist arrivals in developing countries', *Third World Quarterly*, vol 29, pp873–901

Hall, C. M. (2008) 'Tourism and climate change: Knowledge gaps and issues', in J. Saarinen and K. Tervo (eds) *Tourism and Global Change in Polar Regions: An International Conference, 29 November – 2 December 2007*, Thule Institute, Oulu University Press, Oulu, Finland

Heininen, L. (2005) 'Impacts of globalization, and the Circumpolar North in world politics', *Polar Geography*, vol 29, pp91–102

Huebner, A. (2009) 'Tourist images of Greenland and the Arctic: A perception analysis', *Polar Record*, 45, pp153–166

IAATO (International Association of Antarctica Tour Operators) (2008) *IP85 IAATO Overview of Antarctic Tourism 2007–2008 Antarctic Season and Preliminary Estimates for 2008–2009 Antarctic Season*, Antarctic Treaty Consultative Meeting, Kyiv, Ukraine

IPCC (Intergovernmental Panel on Climate Change) (2007) 'Summary for policy makers and technical summary', in S. Solomon (ed) *Climate Change 2007: The Physical Science Basis – Contribution of Working Group 1 to the Fourth Assessment Report of the Intergovernmental Panel on Climate Change*, Cambridge University Press, Cambridge

Johnston, M. (2006) 'Impacts of global environmental change on tourism in the polar regions', in S. Gössling and C. M. Hall (eds) *Tourism and Global Environmental Change: Ecological, Social, Economic and Political Interrelationships*, Routledge, London

Kerr, J. and Packer, L. (1998) 'The impact of climate change on mammal diversity in Canada', *Environmental Monitoring and Assessment*, vol 49, pp263–270

Lamers, M. (2009) *The Future of Tourism in Antarctica: Challenges for Sustainability*, Universitaire Pers Maastricht, Maastricht, The Netherlands, p54

Lamers, M., Haase, D. and Amelung, B. (2008) 'Facing the elements: Analysing trends in Antarctic tourism', *Tourism Review*, vol 63, pp15–27

Lynch, H. J., Naveen, R. and Fagan, W. F. (2008) 'Censuses of penguin, blue-eyed shag and southern giant petrel populations on the Antarctic Peninsula, 2001–2007', *Marine Ornithology*, vol 36, pp83–97

McCarty, J. P. (2001) 'Ecological consequences of recent climate change', *Conservation Biology*, vol 15, pp320–331

Nordic Council (2003) *Towards a Sustainable Arctic Tourism: An Integrated Strategy for the Sustainable Development of Tourism in the Nordic Arctic*, Nordic Council of Ministers, Tourism Ad Hoc Working Group, Virum, Ramboll

Pagnan, J. (2003) 'Climate change impacts on Arctic tourism – a preliminary review', in *Proceedings of the First International Conference on Climate Change and Tourism*, Djerba, Tunisia, April 2003, World Tourism Organization, Madrid

Perry, A. (2006) 'Will predicted climate change compromise the sustainability of Mediterranean tourism?', *Journal of Sustainable Tourism*, vol 14, pp367–375

Sala, O. E., Chapin, F., Armesto, J., Berlow, E., Bloomfield, J., Dirzo, R., Huber-Sanwald, E., Huenekke, L., Jackson, R., Kinzig, A., Leemans, R., Lodge, D., Mooney, H., Oesterheld, M., Poff, N., Sykes, M., Walker, B., Walker, M. and Wall, D. (2000) 'Global biodiversity scenarios for the year 2100', *Science*, vol 287, pp1770–1774

Schiermeier, Q. (2007) 'The new face of the Arctic', *Nature*, vol 446, pp133–135

Scott, D. (2006) 'Global environmental change and mountain tourism', in S. Gössling and C. M. Hall (eds) *Tourism and Global Environmental Change: Ecological, Social, Economic and Political Interrelationships*, Routledge, London

Scott, D., Amelung, B., Becken, S., Ceron, J.-P., Dubois, G., Gössling, S., Peeters, P. and Simpson, M. (2008) *Climate Change and Tourism: Responding to Global Challenges*, UNWTO/WMO/UNE, Madrid

Snyder, J. (2007) *Tourism in the Polar Regions: The Sustainability Challenge*, United Nations Environmental Programme/The International Society, Paris

Stern, N. (2006) *The Economics of Climate Change: The Stern Review*, Cambridge University Press, Cambridge

Stewart, E. and Draper, D. (2008) 'The sinking of the *MS Explorer*: Implications for cruise tourism in Arctic Canada', *Arctic*, vol 61, pp224–228

Stewart, E., Draper, D. and Johnston, M. (2005) 'A review of tourism research in the polar regions', *Arctic*, vol 58, pp383–394

Stewart, E., Howell, S., Draper, D., Yackel, J. and Tivy, A. (2007) 'Sea ice in Canada's Arctic: Implications for cruise tourism', *Arctic*, vol 4, pp370–380

Stirling, I. and Derocher, A. E. (1993) 'Possible impacts of climatic warming on polar bears', *Arctic*, vol 46, pp240–245

Stonehouse, B. and Snyder, J. (2007) 'Polar tourism in changing environments', in J. Snyder and B. Stonehouse (eds) *Prospects for Polar Tourism*, CABI, Wallingford, UK

Sysselmannen På Svalbard (2006) *Tourism Statistics for Svalbard*, Governor of Svalbard, Longyearbyen

White, K. (1994) 'Tourism and the Antarctic economy', *Annals of Tourism Research*, vol 21, pp245–268

WTO (World Tourism Organization) (2001) *Tourism 2020 Vision: Global Forecasts and Profiles of Market Segments*, vol 7, World Tourism Organization, Madrid

Part IV
POLICY
AND
GOVERNANCE
DIMENSIONS

Welcome to Antarctic Treaty Historic Site No. 61 British Base A, Port Lockroy

11

Stakeholder Perspectives on the Governance of Antarctic Cruise Tourism

Daniela Liggett, Alison McIntosh, Anna Thompson,

Bryan Storey and Neil Gilbert

Introduction

Over the last two decades, Antarctic cruise tourism has grown exponentially, from a few thousand tourists in the 1990s to over 44,000 in the 2007/2008 season (IAATO, 2008a). Approximately 95 per cent of Antarctic tourists explore the Antarctic by cruise ship (Dingwall and Cessford, 1996, p65; Hemmings and Roura, 2003, p18). In this way, ship-based tourism continues to hold an incontestable first place when ranking the numbers of Antarctic tourists by mode of transport. Until recently, Antarctic cruise tourism has prided itself on an exceptional safety record. However, as Table 11.1 exemplifies, various accidents and incidents within the last two Antarctic seasons (2007/2008 and 2008/2009) mar this record.

Despite no actual loss of human life, the grounding of three tourist vessels and the sinking of the *Explorer* in the Antarctic Peninsula region are symptomatic of wider issues that raise questions about the governance of Antarctic cruise tourism. Other matters that have played a role in drawing attention to the need for increased regulation of Antarctic tourism are the growth in overall numbers of Antarctic tourists, the potential for shore-based activities to be developed further, and the wholly commercial utilization of Antarctica through tourism (Bastmeijer et al, 2008; Haase, 2008).

Nominally, Antarctic tourism is regulated primarily through the Antarctic Treaty System (ATS) and the International Association of Antarctica Tour Operators (IAATO),[1] although the practical management of Antarctic tourism is carried out largely through the IAATO. The IAATO is the tourism industry association for the region and was established by seven US-based Antarctic tour operators in 1991 to better coordinate Antarctic tourism with the aim of maintaining and guaranteeing environmentally and ethically responsible and safe operations (Splettstoesser, 2000; IAATO, 2006). At present, the IAATO has more than 100 members, the majority of whom operate Category 1 vessels with a capacity to carry 13 to 199 passengers (IAATO, 2009b).

Table 11.1 *Incidents and accidents over the last two Antarctic seasons (2007–2009)*

Date	Vessel (operator)	Location	Incident	Damage	Source
30 January 2007	Nordkapp (Hurtigruten)	Neptune's Bellows, Deception Island	Vessel grounds at the entrance to the caldera as a result of human error	Damage to parts of the hull and tanks	(Norway, 2007)
23 November 2007	Explorer (GAP Adventures)	Bransfield Strait	Vessel strikes submerged ice and damages hull	Complete loss (vessel sinks)	(Reel, 2007)
28 December 2007	Fram (Hurtigruten)	Brown Bluff	Vessel drifts into a glacier after an electricity outage	Damage to one lifeboat	(Gillies, 2008)
4 December 2008	Ushuaia (Antarpply Expeditions)	Wilhelmina Bay, near Cape Anna	Vessel grounds at the entrance of Wilhelmina Bay	Damage to two diesel tanks carrying marine gas oil (MGO)	(IAATO, 2008b)
17 February 2009	Ocean Nova (Quark Expeditions)	Marguerite Bay, west of Debenham Island	Vessel grounds circa 2km from the Argentinean San Martin station	Limited damage to the hull	(Quark Expeditions, 2009)

The ATS forms the basis of tourism regulation through annual Antarctic Treaty Consultative Meetings (ATCMs) attended by the Antarctic Treaty Consultative Parties (ATCPs) and other non-consultative parties, as well as observers. The 1959 Antarctic Treaty, which lies at the heart of the ATS, was born out of successful cooperation of international scientific teams during the 1957 to 1958 International Geophysical Year and the potential danger of involving Antarctica in the Cold War (Buck, 1998; Polk, 1998). Consequently, the Antarctic Treaty pursues the principle objectives of promoting scientific activities in Antarctica and maintaining the status of the continent as a demilitarized and nuclear-free zone. Neither tourism nor environmental protection finds specific mention in the text of the Antarctic Treaty.

As a result of this lack of mention in the Antarctic Treaty, the status of Antarctic tourism has been questioned for some time (Beck, 1994), although now tourism in the Antarctic is nearly unanimously considered a legitimate activity (Beck, 1990; Cessford, 1997; Scott, 2001; Bastmeijer and Roura, 2004; Murray and Jabour, 2004; Johnson and Kriwoken, 2007).

Nonetheless, controversy surrounding the operation of tourism in the Antarctic and its regulation remains. This controversy is nurtured partially by moral and largely academic questions regarding the desirability and appropriateness of tourism in Antarctica (Prosser, 1995), and partially by the regulatory distinction between tourism and other human activities made by some Antarctic Treaty Parties (Pineschi, 1996), which is conceptually difficult to defend.

Decision-making within the ATS embraces a consensus-based approach (Scully, 1990). As stated in Article IX, Section 4 of the Antarctic Treaty, for any regulatory measure to become effective, approval is required by all Antarctica Treaty Consultative Parties who participated in the meeting when a specific measure was considered (Antarctic Treaty Consultative Parties, 1959). The IAATO bases its decision-making also on a participatory, consultative and collective approach (Haase et al, 2009). However, as Article V, Section F in the IAATO bylaws prescribes, a two-thirds majority is sufficient to pass any issue (IAATO, 2009a). As will become clear in this chapter, IAATO's approach to decision-making represents a faster and more flexible process than under the auspices of the Antarctic Treaty Consultative Parties. This chapter will highlight that, notwithstanding the aforementioned managerial issues, tourism regulation remains controversial with significant concerns expressed by Antarctic stakeholders, including the Antarctic Treaty Consultative Parties, over self-regulation and the lack of progress regarding the development of an ATS regulatory alternative.

'Governing the governors':
A story of controlling self-regulation

Antarctic cruise tourism is regulated *in situ* primarily through the IAATO. In light of the emotionally laden imperative of environmental conservation in Antarctica and the unique governance system for the area south of 60°S latitude, a self-regulatory regime for Antarctic tourism is exposed to constant scrutiny and pressure from policy-makers, environmentalists, national Antarctic programmes, as well as the wider public, mostly expressed through the media (Haase, 2008). At the same time, the consensus-based approach to decision-making within the ATS (Lee, 2005) and the nature of Antarctica as an international commons (Buck, 1998) complicate the governance of Antarctic tourism through official government channels (Beck, 1990, 1994; Richardson, 1999; Molenaar, 2005). The IAATO assumed the responsibility for filling the void resulting from an absence of tourism regulation *in situ*, but has since had to battle relentless criticism for the unwanted consolidation of for-profit business and principled governance (Haase, 2008).

Despite the IAATO's willingness to self-regulate, power has not been relinquished by the ATCPs, and it is unlikely that an industry association will ever be solicited to be the sole regulator of their own activities in the Antarctic. Without the official authorization and credible sanctioning power behind them, the IAATO has to operate in a fuzzy realm of 'soft management' through goodwill, peer pressure and public image. The key question here is: can a soft industry-based approach to governing Antarctic cruise tourism be successful in the long term and work towards the greater common good? On the other hand, in the absence of industry self-regulation, would the ATCPs be a viable alternative as sole regulators of Antarctic tourism? These are pertinent and controversial questions, particularly with regard to the rapid growth in the Antarctic cruise tourism sector and the recent rise in the number of incidents and accidents that Antarctic cruise vessels have been involved in. This chapter intends to shed some light on the controversies surrounding the regulation of Antarctic cruise tourism drawing from stakeholder[2] perspectives on the ethos and governance of Antarctic tourism.

Research approach

The information presented in this chapter is based on semi-structured stakeholder interviews conducted between January 2006 and March 2007. The interviews were transcribed verbatim and were analysed in their entirety following an iterative inductive approach based on a modified constructivist version of grounded theory (Charmaz, 2002; Warren, 2002; Pidgeon and Henwood, 2004). Key categories of data were both emergent and expected and aided the segmentation of the transcripts into topical areas. In the following sections, comments and statements from Antarctic tourism stakeholders will be used to illustrate their viewpoints with regard to two main topics:

1   Antarctic tourism practice and ethos: perspectives on self-regulation and the characteristics and 'culture' of Antarctic tourism practice; and
2   perspectives on Antarctic tourism regulation: the current regulation of Antarctic tourism through the ATS and IAATO.

Here, a simple nomenclature has been adopted to differentiate between comments from stakeholders who are:

• representatives of environmental non-governmental organizations (NGOs) and others monitoring tourism developments (M);
• official representatives from Antarctic Treaty Parties or other government bodies involved in the regulation of Antarctic tourism (R); and
• organizers of Antarctic tourism (i.e. operators) (O).

A detailed account of the interview methodology and paradigmatic considerations, as well as a more sophisticated nomenclature of Antarctic tourism stakeholders, is provided in Haase et al (2007) and Haase (2008).

The ethos, practice and self-regulation of Antarctic cruise tourism

To date, the IAATO has succeeded in developing and enforcing soft management strategies (e.g. through voluntary codes of conduct) that ensure high operational standards and has found acceptance among the majority of tour operators as indicated by IAATO membership numbers (Molenaar, 2005; Landau and Splettstoesser, 2007). In fact, at the time of writing, all major commercial Antarctic cruise operators are members of IAATO and follow IAATO's guidelines and procedures. Nonetheless, questions are raised about the limitations of a self-regulatory approach, especially in view of the growing demand for, and supply of, Antarctic cruise tourism, as well as the consequential increasing potential for serious accidents. This section looks at the ethos and practice of Antarctic tourism from the viewpoint of those operating cruises to Antarctica and from those monitoring it, or those with official regulatory capacity. Furthermore, the motivation for, and the perceived success of, self-regulation will be discussed.

From the perspective of cruise operators, the lack of efficient regulation of Antarctic tourism through the ATCPs is regarded as the main reason for self-organization and self-regulation of Antarctic tourism (O3, O10):

> *The main importance for IAATO [is] to ... take over the role of ... a regulating body ... because everybody has the same interests, everybody wants to protect Antarctica as it is now, and creat[e] ... ambassadors for the continent to be able to keep it the way it is.* (O)

Viewed from the eyes of Antarctic tourism operators, the IAATO is a 'very democratic and remarkably represented ... socialist organization' that relies on voluntary action (O). The IAATO's clear strength is seen in its ability to have competitors jointly design and agree on general operating strategies and policies. Interestingly, the IAATO is still fundamentally a small-operator's association.[3] Small cruise operators form IAATO's 'passionate and active core' (O). These small operators are the driving forces behind committee work for the organization and, consequently, decision-making. As Haase (2008) outlines, the organizers see the foundation of their cooperation in 'a shared passion and "love" for the Antarctic ... shared ethics and values ... well-established communication', as well as peer pressure and the operators' proactiveness with regard to new developments.

Many environmentalists, policy-makers and academics remain concerned over the self-interest of Antarctic tour operators forming the basis for a preference for self-regulation, given that the economic imperative to make profit would be difficult to align with restrictive precautionary approaches to tourism regulation (Bastmeijer and Roura, 2004). On the other hand, the tour operators, while admitting their economic interest in Antarctica, maintain that their self-interest demands an environmentally conscientious approach to the regulation and operation of Antarctic tourism:

It still [has to be] economically viable for the operators [to go to Antarctica], but it has to balance that with what is environmentally sustainable. If you look at it this way … there is no reason for the operators to want to destroy the environment because that is all they are selling. (O)

Despite a generally sceptical view of linkages between industry self-interest and environmental conservation efforts, academics (Riffenburgh, 1998; Murray and Jabour, 2004) and some government officials commend the tour operators on their proactive approach and agree that self-interest might result in environmentally responsible operations:

So, at the moment, to some extent we are relying upon the goodwill of the tour operators. Now having said that, we all need to recognize, too, that it is in the operators' best interest, their own business best interest, to make sure these sites are clean, attractive, unspoiled because that is what people want to see. If they were causing damage to the sites, it is not in their own interest to do that because it will hurt their business. (R)

In the same sense, the operators argue that whereas they might be classified as an industry association, they 'operate from the point of view of being an environmental stewardship organization' (O) as 'One would like to think that there is a desire to do what is right and to be at harmony with the place' (O). The practice of environmentally conscientious tourism is rooted in the profound love and passion for the Antarctic that many operators expressed. Congruent with an intrinsically emotional basis of, and bottom-up approach to, operating cruise vessels in Antarctica, the compliance with self-imposed standards and regulatory mechanisms was achieved primarily through peer pressure:

You have to look good in front of your peers. You don't want to look like a bad neighbour. If you talk about self-regulation, it works in many ways on a very visceral level. It is not intellectual… It's on an emotional level, because you don't want to be perceived among your peers and your colleagues as being a jerk… This is our family, a family of people that go to Antarctica, Antarctic tour operators. You don't want to look bad in front of your colleagues and peers, and so in some ways the motivation is very emotional and very basic; but the ultimate goal is intellectual and lofty and important. (O)

The regulators and monitors interviewed, as well as academic literature (Richardson, 1999; Bastmeijer and Roura, 2004; Landau and Splettstoesser, 2007), seem to agree with this poignant self-assessment of the cruise operators and commend the flexibility, responsibility and responsiveness to new developments of the IAATO. IAATO members are considered as having the necessary expertise (M; R) and a desirable proactive attitude towards the practice of Antarctic tourism (R). From an operational point of view, the operators praise the excellent cooperation and communication among expedition leaders, which is attributed largely to the dedication and experience of the staff on Antarctic cruises. Aside from improving the experience for the paying passengers, effective communication and the sharing of hazard information between vessels decrease the risk of accidents. In addition, the tour operators argue that any incidents and accidents would have serious adverse impacts upon their business. Therefore, risks are judged conservatively and are avoided whenever possible:

> ... *the protectionists ... often think that the ship operators don't care, but we care a lot because it is ruining our business if we hit something ... it is ruining your whole company if you have an accident with the ship. So, we are extremely careful.* (O)

Nonetheless, recent events have marred the previously spotless record of Antarctic cruise operators. Incidents like those involving the *Nordkapp*, *Explorer*, *Fram*, *Ushuaia* or *Ocean Nova* exemplify the risks of operating in Antarctica and caution that despite the expertise of Antarctic cruise operators and stringent self-regulatory guidelines, the risk of serious accidents cannot be eliminated. The continued growth of Antarctic cruise tourism and the potential for serious accidents is of concern to regulators and monitors alike and receives mention in the academic literature as a policy problem (Hall, 1992; Dingwall and Cessford, 1996; Polk, 1998; Hemmings and Roura, 2003; Bastmeijer and Roura, 2004; Molenaar, 2005; Johnson and Kriwoken, 2007). Further still, the continuing growth in the industry will increasingly challenge the capacity of Antarctic tourism operators to self-regulate. In light of the rising numbers of Antarctic tourists as well as the risk of incidents, the question arises as to how much longer it will be viable for Antarctic cruise tourism to be operated, managed and regulated almost entirely through one organization.

The regulation of Antarctic cruise tourism through Antarctic Treaty Parties

Within the ATS, Antarctic tourism regulation is facilitated through a range of mostly hortatory measures adopted during ATCMs,[4] as well as conventions and agreements that have been added to the ATS. Of the latter, the Protocol on Environmental Protection to the Antarctic Treaty does not only represent a benchmark in the evolution of the ATS (Njåstad, 2007), but also in the manner in which the Antarctic Treaty Parties addressed Antarctic tourism, which found specific mention in the protocol's Articles 3, 8 and 15 and Annexes III and VI. However, normative, operational and sovereignty issues with regard to tourism regulation through the Antarctic Treaty Parties remain (Haase, 2008). Tourism regulation through the ATS lacks a systematic and comprehensive approach (Beck, 1994; Molenaar, 2005); the implementation and enforcement of regulatory mechanisms are burdened by ambiguous definitions (Kriwoken and Rootes, 2000; Murray and Jabour, 2004; Lamers and Amelung, 2007) and varying levels of national commitment. Decision-making processes within the ATS are slow and cumbersome (Huber, 2006), and the regulatory regime is weakened by sovereignty issues (Beck, 1990; Scott, 2001; Bastmeijer and Roura, 2004; Molenaar, 2005; Enzenbacher, 2007). Despite generally acknowledging the importance of addressing Antarctic tourism issues from a strategic perspective and designating time during the recent annual ATCMs to discuss tourism issues, ATCPs have been noticeably restrained concerning the adoption of stringent regulatory mechanisms focused on Antarctic tourism. This restraint to adopt more stringent measures has largely arisen through a lack of consensus on whether tourism needs to be regulated through the ATS and then how it might be regulated. Considering the parties' hesitancy so far, questions arise regarding the efficacy of tourism regulation through the Antarctic Treaty Parties. The remainder of this section will discuss stakeholder perspectives regarding the success and suitability of Antarctic tourism regulation through ATCPs. Stakeholder opinions concerning the potential for a self-regulatory regime and the ATS to co-share regulatory responsibilities will also be considered.

The regulators and monitors commend the role that the IAATO plays with respect to the management of Antarctic tourism on the ground. Nonetheless, they stress the importance of tourism regulation remaining the responsibility of the Antarctic Treaty Parties. Regulators consider it 'the obligation of governments to regulate... The governments would never want to give up their control of the process' (R). Currently, tourism regulation through the ATS is deemed to represent the most practical option:

> *[The ATS is] the best immediate potential mechanism through which to regulate it. One can say it doesn't regulate it very well right now, but it is potentially able to regulate it. When you look around and look at the alternatives, they are fairly few and far between.* (M)

Despite acknowledging the significance of the Antarctic Treaty Parties as the 'rightful' gatekeepers to Antarctica, the above statement is not very enthusiastically shared by all tourism operators, who view industry self-regulation through the IAATO as superior in terms of its flexibility, its positive track record and its cooperative, proactive approach to tourism management *in situ*:

> *Certainly, at its current scale, self-regulation is an ideal solution because it is so efficient and because it is so fine tuned. It is so sensitive to our circumstances. We don't wait for all the Treaty Parties to ratify that 'no-you-can't-walk-that-path', or you know. We just say: 'Oh, this path, we are not going to use that anymore.' All the expedition leaders get notified: 'You don't use that path anymore, you don't use that landing site anymore. You go over here instead.'... Self-regulation is great, as long as everyone plays the game. Now, pretty much everyone does.* (O)

The Antarctic Treaty Parties seem to lack this efficiency with respect to tourism regulation that tour operators praise the IAATO for. Decision-making within the ATS is viewed as slow and reactionary as new developments are not so much anticipated and planned for as they are regarded retrospectively (Dinuzzi, 2006). Intuitively, the consensus requirement may be seen as the culprit contributing to slow and cumbersome decision-making; but as the regulators stress, the consensus rule fulfils a necessary and beneficial role as a guardian of cooperation in that it facilitates reaching agreements rather than compromises. As such, the consensus rule is viewed as increasing the level of dedication and commitment by the Antarctic Treaty Parties to any decision concluded.

The non-binding nature of most ATS regulation (Bastmeijer and Roura, 2004) can be viewed as another side-effect of the consensus rule due to the perceived difficulties of achieving agreement on mandatory rules. In fact, according to some of the regulators and monitors interviewed, hortatory regulatory instruments may suffice as, on state level, compliance with international agreements is generally high. Whether hortatory or mandatory in character, the implementation and enforcement of any regulatory mechanism is of utmost importance. However, effective enforcement and monitoring will continue to be a challenge on and around the climatically extreme, physically remote and internationally governed Antarctic continent. The lack of an Antarctic police force (Prosser, 1998) and national differences with respect to the implementation of protocol provisions (Richardson, 1999; Kriwoken and Rootes, 2000) complicate the enforcement and monitoring of regulatory instruments *in situ*. For these reasons, monitoring on a continent-wide basis is deemed not feasible and too costly. Instead, monitoring on a regional or sub-regional basis is envisaged as a feasible option and necessary action to ensure compliance with ATS regulation:

> *For tourism-associated impacts and so on, the obligation might well be imposed over the entire region, but it would have to be dealt with in more manageable lumps. I think it would have to be dealt with in a regional or sub-regional way. The mechanics of doing it would be at a smaller scale than the general obligation. It isn't quite as complicated when you look at it at the moment because most of the activity is at the northern/western side of the Antarctic Peninsula.* (M)

However, effective monitoring will remain a challenge even on a regional or sub-regional basis due to its prohibitive costs (if pursued as a goal in itself), 'communication inadequacies ... legal uncertainties' (Beck, 1994) and the lack of onsite visitor management (Cessford, 1997; Mason and Legg, 1999). This gap could be closed, at least partially, through a strong and constructive partnership between the Antarctic Treaty Parties and the IAATO. The tour operators argue that their self-regulatory approach is 'reinforced through a self-monitoring system of mutual observation ... self-criticism, peer pressure and ultimately the possibility of putting non-compliant IAATO members on probation' (Haase et al, 2007). Notwithstanding the potential of a self-regulatory apparatus to monitor *in situ* compliance with ATS regulation, it seems that *in lieu* of alternative currently feasible solutions, the Antarctic Treaty Parties depend on the goodwill of tourism organizers.

Surprisingly, some operators criticize the Antarctic Treaty Parties for this dependence on the goodwill of the tourism organizers as it resembles inactivity and lack of regulatory creativity, which is perceived to be the result of a lack of experience with regard to Antarctic tourism operations. According to a tourism operator, a stricter and more robust national permitting process and the implementation of compliance and monitoring schemes are desired (Haase, 2008). Better enforcement of existing regulatory mechanisms may be wanted by some tourism organizers because of their confidence regarding the high standard of their own operations (Haase, 2008) and because of the need to create a level playing field, which actually reinforces regulatory efforts through both the ATS and the IAATO. According to tourism organizers, legal backing from the ATCPs is needed to give the IAATO some teeth:

At the moment, if I am an IAATO member and I break the rule, what is going to happen to me? Nothing, because there is nothing IAATO can do ... look at the problem that IAATO is faced with. I expel you and you are still going to operate. Are you better on the inside or the outside? You break the rules; sure they will give you a slap on the hand, but then they go: 'Oh, but we are better off to have you in the fold than outside.' So, if you expelled me, I would say: 'Oh well, I will carry on.' So, where is IAATO's strength? The governments haven't given [IAATO] the ability to regulate, so how can it possibly? (O)

The above statement indicates that a cooperative effort joining Antarctic Treaty Parties and the IAATO in their efforts to regulate Antarctic tourism activities might be needed. The operators call for support that surpasses a mere acknowledgement of the self-regulatory system and encompasses the delegation of some regulatory power to the IAATO. Some tourism operators suggest that this delegation of power might be achieved through relatively simple measures, such as a stricter regulation of station visits, which gives preference, or even limits visits, to IAATO members. Nonetheless, as a tourism operator claims: 'IAATO itself would have to pick its act up a bit and become a lot more responsive and responsible' (O) to merit any legal and political support through the ATS.

A unanimous commitment to regulating Antarctic tourism is needed if the ATCPs wish to claim authority as the international gatekeepers to the Antarctic. Since the legitimacy of the ATS with regard to governing human activities in the Antarctic is recognized by most stakeholders, the Antarctic Treaty Parties hold in their hands the power and opportunity to set an example for thoughtful and effective governance of polar cruise tourism. However, some of the above-mentioned system-inherent problems will have to be overcome for the ATS to maintain its status and regulatory power.

Ways forward – practically and conceptually

A key conclusion in this chapter is that Antarctic tourism regulation in its current form is assessed critically by all stakeholder groups with a specific focus on the 'lack of effective mechanisms for monitoring operations and policing infringements' (Haase, 2008). There is much room for improvement, not only from the side of the Antarctic Treaty Parties in terms of, for instance, strengthening the implementation, monitoring and enforcement of regulatory guidelines, but also from the side of the IAATO. A number of tour operators make concrete suggestions as to how the self-regulatory regime could be strengthened. Having independent observers onboard IAATO vessels regularly, the adoption of an accreditation scheme, designated staff training programmes, and higher staff-to-tourist ratios onshore are some of the most frequently mentioned recommendations (Haase, 2008). Some drastic measures are suggested by one operator who would like to see the largest part of the Antarctic Peninsula closed off to allow the ecosystem to recover from human impacts, an idea which, unsurprisingly, has not found wide support amongst other tour operators (O).

Site-specific tourism regulation is considered to be the most cost-efficient and effective way to address tourism issues in Antarctica. Site guidelines for 25 popular landing sites have already been put in place through the ATS (see ATS Resolutions 5-2005, 2-2006, 1-2007, 2-2008 and 4-2009), but are only of a hortatory nature and need to be given regulatory 'teeth'. A site-specific approach (i.e. visitor management) allows for an improved control over, and monitoring of, visitor numbers at selected sites, which could be specifically targeted to each of the limited number of exist-ing landing sites around the Antarctic continent. In this sense, the number of site-specific guidelines embraced by ATCPs should continuously be expanded to include all frequently visited sites. In addition, the use of Antarctic Specially Protected Areas (ASPAs) and Antarctic Specially Managed Areas (ASMAs) to further control activi-ties at key sites deserves mention. Largely, ASPAs provide a mechanism for prohibit-ing access to sites that are either deemed to have been affected or at which ongoing human visitation would cause unacceptable impacts. ASPA designation would allow for site recovery or at least limit further impacts. On the other hand, ASMAs offer a tool to increase coordination among operators at one or more visitor sites as they allow setting common minimum standards of operation through codes of conduct, guidelines or even mandatory measures.

As shown in this chapter, IAATO decisions and structure emphasize the potential effectiveness of peer pressure and the ability of individuals to collaborate, at least for the time being. However, how tenuous is the future of an organization that is based on 'goodwill'? How can 'goodwill' and peer pressure succeed in retaining high operating and compliance standards in light of the current economic crisis and its potentially dire implications for membership numbers or diminishing profit margins, which may start to impact upon environmental behaviours? These pertinent ques-tions cannot be answered clearly at the moment as research into these current issues is scarce and complicated by the dynamic nature of Antarctic tourism development. Evidently, more research combining behavioural psychology and tourism studies is needed to analyse the potential of peer pressure and voluntary codes of practice with regard to the compliance levels and the operational standards of tour operators.[5]

With no incidents or discernable environmental impacts, the debate over whether tourism is a concern or not can rage on; but the increase in incidents has galvanized many of the ATCPs and provided them with an 'excuse' to overcome a seemingly *laissez-faire* attitude to regulating Antarctic tourism. The increasing number of inci-dents will begin to break down the tolerance of the Antarctic Treaty Parties. So far, no human lives have been lost; but for how much longer is this going to be the case? The environmental implications of the recent series of incidents have been relatively limited; but there is no guarantee that future accidents will not be tied to environ-mental disasters. Clearly, a proper response plan to environmental problems arising from incidents involving cruise vessels is needed. Such a plan should be embed-ded within a wider strategy that formalizes and legalizes a cooperative approach to the regulation and management of Antarctic tourism, involving both Antarctic Treaty Parties and the IAATO. Conceptually and practically, explicit definitions are required of what Antarctic tourism regulation should be, who the main stakeholders are and what their responsibilities should entail. Furthermore, clarification is needed regarding who should make decisions regarding those responsibilities, and how and by whom regulatory measures should be enforced. As a result of unequivocal sovereignty elsewhere in the world, the regulation of tourism in other destinations can be much more clearly enforced and its impacts more readily measured. Tourism regulation and management in extreme and remote destinations such as Antarctica require the consideration of human ethics and values. Consequently, there is a visible need for the social sciences, biosciences and Earth system sciences to be implemented together and then collectively used to inform policy-making.

Notes

1   Despite the existence of other self-regulatory systems with a connection to Antarctic tourism (Molenaar, 2005; Dinuzzi, 2006), this chapter will focus on the IAATO as the most important, active and influential self-regulatory organization in the realm of Antarctic tourism.
2   In the context of this chapter, Antarctic tourism operators, Antarctic Treaty Parties and their representatives, environmental NGOs and others monitoring tourism can be considered as key stakeholders.
3   Here, tourism organizers operating vessels with a capacity of less than 200 passengers.
4   A general overview of all regulatory mechanisms with direct or indirect relevance for Antarctic tourism is provided by Molenaar (2005) and Haase (2008).
5   A range of studies by Goldstein et al (2007), Goldstein and Cialdini (2007), Kandel and Lazear (1992) and Sirakaya (1997) provide some good examples outlining how self-perception, imitation of the behaviour of others, the potential of bad publicity and advocacy of good practice can increase compliance with voluntary guidelines.

References

Antarctic Treaty Consultative Parties (1959) 'The Antarctic Treaty', *University of Miami Law Review*, vol 33, Washington, DC, pp515–521
Bastmeijer, K. and Roura, R. (2004) 'Regulating Antarctic tourism and the precautionary principle', *The American Journal of International Law*, vol 98, pp763–781
Bastmeijer, K., Lamers, M. and Harcha, J. (2008) 'Permanent land-based facilities for tourism in Antarctica: The need for regulation', *Reciel*, vol 17, pp84–99
Beck, P. J. (1990) 'Regulating one of the last tourism frontiers: Antarctica', *Applied Geography*, vol 10, pp243–356
Beck, P. J. (1994) 'Managing Antarctic tourism: A front-burner issue', *Annals of Tourism Research*, vol 21, pp375–385
Buck, S. J. (1998) *The Global Commons: An Introduction*, Island Press, Washington, DC
Cessford, G. (1997) 'Antarctic tourism: A frontier for wilderness management', *International Journal of Wilderness*, vol 3, pp7–11
Charmaz, K. (2002) 'Qualitative interviewing and grounded theory analysis', in J. F. Gubrium and J. A. Holstein (eds) *Handbook of Interview Research: Context and Method*, Sage, Thousand Oaks, London, New Delhi
Dingwall, P. R. and Cessford, G. R. (1996) 'Pole positions', *Ecodecision*, vol 20, pp65–68
Dinuzzi, R. (2006) 'Regulating tourism in Antarctica', in G. Tamburelli (ed) *The Antarctic Legal System and Environmental Issues*, Giuffrè, Milano

Enzenbacher, D. J. (2007) 'Antarctic tourism policy-making: Current challenges and future prospects', in G. Triggs and A. Riddell (eds) *Antarctica: Legal and Environmental Challenges for the Future*, British Institute of International and Comparative Law, London

Gillies, E. (2008) 'Hurtigruten's *M/S Fram* heads to Ushuaia', www.wheretogonext.com/release.html?releaseID=124702, accessed 1 May 2008

Goldstein, N. J. and Cialdini, R. B. (2007) 'The spyglass self: A model of vicarious self-perception', *Journal of Personality and Social Psychology*, vol 92, pp402–417

Goldstein, N. J., Griskevicius, V. and Cialdini, R. B. (2007) 'Invoking social norms: A social psychology perspective on improving hotels' linen-reuse programs', *Cornell Hotel and Restaurant Administration Quarterly*, vol 48, pp145–150

Haase, D. (2008) *Tourism in the Antarctic: Modi Operandi and Regulatory Effectiveness*, PhD thesis, University of Canterbury, Christchurch, New Zealand

Haase, D., Storey, B., McIntosh, A., Carr, A. and Gilbert, N. (2007) 'Stakeholder perspectives on regulatory aspects of Antarctic tourism', *Tourism in Marine Environments*, vol 4, pp167–183

Haase, D., Lamers, M. and Amelung, B. (2009) 'Heading into uncharted territory? Exploring the institutional robustness of self-regulation in the Antarctic tourism sector', *Journal of Sustainable Tourism*, vol 17, pp411–430

Hall, C. M. (1992) 'Tourism in Antarctica: Activities, impacts, and management', *Journal of Travel Research*, pp2–9

Hemmings, A. D. and Roura, R. (2003) 'A square peg in a round hole: Fitting impact assessment under the Antarctic Environmental Protocol to Antarctic tourism', *Impact Assessment and Project Appraisal*, vol 21, pp13–24

Huber, J. (2006) 'Notes on the ATCM recommendations and their approval process', in Tamburelli, G. (ed) *The Antarctic Legal System and Environmental Issues*, Giuffrè, Milano

IAATO (International Association of Antarctica Tour Operators) (2006) 'About IAATO: Objectives', www.iaato.org/objectives.html, accessed 26 August 2006

IAATO (2008a) *IAATO Overview of Antarctic Tourism: 2007–2008 Antarctic Season and Preliminary Estimates for 2008–2009 Antarctic Season*, IAATO, Kyiv, Ukraine

IAATO (2008b) 'IAATO update on the incident involving the *M/V Ushuaia*', www.iaato.org/press/MV_Ushuaia_Situation_Report_Dec_16_2008_1500UTC.pdf, accessed 10 February 2009

IAATO (2009a) 'About IAATO: Bylaws', www.iaato.org/bylaws.html, accessed 1 May 2009

IAATO (2009b) *IAATO Membership Directory: 2009–2010*, http://apps.iaato.org/iaato/directory, accessed 2 May 2009

Johnson, M. P. and Kriwoken, L. K. (2007) 'Emerging issues of Australian Antarctic tourism: Legal and policy directions', in L. K. Kriwoken, J. Jabour and A. D. Hemmings (eds) *Looking South: Australia's Antarctic Agenda*, Federation Press, Sydney, New South Wales

Kandel, E. and Lazear, E. P. (1992) 'Peer pressure and partnerships', *The Journal of Political Economy*, vol 100, pp801–817

Kriwoken, L. K. and Rootes, D. (2000) 'Tourism on ice: Environmental impact assessment of Antarctic tourism', *Impact Assessment and Project Appraisal*, vol 18, pp138–150

Lamers, M. and Amelung, B. (2007) 'Adventure tourism and private expeditions in Antarctica: Framing the issue and conceptualising the risk', in J. Snyder and B. Stonehouse (eds) *Prospects for Polar Tourism*, CABI, London

Landau, D. and Splettstoesser, J. (2007) 'Management of tourism in the marine environment of Antarctica: The IAATO perspective', *Tourism in Marine Environments*, vol 4, pp185–193

Lee, M. L. (2005) 'A case for world government of the Antarctic', *Gonzaga Journal of International Law*, vol 9, pp73–95

Mason, P. A. and Legg, S. J. (1999) 'Antarctic tourism: Activities, impacts, management issues, and a proposed research agenda', *Pacific Tourism Review*, vol 3, pp71–84

Molenaar, E. J. (2005) 'Sea-borne tourism in Antarctica: Avenues for further intergovernmental regulation', *International Journal for Marine and Coastal Law*, vol 20, pp247–295

Murray, C. and Jabour, J. (2004) 'Independent expeditions and Antarctic tourism policy', *Polar Record*, vol 40, pp309–317

Njåstad, B. (2007) 'Protocol on Environmental Protection to the Antarctic Treaty', in B. Riffenburgh (ed) *Encyclopedia of the Antarctic*, Routledge, New York, NY

Norway (2007) 'The M/S Nordkapp incident', WP 37 rev 1, XXX Antarctic Treaty Consultative Meeting, 30 April–11 May, New Delhi, India

Pidgeon, N. and Henwood, K. (2004) 'Grounded theory', in M. A. Hardy and A. Bryman (eds) *Handbook of Data Analysis*, Sage, London, Thousand Oaks, CA

Pineschi, L. (1996) 'The Madrid Protocol on the Protection of the Antarctic Environment and its Effectiveness', in F. Francioni and T. Scovazzi (eds) *International Law for Antarctica*, Kluwer Law International, The Hague and Cambridge

Polk, W. A. (1998) 'Welcome to the Hotel Antarctica: The EPA's interim rule on environmental impact assessment of tourism in Antarctica', *Emory International Law Review*, vol 12, pp1395–1442

Prosser, R. (1995) 'Power, control and intrusion, with particular reference to Antarctica', in D. E. Cooper and J. Palmer (eds) *Just Environments: Intergenerational, International, and Interspecies Issues*, Routledge, London and New York

Prosser, R. (1998) 'Tourism', in R. Chadwick (ed) *Encyclopaedia of Applied Ethics*, Academic Press, San Diego, CA

Quark Expeditions (2009) 'Update on the incident involving the *M/V Ocean Nova*', www.iaato.org/press/OceanNovaUpdate4Feb1809.pdf, accessed 12 March 2009

Reel, M. (2007) 'Cruise ship sinks off Antarctica', *Washington Post*, pA01, www.washingtonpost.com/wp-dyn/content/story/2007/11/24/ST2007112400367.html, accessed 17 February 2009

Richardson, M. G. (1999) 'Regulating tourism in the Antarctic: Issues of environment and jurisdiction', *Antarctic Project Report (Fridtjof Nansen Institute)*, vol 2/99, pp1–19

Riffenburgh, B. (1998) 'Impacts on the Antarctic environment: Tourism vs government programmes', *Polar Record*, vol 34, pp193–196

Scott, S. V. (2001) 'How cautious is precautious?: Antarctic tourism and the precautionary principle', *The International and Comparative Law Quarterly*, vol 50, pp963–971

Scully, R. T. (1990) 'The Antarctic Treaty as a system', in R. A. Herr, H. R. Hall and M. G. Haward (eds) *Antarctica's Future: Continuity or Change?*, Australian Institute of International Affairs, Hobart, Tasmania

Sirakaya, E. (1997) 'Attitudinal compliance with ecotourism guidelines', *Annals of Tourism Research*, vol 24, pp919–950

Splettstoesser, J. F. (2000) 'IAATO's stewardship of the Antarctic environment: A history of tour operator's concern for a vulnerable part of the world', *International Journal of Tourism Research*, vol 2, pp47–55

Warren, C. A. B. (2002) 'Qualitative interviewing', in J. F. Gubrium and J. A. Holstein (eds) *Handbook of Interview Research: Context and Method*, Sage, Thousand Oaks, London, New Delhi

12

Port Readiness Planning in the Arctic: Building Community Support

John S. Hull and Simon Milne

Introduction

In the 21st century, visitor numbers to polar regions are expanding rapidly (Snyder, 2007; Dawson et al, 2007) This growth is due, in large part, to a growing interest among visitors in exploring some of the last tourism frontiers on Earth (Hall, 2007) and also to accelerated changes in biological, climatic and oceanographic conditions that stem from natural and human-induced climate change (Stewart and Draper, 2006; Snyder and Stonehouse, 2007) Rising temperatures and melting sea ice are expanding the number of accessible destinations, lengthening tourism seasons, and opening previously remote and austere environments to the global cruise ship industry (Stonehouse and Snyder, 2007).

Historically, limited accessibility has been a major challenge in developing tourism in polar regions. As Hall and Johnston (1995, p4) stated more than a decade ago: 'access in the Arctic though difficult is available by air, land and sea'. The Arctic Climate Impact Assessment (ACIA, 2005) has confirmed that the temperature in the Arctic is rising twice as fast as in lower latitudes. Hall and Higham (2005, p13) argue that 'all demand and supply facets of tourism are regarded as being affected by global climate change, but just as importantly, tourism has direct and indirect effects on climate change itself'. As a result of climate change, melting sea ice is increasing the accessibility of cruise ships to the Arctic and extending the tourism season as a result of a 15 to 20 per cent loss of summer sea ice coverage (Hassel, 2004; Stewart and Draper, 2006; Dawson et al, 2007) In 2004, over 1.2 million passengers travelled to polar regions by cruise ship, raising concerns about the carrying capacity of these destinations (International Ecotourism Society, 2004; Stewart and Draper, 2006; Snyder, 2007)

The Province of Newfoundland and Labrador on Canada's east coast is an important growth market for polar cruising, with several specialized tours focusing on the Labrador coast (see Figure 12.1) (Bermello and Ajamil, 2002; CLIA, 2009). The peninsula of Labrador is bounded by the Gulf of St Lawrence in the south, the North Atlantic in the east, and the Hudson Strait and Hudson Bay in the north. The peninsula is located within the Arctic and sub-Arctic biomes of North America (Grenfell, 1895). Both biomes are characterized by a cold harsh climate with low temperatures and low precipitation, resulting in long winters and short cool summers in the north, with short warm summers in the south (Bone, 1992). Along the Labrador coast, the sub-Arctic climate extends south to the island of Newfoundland due to the southward flow of the cold Labrador Current (de Boileau, 1969).

Figure 12.1 *The Province of Newfoundland and Labrador, Canada*

Source: Natural Resources Canada (2009)

Over the last five years, the province has experienced steady growth in cruise ship visitors. During the 2004 cruise season, 39 ports throughout the province hosted 22 cruise ships with 38,842 passengers. In 2009, 33 ports of call hosted 24 cruise ships with 47,696 passengers, representing a 19 per cent growth rate over the five-year period (CANAL, 2004, 2009). The Cruise Association of Newfoundland and Labrador (CANAL) estimates that the overall direct and indirect economic impact from the cruise industry in the province has surpassed Cdn$10.7 million (CANAL, 2009). In an effort to better respond to the growth of the industry, CANAL launched a Port Readiness Programme in May 2005. The aim of the programme is to improve the quality of service and increase the number of cruise ship calls to provincial ports by informing communities of the opportunities for local revenue generation, employment enhancement and excursion planning (Hull et al, 2005).

The purpose of this chapter is to first review the growth of cruising in Newfoundland and Labrador, providing an understanding of the development of the province as a cruise ship destination. The next section presents the methodology for the Port Readiness Programme's needs assessment, administered to 40 provincial ports of call. This section presents background on and documents the results of the needs assessment. Finally, a series of recommendations for future planning and development are proposed for port readiness not only in Newfoundland and Labrador, but also for other Arctic destinations.

The Newfoundland and Labrador context

Newfoundland and Labrador have a rich natural and cultural history that has captured the imagination of cruise travellers for over a century. Explorers, Moravian missionaries, fishing and trapping merchants, wilderness adventurers and naturalists have been lured to the province and left a legacy of journals, images and maps of the region (Grey, 1858; Wallace, 1907; Grenfell, 1909). These accounts have helped to foster the province's international market awareness as a destination for expedition cruising and nature-based adventure based around the northern wilderness and the unique cultures found there. Cruise consultants acknowledge that Newfoundland and Labrador are well positioned to capture an increasing number of cruise ship calls as a result of their many scenic destinations, rugged coastlines, protected areas, abundant wildlife and rich cultural heritage. The province's advantageous geographic location also provides an access point for tours to the Canadian Arctic (Hull, 2001; Bermello and Ajamil, 2002; Global Destinations Development, LLC, 2006; Lemelin and Maher, 2009).

Historically, the growth of formal cruising routes in Newfoundland and Labrador began during the 19th and 20th centuries. By 1863, coastal steamers based in St John's, Newfoundland, were completing northern runs as far as Battle Harbour, Labrador. In 1897, the steamer service expanded rapidly with the Reid Newfoundland Company's *SS Bruce*, offering steamer services linked to the newly completed Newfie Bullet train service across the Island of Newfoundland (Hull et al, 2005). By 1900, the company's steamer service had expanded to more than eight boats, known as the *Alphabet Fleet*, serving Placentia Bay, Notre Dame Bay,

Conception Bay, Trinity Bay, the Great Northern Peninsula and the polar regions of Labrador (Hanrahan, 2007, p5):

> *The SS Home ... was built in 1900. The SS Home was well-loved by Labradorians and the Newfoundland families who spent their summers fishing in Labrador... The SS Home called at Henley Harbour and Cape Charles and right up to Hopedale, Labrador.*

These coastal steamships initially served small numbers of travellers to the region, with a primary focus on the transport of mail, freight, local residents and fishing families. A nurse at the Grenfell Medical Mission described the ship on her voyage to Labrador as:

> *Evidently built, not for comfort nor for beauty, but for service and for safety ... to battle the wildest and roughest seas and to carry essential cargo to the waiting fishing folk.* (Banfill, 1952, p4)

By 1905, provincial service expanded with *The Newfoundland Guidebook* (Prowse, 1905, pp92, 114), promoting the province as a destination for fishing 'in pristine, fast flowing rivers and sightseeing on cruise ships to spectacular northern landscapes as part of an Arctic expedition'. There were two main ports – Port-aux-Basques and St John's – serving Labrador:

> *The east coast boat starts from St John's every fortnight and after calling at numerous places on the east side of the Island of Newfoundland, she meets the western boat at Battle Harbour and then goes all down the Labrador on the Atlantic side as far as Nain. She visits up both Hamilton Inlet and Sandwich Bay. The point at which she turns to the southward is about two-thirds of the way to the Hudson Bay Straits.*

During the 1920s, an expanded steamer service to Labrador was initiated from the Province of Quebec. In 1920, the Clarke Brothers, from Montreal, founded the Clarke Steamship Lines and initiated a number of pleasure cruises that serviced the Gulf of St Lawrence, visiting ports in Newfoundland and Labrador. An entry from the *Clarke Day Book* (Clarke Steamship Company, undated) reports:

> *The scenic splendours of the Gulf of St Lawrence, which had first attracted the Clarke brothers, prompted the new line to develop pleasure cruises from Montreal to many picturesque ports on the Gulf. These cruises, operated by the S.S. New Northland and later by the S.S. North Star, brought thousands of tourists to this region for the first time. Labrador, the unknown country, became more than just a synonym for Polar Regions. The new cruises did much to make the people aware of the work of the Grenfell Medical Missions in the North Country and aided that enterprise in many ways, focusing attention on a region, which proved to be so rich in natural resources.*

The early 20th century up to the outbreak of World War II featured an era of honeymoon, pleasure and rest cruises on the St Lawrence River. The Clarke Steamship promotional brochure from 1934 advertised 12-day cruises starting at Cdn$85 and up as 'a northern adventure'. This service continued after the war until the 1960s (Clarke Steamship Company, undated, 1934):

> *Things you will see in these outposts of civilization … among them are fishermen tending the cod traps, salting and spreading of the fish … Northern Lights … majestic icebergs, playful seals and occasionally the spout of a whale.* (Clarke Steamship Company, 1934, pp1–5)

At the beginning of the 21st century, steamship lines, subsidized by the provincial and federal government, continued to play an important role as a means of transportation for visitors to access the isolated outposts on the Labrador Coast (Porter, 1988; Hull, 1999). *The Northern Ranger* offered a regional service to over 45 communities as part of the Viking Trail Tourism Association's guided Cruising Labrador programme. The year 2002 was reportedly the best of the association's programme, with 184 passengers on ten sailings (VTTA, 2003). In addition, *The Sir Robert Bond* offered a service from Lewisporte on the Island of Newfoundland to Happy Valley/Goose Bay, Labrador (Labrador Marine Service, 2009). As of 2009, seven international cruise lines – Cruise North Expeditions, Silver Sea, Polar Star Expeditions, Adventure Canada, Clipper Adventure, Holland America and the Hurtigruten – have entered the market and now offer polar, expedition and adventure cruising opportunities to the Labrador coast, transporting over 2100 passengers to the region (CANAL, 2009)

The growth of the cruise ship industry in Newfoundland and Labrador illustrates the steady development of cruising over two centuries from southern regions of the province to northern ports. In the 19th century, early steamers, subsidized by the provincial government, were locally owned and operated by businessmen from St John's, who marketed the Labrador region as an Arctic destination for pleasure and adventure.

Over the course of the 20th century, outside interests from large urban centres in central Canada, North America and Europe entered the market, building bigger ships, transporting thousands of travellers from these markets, and customizing their product for an increasingly discerning cruise traveller interested in pleasure and educational experiences focused on learning about a northern way of life. Today, Adventure Canada offers 'adventurous experiences with a team of naturalists, historians, photographers, musicians and guides … to impart knowledge and experience of the natural world and local culture, and give life to times past' (National Geographic, 2009, p16). CANAL now markets the cruise experience in the province as 'Far from the ordinary, close to you', reflecting the uniqueness of the destination and its proximity to the major cruise markets, the US and the UK (Barron and Greenwood, 2006; CANAL, 2009).

Building port readiness: Approach and findings

For many coastal communities in eastern Canada, the decline of the fisheries over the last two decades has forced many communities to adopt alternative regional economic development options that have included tourism (Hull, 1998). One of the fastest growing market segments for tourism is the cruise industry (Dowling, 2006). In an effort to meet market demand, destinations such as Newfoundland and Labrador have expanded attractions, recreational activities, accommodations and convenient modes of travel to appeal to an increasing clientele interested in sightseeing, nature, adventure and the culture of the region. Labrador has been recognized as a popular destination for expedition cruise ships (EPG Canada, 1996; Hull, 2001; CANAL, 2009). The unique local communities and spectacular coastal scenery is of increasing interest to international cruise operators who offer comfortable transport, accommodation and authentic experiences for tourists to these remote destinations that often lack basic goods and services. In addition, the increasing global awareness of climate change has motivated many tourists to visit polar regions, such as Labrador, to witness firsthand the impacts of rising temperatures upon the local environment. The small size of the ships and the disembarking visitors are attractive to local communities who are interested in capturing local economic benefits while minimizing negative environmental and social impacts (Snyder, 2007). CANAL's Port Readiness Programme was launched in 2005 to provide increased support to local communities in welcoming and managing an increasing number of tourists to the region.

Three approaches were adopted to support the collection of primary and secondary information for the Port Readiness Programme needs assessment. First, a product-market match method was adopted for analysing the development of the cruise industry in Newfoundland and Labrador. In tourism planning, the sustainability of the industry is dependent upon balancing demand (market) and supply (product) (Inskeep, 1991; Gunn, 2002). The needs assessment targeted representatives from the cruise ship industry (the market) and key stakeholders in the 40 ports of call (the product) to analyse the present state of affairs and provide a comprehensive analysis of the tourism system.

The data presented in this chapter is limited to the supply side of the tourism system and integrates accounts from the ports to understand present needs, distribution, patterns and flows, as well as community resident expectations and satisfaction linked to the growth of the industry. Gilbert (1990, p20) defines the tourism product as 'an amalgam of different goods and services offered as an activity experience to the tourist'. In a context of port readiness, the goods and services associated with onshore experiences and excursions are dependent upon not only the classification of the ship (i.e. size and number of passengers), but also the market segment in which the ship is positioned (i.e. standard, premium, luxury) (Ward, 2005; Barron and Greenwood, 2006).

In the spring of 2005, an online web-based survey was administered by the New Zealand Tourism Research Institute's (NZTRI's) Tourism and Community's Research Programme Area to key stakeholders in provincial ports. The purpose of the survey was to provide insights into the needs of the ports and to understand how they are, in turn, meeting the expectations and requirements of the cruise ship industry. Specific information was collected on port participation rate in the cruise sector; key industry partners; tourism products/services in ports of call; market readiness; and strengths, weaknesses, opportunities and threats targeted at the cruise sector.

Web-based surveying offers a number of distinct advantages over more traditional mail and phone techniques by reducing the time and cost of conducting a survey and avoiding the often error-prone task of data entry (Solomon, 2001). While the web is still being developed and studied as a tool for scientific research, researchers are increasingly acknowledging web-surveying as being at least as reliable as paper-based surveys (Gosling et al, 2004; Denscombe, 2006). The surveys were pre-tested for clarity and readability and then approved by CANAL.

A list of key stakeholders in ports of call was generated from CANAL and from phone research conducted by the research team. Key stakeholders included representatives of public and private organizations currently involved in cruise ship planning in the province. Emails were sent to key stakeholders inviting them to participate in the survey. In a number of cases, the port surveys were also faxed to individuals who did not have access to the internet. In the latter case, stakeholders were invited to complete the survey and fax it back to the CANAL office, where they were collected for analysis. These surveys were then entered into the online web-based survey by the research team. One week after the web-based survey was launched on the website, the research team conducted email and phone follow-up, with ports encouraging individuals to participate in the survey. Ninety-seven individuals representing 40 provincial ports were invited to complete the port survey. Final results reveal that 34 responded (35 per cent) representing 24 ports (60 per cent). This response rate is higher than one would expect from a mail or phone survey and within the range reported in web-based surveying. Researchers note that it is often possible to double the response rate of web-based surveys with follow-up memos (Solomon, 2001) as administered as part of the data-gathering efforts for the Port Readiness Programme. Incentives can also be an effective tool to increase response rates (Dickson and Milne, 2008) and are a factor that may be used in follow-up survey work.

A review of literature – historical accounts, government and cruise reports, journals, books and web-based research – provided important contextual information on the history of cruising, and on the present impacts and growth of the industry. Through a product market match approach, web-based port surveys and a secondary review of literature, the research team was able to identify the needs and expectations in the ports of call; document the present state of affairs of the industry; and provide baseline data for recommending future planning and development for the provincial cruise product.

Port participation rates and key industry partners

Communication and coordination are fundamental to successfully hosting a cruise ship. The involvement of key industry stakeholders is essential to ensure that cruise operator and passenger needs and expectations are satisfied. The organization of a local cruise committee, composed of port authorities, provincial/municipal governments, shipping agencies, tour operators, retail operators and other organizations, is a first step in ensuring local participation and that appropriate activities are planned and communicated to all industry stakeholders (Hull et al, 2005). In evaluating the participation rate of provincial ports and the degree of local coordination, the following results were summarized.

Over two-thirds (69.7 per cent) of the respondents indicated that they live in communities where cruise ships dock. Almost 22 per cent of respondents in these communities have never welcomed cruise ships, with approximately 8 per cent living in communities who have hosted cruise ships in the past. The number of port calls at a destination is a reflection of the growth and size of the cruise industry and the market demand for new and different locales (Dickinson and Vladimir, 2008). The large number of Newfoundland and Labrador ports welcoming cruise ships reflects a diverse industry that is catering to a variety of ships and cruise lines serving different market segments. This is a result of the geographic location of the province and its positioning as a stopover for larger ships on transatlantic voyages and Canada–New England itineraries at the main ports of St John's and Corner Brook, as well as its growing popularity for small- and medium-sized ships, offering more exclusive polar, adventure and expedition cruises to more remote northern ports and around the island of Newfoundland (CANAL, 2009).

The general profile of key industry partners involved in port readiness programming at Newfoundland and Labrador ports of call is presented in Table 12.1.

Table 12.1 *Responses to port survey (N = 34)*

Representative category	Number of responses	Response rate (%)
Port authority/development association/ waterfront committee	15	44
Municipality	9	26
Federal government/public institution	4	12
Private businesses/tour operators	2	6
Unknown	4	12
Total responses	34	100

Source: CANAL (2005)

The results reveal that there is strong participation of port authorities, development associations and waterfront committees in port readiness planning. However, the participation of individual private businesses and tour operators is relatively low. The provincial tourism industry is composed of approximately 2400 tourism businesses (DTCR, 2009). As a result of historical settlement patterns linked to the fisheries, the majority of these businesses are located in coastal communities, suggesting that there is potential for increased participation of private enterprise with the cruise sector.

Identifying key industry partners in the public and private sector is critical in developing a coordinated Port Readiness Programme that is responsive to the needs of the industry. The presence of key stakeholders – port contacts, shipping agents, harbour authorities and cruise committees – play a major role in coordination, logistical support and communications with the cruise industry (Hull et al, 2005; Marquez and Eagles, 2007). Municipalities (71 per cent) and local tourism associations (50 per cent) are perceived to be providing the majority of public-sector support in Newfoundland and Labrador (see Table 12.2). Less than 50 per cent of provincial ports are supported by a local harbour authority (47 per cent), cruise committee (32 per cent), port contact (32 per cent) or shipping agent (26 per cent). The results illustrate a need for the creation of local institutional organizations and employment positions that can better serve the industry and provide the necessary support services for ports.

Table 12.2 *Key public partners working with the Newfoundland ports at present (N = 34)*

Key community partners	Yes (%)	No (%)
Port contact	32	68
Shipping agent	26	74
Cruise committee	32	68
Harbour authority	47	53
Municipality	71	29
Chamber of commerce	21	79
Local tourism association	50	50
Protected areas/historic site	44	56
Others	32	68

Source: CANAL (2005)

The survey revealed that less than one in five (20 per cent) of the respondents are aware of local attractions, transport companies, tour operators, food service and other private operators who provide support services to cruise ships when they arrive in provincial ports. If the cruise industry is to become more of a driver for local economic development, strong itineraries and private business need to keep pace with sufficient investment to accommodate the sector's growth through broader, more integrated, management approaches (Stewart and Draper, 2006; Dickinson and Vladimir, 2008).

Tourism products/services in ports of call

Successful cruise destinations have a number of basic features in common that include appeal as a travel and leisure destination; adequate port infrastructure to support vessel operations and movement of passengers; competitive cost; and a strategic fit depending on the size of the ship that is welcomed in port, as well as the itineraries the cruise ship has organized (Bermello and Ajamil, 2002; Barron and Greenwood, 2006). Understanding the availability of tourism products and services in communities is an important step in evaluating the quality of programming, the economic impacts and the sustainability of the cruise industry over the long term (Hull et al, 2005).

In 2007, an economic impact study of the cruise industry in Newfoundland and Labrador indicated that cruise lines spent Cdn\$3.5 million dollars on administrative and professional expenses with businesses in the province, and Cdn\$1 million in operational expenses, including machinery and equipment. Cruise passengers spent Cdn\$1.7 million on goods and services. Of that total, 47 per cent of passenger spending accounted for shore excursions. Average expenditure per passenger was Cdn\$48.83 in larger ports and Cdn\$16.11 in smaller ports. Crew spent an estimated Cdn\$400,000 for tours and transportation, food and beverages, and other retail. The total direct expenditure of the cruise industry in the province was estimated at approximately Cdn\$5.8 million (BREA, 2008). Table 12.3 provides a summary of the tourism products and services from respondents, which have served to lure and facilitate cruise lines and their passengers to a number of destinations in Newfoundland and Labrador.

The data reveal that the majority of Newfoundland and Labrador communities provide a diversified base of visitor services that can be offered to cruise ships in ports-of-call. Services that performed best include visitor information centres (79 per cent), attractions (82 per cent), accommodation (68 per cent), restaurants (76 per cent), docking facilities (61 per cent), and shopping opportunities in the form of arts and craft shops (73 per cent) and retail shops (71 per cent). Services that exhibited a need for improvement in order to better meet the needs of the cruise sector include: transportation services (47 per cent); excursions (50 per cent); local certified guides (41 per cent); as well as the majority of port services linked to local hospitality and way-finding for passengers. By improving on these services, ports have potential to increase the local economic impact of cruise ships when they are in port.

It is evident that in ports there is a lack of coordination between public and private industry partners to support the integrated management of the cruise industry. Stewart and Draper (2006, p82) point out that, in general, 'the planning and development of cruise tourism is just beginning to be recognized', arguing that 'there is a need for more integrated coastal management strategies that foster a process through which decisions are made for sustainable use, development and protection of areas and resources'. Training programmes are needed to assist local communities and operators in working together to develop and coordinate organized excursions and support services. There is also a need to enhance the quality of the physical infrastructure and to improve the availability of transportation services as part of an overall sustainable development strategy (Hull et al, 2005; Marquez and Eagles, 2007; Maher and Meade, 2008).

Table 12.3 *Tourism products and services provided by provincial ports (N = 33)*

Services provided	Yes (%)	No (%)
Community services		
Visitor information centre	79	21
Tourism attractions	82	18
Accommodation	68	32
Transportation	47	53
Restaurant	76	24
Port services		
Harbour front beautification	39	61
Docking facilities	61	39
Flags of visiting nationalities	21	79
Currency exchange	27	73
Traffic control	36	64
Public safety/security	36	64
Official presentation onboard ship	36	64
Dockside welcome/entertainment	45	55
Media/press releases	30	70
Town services/attractions maps	48	52
Local business welcome signs	24	76
Local information services onboard	27	73
Local information services dockside	42	58
Directional signage	39	61
Other services		
Arts and crafts shops	73	27
Retail shops	71	29
Public washroom facility	65	35
Public telephone facilities	62	38
Cell phone access	56	44
Excursions	50	50
Internet access	71	29
Local certified guides	41	59

Source: CANAL (2005)

Market readiness

Market readiness can be defined as:

> *... the state of preparedness of a destination or tourism operation in meeting the expectations of its customers. It refers to the whole spectrum of things affecting customer satisfaction – quality of facilities and services, range of services provided, information services, business policies and practices that affect the customer directly or indirectly.* (EPG Canada, 2004, p361)

A regional viability audit of the Newfoundland and Labrador cruise industry in 2006 (Global Destinations Development, LLC, 2006) reported that the province had many viable destinations waiting for larger market forces to drive ship business to the region. Based on global trends, research indicated that CANAL should focus on expanding its large and medium cruise ship markets in response to a 25 per cent forecasted growth in these markets. It was identified that the good condition of the two large ship ports of St John's and Corner Brook support capacity development for larger ship markets. The small cruise ship market, however, indicated no similar growth plans. As a result, CANAL and the Canadian government have been focusing on expanding regional marketing programmes rather than port capital improvements (Global Destinations Development, LLC, 2006). The following data results analyse the 'port readiness' of communities in a context of quality of port infrastructure, customer service and tourism product to ensure that ports are prepared for potential cruise ship calls as a result of marketing efforts.

Quality of services

In reviewing the quality of port services (see Figure 12.2), approximately 55 per cent of respondents indicated that they perceive their port infrastructure to be of average, low or lowest quality, while a majority of respondents (53 per cent) also indicated that the level of customer service was of average, low or lowest quality. In contrast, 58 per cent of respondents indicated that they felt that their tourism product is of high or the highest quality. The results illustrate that respondents are most confident of their tourism product offerings, while the majority of ports are concerned about their quality of port infrastructure and the level of customer service that they provide to visiting cruise ships. The results suggest that CANAL's decision to focus on marketing over the next five years will require that 'market-ready' ports be strategically identified as part of the future development of the sector.

Community interest, coordination and leadership

The majority of respondents identified community interest, degree of coordination and leadership potential in advancing cruise ship priorities as factors of critical importance in ensuring positive future cruise ship development (Hull et al, 2005). In general, there was believed to be considerable community interest in advancing cruise ship priorities (64.5 per cent). Respondents were less positive about the present leadership available to advance cruise directives (51 per cent). The degree

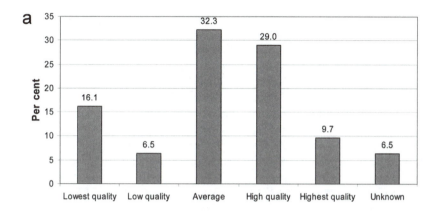

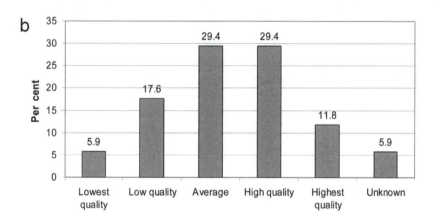

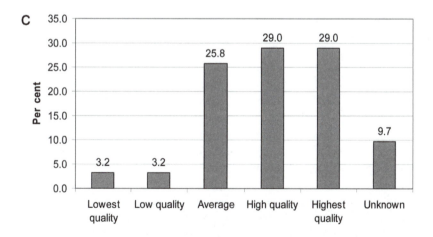

Figure 12.2 *(a) Quality of port infrastructure (N = 31); (b) quality of customer service (N = 34); (c) quality of tourism product in your community (N = 31)*

Source: CANAL (2005)

of coordination currently provided by communities for cruise ships (48.4 per cent) received the lowest rankings by respondents, suggesting that there is a need to focus on heightening local awareness and building community capacity to better meet the needs of cruise ships and their passengers through the organization of local cruise committees as part of CANAL's Port Readiness Programme.

Tourism researchers point out that collaboration and integrated planning are critical in minimizing the fragmented nature of tourism development. There has been little coordinated planning for sustainable development of cruise tourism in Arctic Canada to date (Jamal and Getz, 1995; Stewart and Draper, 2006), compared to the European Arctic and Antarctica, where organizations such as the Association of Arctic Expedition Cruise Operators (AECO) and the International Association of Antarctica Cruise Operators (IAATO) operate (AECO, 2009; IAATO, 2009)

Strengths, weaknesses, opportunities and threats (SWOT)

A SWOT analysis is an important first step of the strategic planning process. The analysis is often conducted by organizations to identify internal (strengths and weaknesses) and external (opportunities and threats) environmental factors that will affect future decision-making and planning (QuickMBA, 2009). A SWOT analysis was administered as part of the port survey to achieve an initial understanding of the available resources, capabilities and challenges facing Newfoundland and Labrador ports in working with the cruise industry (Hull et al, 2005).

Respondents identified the following strengths and weaknesses of their ports in working with the cruise ship industry. The data has been sorted by key word and organized into categories for analysis. The following ten resources/capabilities presented in Table 12.4 were listed by respondents as strengths (i.e. resources and capabilities) in working with the cruise industry.

Well-developed local attractions (21.8 per cent) and the provision of a variety of services (20 per cent) were identified as the potential greatest strengths of ports. Key local attractions that were mentioned included natural, cultural and recreational experiences. One respondent commented:

> We have a vast cultural and geographical product, including hiking trails, unique geological features, mineral and mining history, the French Shore history, Dorset Sites and Beothuk history. (Respondent 25, Regional Development Agency)

In addition, respondents also described their natural and cultural attractions as 'authentic', 'well-defined' and 'tremendous'. These statements were also made about customer service offerings. One respondent commented:

> The port is known to the cruise industry and has provided excellent service to its visiting cruise ships. It has the majority of products and services necessary to supply the needs of the industry. (Respondent 2, port authority representative)

Table 12.4 *The strengths of provincial ports in hosting cruise ships (N = 26)*

Resources/capabilities	Key word mentions	Percentage
Well-developed attractions/tourism products	12	21.8%
Variety of services	11	20%
Community interest/organization to meet cruise needs	8	14.5%
Natural harbour/easy navigation and access	8	14.5%
Scenery	7	12.7%
Friendly people	3	5.5%
Brings in revenue/employment	2	3.6%
Established reputation	2	3.6%
Climate for business opportunities	1	1.9%
Established marketing programme	1	1.9%
Total mentions	55	100%

Source: CANAL (2005)

Community interest in the cruise industry (14.5 per cent) as well as the physical ease of access to ports (14.5 per cent) (natural deep-water harbours) were also important resources identified by respondents. One respondent added:

> *We have a protected harbour, good bird-watching, walking trails and a strong tourism committee interested in working with visiting cruise ships.* (Respondent 18, local tourism committee member)

Another commented:

> *Local groups are willing to work together to improve the cruise industry in the community.* (Respondent 28, regional public administrator)

The respondents' statements suggest that there are a number of ports that feel they are market ready and that have the motivation, organization, and physical infrastructure in place to continue to improve and expand the quality of their services to the growing cruise ship market.

In identifying the weaknesses, respondents identified four major concerns (see Table 12.5)

Table 12.5 *The weaknesses of provincial ports in hosting cruise ships (N = 21)*

Resources/capabilities	Key word mentions	Percentage
Poor docking facilities and physical infrastructure	16	48.4%
Lack of proper port services (shopping/ excursions)	12	36.5%
No community coordination and cohesion to work with cruise ships	4	12.1%
Too much government regulation limiting proper development	1	3%
Total mentions	33	100%

Source: CANAL (2005)

The focus on poor docking facilities (48.4 per cent) reflected not only the state of repair of these facilities, but also their limited size and capability. One respondent commented:

> *The port services are almost non-existent and the docking facilities are in a bad state of repair.* (Respondent 1, federal government administrator)

Another added:

> *Larger ships have to anchor at the mouth of the harbour and shuttle their guests. Future harbour improvements will rectify that problem.* (Respondent 22, municipal public administrator)

This comment suggests that there is a need to work with ports to ensure that infrastructure requirements meet the needs of visiting ships. A lack of port services (36.5 per cent) was also an overriding concern of respondents. For many respondents, poor infrastructure facilities were linked to weaknesses in port services. One respondent commented that there is a:

> *Lack of cruise terminal for visiting ships, limited motor coaches, tour buses and tour guides'* (Respondent 7, municipal public administrator)

Another respondent from Labrador added:

> *No infrastructure in place to house cruise ships and tourists. No craft shop available in community. No museum to display our past history.* (Respondent 32, federal public administrator)

The respondents' feedback illustrates the need for a programme in ports to coordinate public-sector and private-sector participation to upgrade facilities. There is also a need to improve the availability of goods and services for cruise ships and their passengers at certain ports.

Respondents identified the following opportunities and threats to their ports in working with the cruise ship industry. Six critical factors were identified as opportunities that will bring about positive change and continued growth to the cruise sector over the next five years (see Table 12.6)

Table 12.6 *The opportunities for cruise ship tourism in provincial ports (N = 22)*

Resources/capabilities	Key word mentions	Percentage
Work together with operators/ associations to offer high-quality/unique products/ services	17	61%
Improve revenue generation and employment opportunities in ports	3	11%
Actively participate in the Cruise Association of Newfoundland and Labrador (CANAL) and the Atlantic Canada Cruise Association (ACCA) to bring benefits to our ports	2	7%
Develop a strong marketing strategy targeted at the travel trade, media relations and the internet	2	7%
Continue to develop our understanding of the cruise sector that has been realized over the last few years	2	7%
Take advantage of the increasing number of cruise visitors to the province	2	7%
Total mentions	28	100%

Source: CANAL (2005)

The majority (61 per cent) of respondents indicated that there is an opportunity for organizations in ports to offer coordinated products and services that will set the province apart as a cruise destination and provide a competitive advantage in the marketplace. One respondent commented that they see an opportunity to:

> *Work with public-/private-sector partners in introducing more unique tours/products that showcase the culture, history, natural heritage and environment of the destination.*
> (Respondent 29, port authority representative)

Another respondent from the Gros Morne region added that there is:

> *Tremendous opportunity for touring, restaurants, internet cafés, transportation, start and finish tours, because it is a known destination as it is a UNESCO World Heritage Site.* (Respondent 17, Municipal Waterfront Committee)

In addition, one respondent stated that taking advantage of these opportunities for coordinated programming will depend upon the:

> *Experience and cooperation of various individuals, groups and associations dedicated to providing the cruise ship industry with a first class experience at our ports.* (Respondent 22, municipal public administrator)

At the same time, respondents identified the following threats and challenges to developing a high-quality product for visiting cruise ships (see Table 12.7)

Table 12.7 *The threats/challenges for provincial ports hosting cruise ships (N = 28)*

Category	Key word mentions	Percentage
The absence of physical infrastructure/ docking facilities.	10	32.3%
The need for more awareness and support from the community	9	29%
The lack of programming and services to welcome cruise ships	7	22.6%
Engage cruise ships to visit our ports	4	12.9%
The lack of funding for cruise initiatives	1	3.2%
Total mentions	31	100%

Source: CANAL (2005))

The absence of physical infrastructure (32.3 per cent), the need for community support for the cruise industry (29 per cent), and the lack of programming and services (22.6 per cent) represented the major concerns of survey respondents. One park manager commented:

> *Port infrastructure needs to be improved and community, in general, should become more involved.* (Respondent 5, federal public administrator)

Another participant emphasized that the involvement of the local council was critical in assisting with infrastructure and service development, arguing that they:

Need more interest by council, need to prioritize waterfront improvement, should consider marina development complete with shore based services. (Respondent 17, Municipal Waterfront Committee)

In addition, one park manager from Labrador emphasized that there is a need to balance cruise ship development and community heritage, stating that there is a need to:

Overcome the challenges of introducing the new world into a community linked to its past roots. Community members have to be comfortable with tourists. (Respondent 32, federal public administrator)

The data reveals that Newfoundland and Labrador support a diversified cruise industry with strong participation from port authorities, development associations and waterfront committees. There is a need for continued participation from private industry, especially for providing quality customer service as part of transportation services, excursions and local guiding in ports of call. Cruise ship tourism provides important economic opportunities for employment, in guiding and for souvenir sales, especially for remote Arctic communities (Marquez and Eagles, 2007) such as those in Labrador.

Greater coordination is required between the key stakeholders as part of CANAL's Port Readiness Programme to respond to provincial marketing efforts. These efforts are focused on expanding the large and medium cruise ship markets, and securing gains in the expedition and adventure cruise markets to Labrador that have been made over the last decade. Marquez and Eagles (2007, p90) point out that the challenge for many ports is that 'the industry faces a lack of coordination, cohesion, and control'.

Even so, the growth of the cruise industry in Newfoundland and Labrador reveals that the province is establishing a name for itself in the marketplace through its well-developed attractions and variety of services that are providing a competitive advantage in the marketplace. As a result, appropriate management strategies are needed that integrate concerns from key stakeholders (i.e. government agencies, regional associations and private industry). These strategies need to incorporate codes of conduct, and education and infrastructure strategies to minimize risk and the negative impacts of increased visitation (Stewart and Draper, 2006; Marquez and Eagles, 2007; Lemelin and Maher, 2009).

Conclusions and recommendations

As interest in changing polar environments grows, CANAL's Port Readiness Programme in Newfoundland and Labrador illustrates the importance of proper planning and development to support sustainable tourism efforts through local coordination and cooperation. At present, the main impacts of the cruise ship industry have been largely evaluated in a context of visitor numbers, and direct and indirect economic impacts of the industry on key ports (CANAL, 2009). Policy-makers point out that 'there is a need to take a long-term view toward adoption of holistic integrated management approaches; for operators to continue to invest in good environmental practice; for political will to safeguard destinations; for greater profit-sharing between shareholders and destination communities; and for both operators and communities to raise environmental awareness and practise environmentally responsible activities' (Johnson, 2002, cited in Stewart and Draper, 2006, p86). The fragility of polar environments and small size of many communities requires that cruise ship industry stakeholders support efforts to protect these resources that are the basis of the industry (Marsh and Staple, 1995; Dawson et al, 2007; Marquez and Eagles, 2007).

In 2004, the province launched its Provincial Product Development Strategy, stating that tourism is growing in Newfoundland and Labrador and that growth is good for the economy, but that there is a risk of homogenization and overdevelopment (EPG Canada, 2004). The strategy states that Newfoundland and Labrador as a destination is 'a special place with a special people that is fundamental to our appeal as a tourism destination' (EPG Canada, 2004, pi). The province offers experiences – dramatic and unique outdoors, wildlife, cultural heritage and people – that are drawing an increasing number of visitors on cruise ships. The authors argue that it is important to take steps to nurture and protect the unique features of 'this special place' (EPG Canada, 2004). Since 2005, CANAL's Port Readiness Programme continues to offer community capacity-building programmes to support the development of a viable cruise industry for sustainable tourism development. The challenge will be to balance economic benefits while preserving the natural and cultural heritage of the region under a changing climate (Dawson et al, 2007).

References

ACIA (Arctic Climate Impact Assessment) (2005) *Arctic Climate Impact Assessment*, Cambridge University Press, Cambridge, UK

AECO (Association of Arctic Expedition Cruise Operators) (2009) 'Welcome to the Association of Arctic Expedition Cruise Operators', www.aeco.no, accessed 25 August 2009

Banfill, B. (1952) *Labrador Nurse*, Ryerson Press, Toronto, Ontario

Barron, P. and Greenwood, A. B. (2006) 'Issues determining the development of cruise itineraries: A focus on the luxury market', *Tourism in Marine Environments*, vol 3, no 2, pp89–99

Bermello, W. and Ajamil, L. (2002) The Province of Newfoundland and Labrador: Cruiseship Marketing Strategy and Destination Analysis, BA Bermello Ajamil and Partners, Inc, Miami, FL, pp193

Bone, R. M. (1992) *The Geography of the Canadian North: Issues and Challenges*, Oxford University Press, Oxford, UK

BREA (Business Research and Economic Advisors) (2008) *The Economic Contribution of the International Cruise Industry in Canada: A Survey-Based Analysis of the Impacts of Passenger, Cruise and Cruise Line Spending*, Business Research and Economic Advisors, Exton, PA, p98

CANAL (Cruise Association of Newfoundland and Labrador) (2004) *Cruise Newfoundland and Labrador, Canada, 2004 Cruiseship Statistics*, CANAL, St John's, Newfoundland

CANAL (2005) *Newfoundland and Labrador Port Readiness Program: Needs Assessment Report*, CANAL, St John's, Newfoundland

CANAL (2009) *Cruise Newfoundland and Labrador, Canada*, www.cruisenewfoundlandandlabrador.com, accessed 7 November 2009

Clarke Steamship Company (undated) *Clarke Day Book*, Montreal, Quebec

Clarke Steamship Company (1934) *Labrador, Newfoundland, Gulf of St. Lawrence Lure Brochure*, Clarke Steamship Company, Montreal, Quebec

CLIA (Cruise Lines International Association) (2009) *The Overview: Spring 2009*, www.cruising.org, accessed 23 August 2009

Dawson, J., Maher, P. and Slocombe, S. (2007) 'Climate change, marine tourism and sustainability in the Canadian Arctic: Contributions from systems and complexity approaches', *Tourism in Marine Environments*, vol 4, no 2–3, pp69–83

de Boilieu, L. (1969) *Recollections of Labrador Life*, Ryerson Press, Toronto, Ontario

Denscombe, M. (2006) 'Web-based questionnaires and the mode effect: An evaluation based on completion rates and data contents of near-identical questionnaires delivered in different modes', *Social Science Computer Review*, vol 24, pp246–254, doi:10.1177/0894439305284522

Dickinson, B. and Vladimir, A. (2008) *Selling the Sea: An Inside Look at the Cruise Industry*, 2nd edition, John Wiley and Sons, Hoboken, NJ, p340

Dickson, G. and Milne, S. (2008) 'Measuring the impact of micro-events on local communities: A role for web-based approaches', in J. Ali-Knight, M. Robertson, A. Fyall and A. Ladkin (eds) *International Perspectives of Festivals and Events: Paradigms of Analysis*, Elsevier, London, pp253–263

Dowling, R. (2006) 'The cruising industry', in R. Dowling (ed) *Cruise Ship Tourism*, CAB International, Wallingford, UK, pp3–17.

DTCR (2009) *Uncommon Potential*, www.tcr.gov.nl.ca, accessed 29 November 2009

EPG Canada (1996) *Newfoundland and Labrador Product Market Match Study*, Queen's Printer, St John's, Newfoundland.

EPG Canada (2004) *A Special Place, a Special People: The Future for Newfoundland and Labrador Tourism – Main Report, March 2004*, Government of Newfoundland and Labrador, St John's, Newfoundland, p363

Gilbert, D. C. (1990) 'Conceptual issues in the meaning of tourism', in C. Cooper (ed) *Progress in Tourism Recreation and Hospitality Management*, vol 2, Belhaven, London, pp4–27

Global Destinations Development, LLC (2006) *Cruise Association of Newfoundland and Labrador: Study of Future Transatlantic and European Cruise Opportunities for Newfoundland and Labrador*, Global Destinations Development, LLC, Miami, FL, p115

Gosling, S. D., Vazire, S., Srivastava, S. and John, O. P. (2004) 'Should we trust web-based studies? A comparative analysis of six preconceptions about internet questionnaires', *American Psychologist*, vol 59, pp93–104, doi:10.1037/0003-066X.59.2.93

Grenfell, W. T. (1895) *Vikings of Today, or Life and Medical Work among the Fishermen of Labrador*, Marshall, London

Grenfell, W. T. (1909) *Labrador, the Country and the People*, Macmillan, New York, NY

Grey, W. (1858) *Sketches of Newfoundland and Labrador*, S. H. Cowell, Ipswich, England

Gunn, C. (2002) *Tourism Planning*, Routledge, New York, NY

Hall, C. M. (2007) 'Foreword', in J. M. Snyder and B. Stonehouse (eds) *Prospects for Polar Tourism*, CAB International, Wallingford, UK, ppxi–xiv

Hall, C. M. and Higham, J. (2005) 'Introduction: Tourism, recreation and climate change', in C. M. Hall and J. Higham (eds) *Tourism, Recreation and Climate Change*, Channel View Publications, Clevedon, pp3–28

Hall, C. M. and Johnston, M. (1995) 'Introduction: Pole to pole, tourism issues, impacts and the search for a management regime in polar regions', in C. M. Hall and M. Johnston (eds) *Polar Tourism: Tourism in the Arctic and Antarctic Regions*, John Wiley and Sons, Toronto, pp1–26

Hanrahan, M. (2007) *The Alphabet Fleet*. St. John's, NL: Flanker Press Ltd.

Hassel, S.J. (2004) *Arctic climate impact assessment – impacts of a warming Arctic: Highlights*. Cambridge, UK: Cambridge University Press.

Hull, J. S. (1998) 'Coping with the closure of the fishery', in J. O. Baerenholdt and N. Aarsaether (eds) *Coping Strategies in the North: Local Practices in the Context of Global Restructuring*, Copenhagen: Nordic Council of Ministers, Copenhagen, pp121–136

Hull, J. S. (1999) 'Charting adventure tourism development in the North: Labrador's wilderness experience', *TEOROS*, summer, pp15–23

Hull, J. S. (2001) 'Opening up the big land to the world: The role of the public sector in adventure tourism development in Labrador', in B. Sahlberg (ed) *Going North: Peripheral Tourism in Canada and Sweden*, ETOUR, Ostersund, Sweden, pp47–78

Hull, J. S., Parsons, R. Wight, T. and M. T. Ash (2005) *Newfoundland and Labrador Port Readiness Program: Needs Assessment Report*, CANAL, St John's, Newfoundland, p85

IAATO (International Association of Antarctic Tour Operators) (2009) 'About IAATO', www.iaato.org/about.html, accessed August 26, 2009

Inskeep, E. (1991) *Tourism Planning: An Integrated and Sustainable Development Approach*, John Wiley and Sons, New York, NY

International Ecotourism Society (2004) 'Special issue: The cruise industry', *Eco Currents*, September, Washington, DC, p7

Jamal, T. and Getz, D. (1995) 'Collaboration theory and community tourism planning', *Annals of Tourism Research*, vol 22, no 1, pp186–204

Johnson, D. (2002) 'Environmentally sustainable cruise tourism: A reality check', *Marine Policy*, vol 26, pp261–270

Labrador Marine Service (2009) *Labrador Marine Serving Labrador Communities since 1998*, www.labradormarine.com, accessed 20 November 2009

Lemelin, H. and Maher, P. (2009) 'Nanuk of the Torngats: Human-polar bear interactions in the Torngat Mountains National Park, Newfoundland and Labrador, Canada', *Human Dimensions in Wildlife*, vol 14, pp152–155

Maher, P. T. and Meade, D. (2008) *Cruise Tourism in Auyuittuq, Sirmilik and Quttinirpaaq National Parks*, Technical Report, ORTM Publication Series 2008-02, UNBC ORTM Program, Prince George

Marquez, J. R. and Eagles, P. F. J. (2007) 'Working towards policy creation for cruise ship tourism in parks and protected areas of Nunavut', *Tourism in Marine Environments*, vol 4, no 2–3, pp85–96

Marsh, J. and Staple, S. (1995) 'Cruise tourism in the Canadian Arctic and its implications', in C. M. Hall and M. E. Johnston (eds) *Polar Tourism: Tourism in the Arctic and Antarctic Regions*, John Wiley and Sons Ltd, Chichester, pp63–72

National Geographic (2009) *Adventure Canada's High Arctic Adventure*, December 2009/ January 2010, National Geographic Adventure Magazine, Washington, DC

Natural Resources Canada (2009) *Atlas of Canada*, Natural Resources Canada, Ottawa, Canada

Porter, H. (1988) 'By coastal boat to Labrador', *Newfoundland Lifestyle*, vol 6, no 5, pp16–17

Prowse, D. (1905) *The Newfoundland Guidebook, Including Labrador and St. Pierre*, Bradbury Agnew, London

QuickMBA (2009) *SWOT Analysis*, www.quickmba.com/strategy/swot, accessed 23 November 2009

Snyder, J. M. (2007) 'The polar tourism markets', in J. M. Snyder and B. Stonehouse (eds) *Prospects for Polar Tourism*, CAB International, Wallingford, UK, pp51–70

Snyder, J. M. and Stonehouse, B. (2007) 'The growing significance of polar tourism', in J. M. Snyder and B. Stonehouse (eds) *Prospects for Polar Tourism*, CAB International, Wallingford, UK, pp3–14

Solomon, D. J. (2001) 'Conducting web-based surveys', *Practical Assessment, Research & Evaluation*, vol 7, no 9, http://PAREonline.net/getvn.asp?v=7&n=19, accessed 23 November 2009

Stewart, E. J. and Draper, D. (2006) 'Sustainable cruise tourism in Arctic Canada: An integrated coastal management approach', *Tourism in Marine Environments*, vol 3, no 2, pp77–88

Stonehouse, B. and Snyder, J. M. (2007) 'Polar tourism in changing environments', in J. M. Snyder and B. Stonehouse (eds) *Prospects for Polar Tourism*, CAB International, Oxon, UK, pp32–48

VTTA (2003) *VTTA Board Meeting, February 13, 2003, New Business: Cruising Labrador Update*, Viking Trail Tourism Association, St Anthony, Newfoundland

Wallace, D. (1907) *The Long Labrador Trail*, The Outing Publishing Co, New York, NY

Ward, D. (2005) *Ocean Cruising and Cruise Ships 2005*, 15th edition, Berlitz Publishing, London

13

Beyond the Cruise: Navigating Sustainable Policy and Practice in Alaska's Inland Passage

Greg Ringer

Introduction

In the middle of a global economic recession, cruise tourism continues to be one of the major growth engines of international travel. With 'average annual increases in passenger numbers of 8.2 per cent over the last two decades' (Mittermeier, 2007, p1), and sustained 'growth in cruise capacity averaging 7.6 per cent annually', (North West Cruise Ship Association, 2009, p1), the resilience of the industry is clearly displayed in Alaska and the Pacific Northwest, one of the fastest growing cruise destinations in the world (see Figure 13.1).

In ports from San Francisco to Seward, passengers are enticed aboard ships with onboard credits and free upgrades to 'Explore breathtaking landscapes and come face to face with the people and wildlife [who inhabit] the stunning alpine meadows and glacial wonders of Denali and the Talkeetna Mountains... This is the perfect non-camping itinerary for those looking for comfort in the natural wonderland of Alaska' (World Expeditions, 2009, p1). For residents, however, the experience of cruise tourism is often less well described: inundated by summer passengers and carrying the costs of funding and maintaining community infrastructure for a seasonal industry that is known to relocate vessels to competing ports whenever financial incentives warrant.

The transition in rural Alaska's economy from natural resource extraction to tourist attraction has engendered a modern 'gold rush' as cruise providers and operators expand their itineraries and marine destinations now compete for passengers. Communities historically dependent on fishing, mining or logging now (re)create their heritage for visitors in search of recreation and education. The result is an ever-evolving landscape of scenic summer attractions and a population that seeks fruition through tourism, yet increasingly finds frustration in the transitory nature of an industry in transition, both regionally and globally (Peck, 2009).

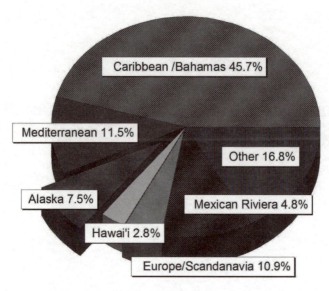

Figure 13.1 *Preferred cruise destinations worldwide, 2008*

Source: J. Hansen, NW Cruise Update, San Francisco, 13 February 2008

The nature of this conflicted relationship for Alaska's cruise communities, and the alternative outcome suggested by more sustainable nautical tourism practices are the focus of this chapter. The intent is to highlight the critical socio-economic and environmental costs of unregulated cruise tourism, and to offer instead a vision and management framework that may reduce operational costs and impacts, and, thereby, profit – and sustain – cruise communities, companies and conservation. In a state already affected by higher gas prices and fewer overland travellers, the decline of ship passengers in the 2009 summer season only adds to the 'rough seas' that confront the state's visitor and hospitality companies today (Jackson, 2009).

Despite the discontent, continued growth in the Alaskan market, surpassing 1 million visitors in 2007 and 2008, is expected, albeit at a much slower pace until the global economy improves (*Chicago Sun-Times*, 2009; SeattleTimes.NWsource. com, 2009). Although 'cruise line revenue is down about 40 per cent for Alaska, compared with 10 to 15 per cent for areas like the Caribbean' (Associated Press, 2009c, p1), a new cruise terminal opened in Seattle for the 2008 season, with 20 more port calls than the previous year, and Ketchikan, in south-east Alaska, now has two cruise berths under construction. Meanwhile, other cruise lines, including Disney, announced plans to base ships in the Pacific for the Inland Passage as well (Cerveny, 2004; Gibson, 2006; Peisley, 2006; Lück, 2007; Servos, 2007; Brida and Zapata-Aguirre, 2008; Chafe, 2008; Hansen, 2008; Ruff, 2008; Westoby, 2008; Browne, 2009).

Sailing on seven- to ten-day itineraries, most Alaskan cruises traditionally follow two major routes that either begin and terminate in the US, or travel one way between Canada and south-central Alaska (see Figure 13.2). The former usually departs from

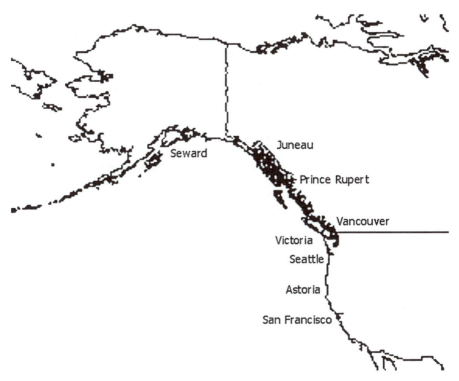

Figure 13.2 *Inland Passage cruise ports, Alaska and Pacific Northwest region*
Source: G. Ringer, 2009

San Francisco or Seattle, with stops in Oregon and Victoria or Prince Rupert, British Columbia, en route to south-east Alaska. One-way cruises sail between Vancouver, British Columbia, and the Alaskan ports of Seward or Whittier, while 'pocket cruises' offer three- to four-day trips solely within Canada to the Pacific ports of Nanaimo, Campbell River and Prince Rupert. These small expedition ships, promoted for their socially and ecologically friendly practices, reduced passenger loads (typically not exceeding 150 tourists) and 'value-added' cruise experience are able to call at ports inaccessible to the larger cruise vessels, including the provincial capital of Victoria (Klein, 2005; Ringer, 2006).

As a result of the growing popularity and operational range of cruise ships, the contribution of the industry is significant for both urban and rural communities along the Inland Passage. The Carnival Corporation alone now carries approximately 560,000 passengers to Alaska each year onboard 1 of 16 ships operated by three subsidiaries: Holland America Line, Princess Cruises and Carnival Cruise Lines. In Canada, the Pacific ports of British Columbia 'accounted for 73 per cent of the [total] Canadian cruise passenger traffic' (BREA, 2008, p5), with almost 2 million visitor arrivals recorded in 2007 during the abbreviated six-month cruise season of May to October. Of this total, approximately 960,554 passenger embarkations, debarkations and port-of-call arrivals (50 per cent) were recorded by Vancouver port authorities. The Port of Victoria reported another 324,000 cruise tourists (17 per cent), with an additional 98,354 from Prince Rupert (5 per cent). For all three ports, the numbers reflect a continued upward trend in cruise tourism in Canada, especially British Columbia. The province 'welcomed more than 1.4 million passengers in 2007' (Cruise BC Association, 2008, p1), while 'cruise passenger arrivals have increased by 24 per cent, or slightly more than 378,000 passengers' (BREA, 2008, p6) over the past five years.

This visitor data also suggests the economic importance of the industry to the province, where spending by cruise passengers, crew and marine recreational providers generated more than Cdn$1.5 billion in direct and indirect spending in Canada in 2007 (BREA, 2008). This income, representing almost Cdn$169 per passenger, helped to create almost 10,000 full- and part-time jobs for local residents. Most of the activity (68 per cent) occurred in coastal British Columbia, which benefited from the Alaska-bound cruise traffic and passenger purchases ashore during scheduled port calls. However, the interior of Canada and Alaska is also positively affected by the cruise market, both as a source of domestic passengers and ancillary business services, and by the increasing number of cruise tourists who take advantage of pre- and post-cruise options to tour national parks in Alaska, northern British Columbia, Alberta and the Yukon Territories. Indeed, the influence, and affluence, of passengers who extend their cruise ashore is a substantial contribution to the economies of many inland communities: 'According to Fairbanks Convention and Visitors Bureau Executive Director Deb Hickok, about half the 400,000 annual summer visitors to the Interior reach Alaska on a cruise (Associated Press, 2009b, p2; see also Ray and Williams, 2003; Cruise BC Association, 2009).

Unfortunately, the average time ashore for the majority of the 1.6 million passengers and crew who disembarked in 2007 was only 4.1 hours, which limits business access, as well as visitor satisfaction and awareness of the destination and available marine resources (see Figure 13.3). Furthermore, nearly 67 per cent of the cruise passengers purchase only duty-free goods in company-affiliated stores, while 90 per cent of those who purchase shore excursions also buy directly from the cruise company, rather than from a local tour operator. As a result, the full benefit of visitor spending in Alaska and British Columbia is diminished by leakage to non-local suppliers and service providers. The economic disparity is compounded by the global recession, as tourism officials in Alaska forecast a 30 per cent drop in summer visits in 2009 (Véronneau and Roy, 2009):

> Cruise lines, in particular, are heralding declines. The Alaska Cruise Association represents nine cruise lines that bring about 1 million visitors to Alaska annually. 'All the indications from them are that bookings and sales are off dramatically', association President John Binkley said. 'Our hope is that the trends are just changing, that people will eventually come, but they're waiting to book... Hopefully, it will start to turn around, and we'll be able to hire more people than we anticipate.' (Koumelis, 2008, p1)

Since each visitor spends an average of US$1000 while in state, the loss of jobs and revenue is expected to be dramatic: 'That money probably rolls around the

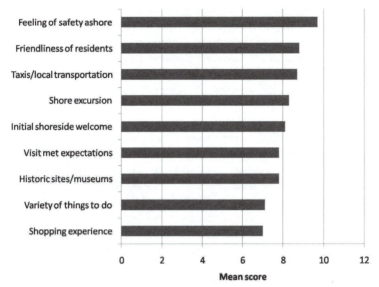

Figure 13.3 *Passenger satisfaction with destination visit, Canada*
(score of 10 = extremely satisfied, 1 = not at all satisfied)
Source: BREA (2008, p15)

economy two and a half, three times ... $1.7 billion easily becomes $3 billion to $5 billion in economic activity' (Koumelis, 2008; see also Associated Press, 2009a; Jackson, 2009). For this reason, while the current economic outlook is questionable, the long-term importance and benefits of cruise tourism to Alaska and the Pacific Northwest region remain unquestioned. Instead, several Alaska law-makers are calling for their state government to provide even more money for the industry, given the financial benefits that extend to Alaska's coastal and interior economies during the summer cruise season. The Government of Canada also negotiated new economic development agreements with the western provinces to take advantage of the industry's presence, and to encourage complementary business activities and tax policies (BREA, 2008; Western Economic Diversification Canada, 2008).

Current policy and practice

Cruise tourism in the Inland Passage is a sector equally dependent on environmental stability and sustainable practices by both vessel operators and destinations. The two parties have certainly made credible progress in actions taken since the mid 1990s to eliminate or mitigate the impacts of cruise tourism on the terrestrial and marine environments upon which this segment depends. These steps include a decline of almost 50 per cent in garbage and human waste produced onboard ships, and an equally dramatic reduction in airborne particulate emissions. Yet, tourism proponents and opponents alike continue to express serious concerns over the accelerated environmental degradation attributed to cruise ships and passengers in the Inland Passage (Johnson, 2002; Ringer, 2006; Mittermeier, 2007).

Reputedly one of Alaska's – and the world's – largest service industries, tourism plays a dominant role in the state's development, where it has long been guided by respect for, and inspiration from, history and culture: 'Businesses that provide knowledgeable guides and highlight cultural events and traditions help preserve community identity while enhancing the experience of their clients' (Adventure Green Alaska, 2009, question 26). At the same time, 'As tourism continues to become an even more important part of the state economy, so too will the need to protect the very things those tourists come to see: mountains, glaciers, forests, ocean, wildlife, and authentic communities' (Adventure Green Alaska, 2009, question 2). As a result, if effective action is not taken immediately to manage cruise numbers, landings and routes in the northern Pacific, critics assert that the industry could endanger the terrestrial and marine ecosystems where it operates, the local infrastructure and transportation network that support it, and the wildlife and biophysical resources on which it depends (Ringer, 2006, 2007; Robertson, 2008; Brida and Zapata-Aguirre, 2008, 2009; Véronneau and Roy, 2009).

Already, they complain that 'Cruise ships emit three times more CO_2 than airplanes' (Environmental Leader, 2008, p1), a source of concern among some in the state capital, Juneau. A major cruise company, 'Carnival Cruise Lines, made up of 11 distinct lines, emits about 401 grams of CO_2 per passenger' (CruiseLineFans. com, 2009, p1) in a city where coastlines are now rising as glaciers and the sea retreat due to climate change from carbon dioxide emissions (Dean, 2009). Environmental pollution is also a continuing source of aggravation for coastal residents and the Alaska Department of Environmental Conservation (ADEC), whose regulators issued ten violation notices and 'cited eight cruise ships for air quality violations in 2008' (Associated Press, 2009b, p1; see also Anderson, 2005; Carnival Corporation, 2005; Carlock, 2006; Rice, 2006; Ringer, 2006, 2007).

These citations, levied against five of the largest cruise companies in the world – Royal Caribbean, Princess Cruises, Holland America Line, Celebrity and the Norwegian Cruise Line – represent a 500 per cent increase from the previous year. Equally problematic for ADEC regulators and 'sustainable tourism' advocates, the legal actions undertaken by the State of Alaska now mean that 'every major cruise line has been convicted on felony charges for dumping wastes into public waters' (Cohen, 2008, p1; see also North West Cruise Ship Association, 2009). John Brinkley, president of the Alaska Cruise Association, believes the number of violations (10 violations out of a total of 224 readings) is relatively insignificant, suggesting that the industry has only 'dropped from an A+ to a solid A' (Associated Press, 2009b, p2). But cruise officials warily note that the 'Alaska cruise industry is having trouble getting traction with [Alaska state] legislators to abolish a strict water-pollution rule approved by voters in 2006' (Bluemink, 2009, p1).

The rule requires cruise ships to obtain new pollution permits, post environmental waste monitors and independent marine engineers (ocean rangers) on every vessel, and discontinue emission and particulate discharges in specified 'mixing zones',[1] or areas where 'Alaska's water quality standards for toxicity, copper, zinc, nickel and ammonia won't apply' (Cohen, 2008, p1). To fund programme administration and enforcement, a gambling tax was instituted on onboard gambling within state waters, as well as the first corporate income tax on cruise ships. A US$50 tax was levied on each passenger as well, in addition to a US$7 passenger tax imposed by the port of Ketchikan, and US$8 per person for cruise ships that visit Juneau (de Place, 2008).

Cruise proponents spent more than US$1 million on advertising costs alone in their failed effort to defeat the initiative, which passed by a slight majority of voters (Karantzavelou, 2006). However, despite fears the new taxes would reduce company profits, and claims that the taxes would dissuade both ships and passengers from visiting, the number of cruise departures, visitors and spending all climbed in 2007 and 2008 instead. Perhaps more importantly, during both years the 'cruise law generated more than $100 million in state tax revenue' (Bluemink, 2009, p1). Of this total, almost 20 per cent was given to coastal port communities for cruise-related construction and infrastructure improvements crucial to their emerging tourism programmes (Klein, 2005; Carnival Corporation, 2006; Cohen, 2008).

Even so, the cruise industry – with the aid of city councils and local organizations in the ports of Seward, Ketchikan, Whittier and Juneau – is again contesting the law as overly stringent and a significant impediment to cruise expansion. The primary complaint remains the lack of 'mixing zones'. Cruise owners further argue that they are required to achieve a higher standard than applied to other industry polluters. Already, they note, initial tests undertaken by federal and state agencies indicate some cruise ships will be unable to satisfactorily reduce copper and ammonia concentrations as mandated by the new regulations. Ironically, ship-owners say that the source of the ammonia is human urine, which is concentrated in higher amounts by the water conservation measures and ultra low-flow toilets installed onboard ships to reduce their ecological impact (Green Meeting, 2008; Environmental Leader, 2009).

The environmental challenges of cruise tourism are further exacerbated by persistent trends and reports of the declining quality of terrestrial and marine ecosystems – which are so vital to the cruise experience. Cruise ships offer millions of people worldwide a chance to learn about the world's oceans and marine resources. At the same time:

> ... *a typical 3000 passenger cruise ship each week generates 210,000 gallons of black water, which is raw sewage; 1 million gallons of grey water, including runoff from showers, sinks and dishwashers; and 37,000 gallons of oil bilge water, which collects in the bottom of ships and contains oil and chemicals from engine maintenance that are toxic to marine life.* (Alaska Oceans Program, 2009, p1)

While cruise ships are exempt from Canadian regulations to protect marine wildlife, they are restricted by federal legislation in Alaskan waters. However, the rules have been weakened in the past decade as legislators respond more favourably to business interests. As a result, there remains a troubling sense that the cruise tourism sector is still unconcerned with its environmental performance, given the failure of ship-owners and other destination stakeholders to acknowledge or prioritize sustainability issues (CELB, 2008).

This deficiency is further reflected in 'a lack of inclusive government guidelines for the Canadian cruise tourism industry' (Marquez, 2006, pviii), an omission attributed to the widely held perception that it is a 'safe and economically viable industry' (Marquez, 2006). Unlike the US, where state legislatures in Alaska, Washington, California and Oregon have restricted cruise emissions and pollution, 'Protection of BC's [British Columbia's] marine environment is left to the federal government, which has taken a "voluntary self-regulation" approach to the industry, issuing pollution prevention guidelines it hopes the industry will respect' (Klein, 2005, p16).

As a result, ships visiting ports in Canada while en route to Alaska or Seattle face less stringent controls, and are able to discharge sewage and sludge banned from US waters. The apparent lack of awareness and enforcement is also evident in the failure of Canadian and US agencies to fully comprehend or evaluate the impacts of cruise tourism on indigenous peoples and their cultural landscape. Yet, Marsh and Staple (1995, p71) urged, more than ten years ago, that 'given the fragility of some of the ... Arctic environments and the vulnerability of small, remote, largely aboriginal communities to impact, great care must be exercised in using the area for cruise tourism'.

Added to these demands, the continued global economic recession will place additional pressure on cruise companies to reduce conflicts and costs. As lines struggle to maintain profitability and compete for tourists, they must also successfully demonstrate their environmental commitment to the growing number of passengers in search of shore and ship activities that blend leisure, native culture, and 'wild and scenic' nature. Already, Royal Caribbean and Cruise West have announced plans to pull five ships from the Alaskan market in 2009 to 2010 due to the financial and environmental costs, and the Alaska Travel Industry Association (ATIA) recently launched an 'emergency campaign' to better promote the state's access, 'With cruise lines and tour operators cutting prices and adding value' (Browne, 2009, p2; see also Arsenault, 2009; Joling, 2009).

It is essential, therefore, that cruise operators and decision-makers now collaborate more effectively in environmental management, including the collection and disposal of waste onboard ships, and focus on 'intra-societal equity rather than merely accept the prospect of short-term economic gain' (Johnson, 2002, p1) when developing cruise- and community-related activities. To do so, Alaska's ports must consciously decide what kind of cruise tourism they desire, in terms of scale and public investment, and how best to balance 'income and growth on the one hand and preservation of local heritage and beauty on the other' (Klein, 2005, p5):

> To address these challenges, major stakeholder groups need to work together to maintain, protect and preserve the quality of natural and cultural resources in cruise destinations. From cruise lines and governments to civil society organizations and shore operators, they all have a stake in ensuring a healthy future for each destination and for cruise tourism around the world. (Mittermeier, 2007, p1)

The cruise lines can help to preserve Alaska's human and natural landscapes through careful promotion, and the selection of socially and environmentally responsible operators and service providers in port. Doing so will further maximize the benefits of their visits for local governments and residents, and provide the best possible long-term learning experience for the passenger. To do so, however, will require a model of stewardship that balances the desired growth in visitor facilities and users with conservation of the resources that maintain the cruise business, so that tourism will continue to provide long-term benefits for visitors, residents and the marine environment alike.

Sustainable Alaskan cruise tourism

The growing cruise demand worldwide presents significant opportunities and challenges to destination planners in terms of local capacity, quality and competitiveness. While Alaska's ports offer tremendous advantages to the cruise tourist in search of natural scenery, native culture and 'mega-charismatic' wildlife (such as grizzly and black bear, moose, whales and bald eagles), many visitors also witness overcrowding, price gouging and environmental harm from unsustainable services and illegal activities. As a result, managers must reconcile these divergent experiences, while protecting the integrity of Alaska's tourist resources in a manner that simultaneously sustains the industry's competitive advantages, entices visitors in search of marine and nature-based learning and recreation, and satisfies local desires for economic sufficiency.

Fortunately, there are signs that a more sensitive – and sensible – approach is gaining adherents, as more stakeholders recognize their shared interest in, and co-responsibility to sustain and protect, the social and ecological integrity of the cruise destination. In collaboration with governments and non-government agencies and tour operators, the cruise industry is proactively seeking to 'ensure a sustainable future for cruise tourism while preserving cruise destinations' (Teixeria, 2006, p1), and the integrity of their cultural and natural heritage. Many cruise lines, including Holland America, have installed certified marine sanitation devices and wastewater purification systems on all of their Alaskan vessels, and aggressively sought to reduce excess plastic and non-recyclable packaging. Others have reduced the use of hazardous materials onboard, replacing them with soy and plant-based cleaning products instead (World Travel and Tourism Council, 2002; Park, 2005; Pedrick, 2005; Horak et al, 2006; Valenti, 2006; Kmet, 2008).

As a concept, 'Sustainable tourism is guided by the principle of a qualitative economical growth' (Lighthouse Foundation, 2008, p2), where the destination's welfare and ecological integrity are integrated within the social and environmental planning that guide and support cruise tourism. Increased traveller demand for 'authentic' experiences and a geographic 'sense of place' have also stimulated greater interest by cruise officials, who desire to satisfy the 55.1 million Americans classified as sustainable tourists or geo-tourists (Crannell, 2008).

Applicable to any form of tourism or destination, the principles of sustainability – and related management guidelines and practices – establish a balance between the multiple socio-cultural, economic and environmental dimensions of tourism development. Measured against a set of standards established by community leaders and cruise operators to preserve Alaska's bio-cultural heritage through nautical tourism, the sector's contribution to the region's attraction value is maximized through the direct participation of cruise tourists in intercultural exchanges and protection of the region's ecosystems 'in such a way that economic, social and aesthetic needs can be fulfilled while maintaining cultural integrity, essential ecological processes, biological diversity and life support systems' (Neto, 2003, p6; World Tourism Organization, 2004; Romero and Castaneda, 2008).

Along the Inland Passage, the primary concerns of Alaska's port communities are now addressed through comprehensive assessments of cruise tourism activities, and analytical measurements of their ecological and social 'footprint'. These examinations may include whether a ship uses local agriculture products in its dining areas, the existence of problems associated with ship-provided recreation, or the presence and efficiency of cruise waste disposal systems and recycling practices. In addition, regulatory criteria and recreational activities are sometimes designed to encourage greater cultural and environmental awareness. For example, many Alaska-bound companies, such as Princess Cruises, provide onboard lecture topics on Alaska's geography and wildlife, or US Forest Service interpreters who share site- and species-specific details. Others have installed scientific equipment and conduct research for universities as part of a broader effort to learn more about critical marine environments and the consequences of climate change.

Community stakeholders (governments, travel providers, visitors and local residents) are also working together to establish appropriate performance standards and quality assurance indicators for visitors and vendors alike. Land- and marine-based tourism activities are frequently monitored to assess successes and areas of improvement, while voluntary protocols, acceptable levels of change, and established 'best practices' encourage compliance by cruise companies intent on reducing costs, yet maintaining quality services. Collectively, these social and environmental indicators measure performance over time, and often suggest emerging issues overlooked by those less concerned with visitor satisfaction with the cruise experience. Ship programmes, tours and operations also contribute to sustainability through local capacity-building and job training, and some smaller cruise lines enable local communities to profit from the increased tourism through business partnerships, and the direct sale of souvenirs and services to ship passengers (CELB, 2008).

As a result, a new 'skill set' is now evolving between port planners and cruise managers, one that emphasizes process, rather than strategy alone. While the motives behind these efforts to craft a sustainable cruise business model may be viewed cynically by some as more promotional than practical, there is a growing consensus that the industry has an important role in community development and conservation. Indeed, this opportunity – and critical need – for cruise lines to both lead and educate in the 21st century was reiterated by Russell Mittermeier, president of Conservation International, who noted:

> *Although cruise tourism has the potential to overwhelm fragile destinations if not managed effectively, the industry is also a great potential ally for conservation because many cruise passengers are attracted by the opportunity to experience new places and cultures.* (Mittermeier, cited in Teixeria, 2006, p3)

Whether, and to what extent, the cruise industry responds to this paradox will ultimately determine whether it successfully sustains Alaska as a destination for tourists in search of 'wildness and authentic' indigenous history.

Conclusions

The constructive measures now under way in Alaska certainly have the potential to make cruise tourism more sustainable and profitable for the companies, ports and Alaska's people. To do so, however, tourism and community leaders must successfully overcome many obstacles if the industry is to satisfactorily:

- develop and market a quality cruise product;
- safeguard affected port destinations;
- ensure personal health and safety concerns;
- satisfy market demand; and
- fully protect the natural environment.

The operation of cruise ships in south-east Alaskan is already inducing changes in the identity, structure and behaviour of both human and biological systems, and communities throughout the state. Whales and other marine life are threatened by cruise boats, habitat loss, and air and water pollution, while greater numbers of cruise ships transiting the same waters and ports reduce vessel safety and the quality of the visitor experience ashore.

The most prominent challenges today, therefore, for state regulators, residents and the cruise lines are twofold:

1　how best to identify and measure the achievement of 'sustainable' indicators; and
2　how to implement these standards agreeably and constructively.

Also needed are interpretive signs and educational programmes that improve passenger awareness of Alaska's natural heritage and human geography, and assist travel providers in reinforcing the importance of protecting the state's marine assets through their private business operations. In this manner, the tourism sector could directly reduce visitor impacts upon marine life, cultural sites, protected parks and subsistence lifestyles.

In order to accomplish these tasks successfully, relevant research data and visitor materials are required that explicitly link marine conservation, outdoor recreation, cultural interpretation and community education. Detailed knowledge of preferred visitor activities and attractions is also essential in order to identify the experiential outcomes desired by cruise tourists, the most appropriate indicators of sustainability for individual destinations, and the management pathways that would best lead to greater support and active involvement by visitors, communities and cruise companies.

Industry and port planners also have need of tools to identify sustainable practices that mitigate or eliminate the harmful aspects of cruise tourism, and an appreciation of collaborative processes that facilitate the direct participation of cruise operators and community guides. This information will necessitate that a number of related issues be addressed as well, including the following:

- Is the perceived erosion of authentic native Alaskan cultures and experiences related to the environmental, ecological and economic damage associated with cruise tourism?
- What can passengers do to reduce their waste and ecological footprint onboard ship and ashore?
- How can cruise passengers best interact with local communities and protected environments in order to educate themselves about their 'host's' identity, and to help conserve community resources?
- How influential are environmental standards and 'green' certifications for passengers when selecting cruise ships and destinations?
- How can resource managers and cruise officials establish and enforce visitor capacity limits (spatial, environmental and experiential) for different recreational locations (land and sea)?

Fortunately, the US Forest Service and other agencies, both public and private, have already taken steps to survey tourists, resource managers and port authorities along the Inland Passage about travel expectations and experiences. As the answers are collected and synthesized industry and community leaders hope to make better informed decisions when they select venues for cruise operations and criteria for accreditation. It should also help them to determine how these operational choices can best reinforce community and conservation values in the Inland Passage (Cerveny, 2004; Greve, 2006; Gil, 2008; Arsenault, 2009; CELB, 2008; Nanos, 2008; Western Economic Diversification Canada, 2008).

The sinking of the *Explorer* in November 2007, by an iceberg near Antarctica, was a wake-up for those still uncertain about the potential social and environmental impacts of cruise tourism in polar waters. While clean-up crews skimmed some of the '50,000 gallons of marine diesel fuel, 6300 gallons of lubricant and 260 gallons of gasoline' (Robertson, 2008, p1) from the sunken ship, much more leaked into the ocean, where it still jeopardizes marine life and birds (Stewart and Draper, 2008).

Regrettably, the environmental impacts of this sinking, though perhaps the most egregious example of the hazards of polar cruise tourism, are not unique. Instead, Alaskan and Canadian residents, environmentalists, governments and local tourism agencies also express rising concern over:

> ... the impact of visitors ashore from the smaller tour boats, fearing they could disturb wildlife, trample on important mosses and lichens and damage the region's unique ecosystems by introducing non-native species. Unwanted species can also hitch rides on ships' hulls and are often dumped out in ballast water, as well as latching onto everything from footwear and machinery to camping gear. (Robertson, 2008, p3)

Added to these worries are the emerging effects of global climate change. Although still debated, there is a growing consensus that even micro-changes in Alaska's weather will strongly affect cruise tourism. Some enthusiasts believe the implications will prove positive for cruise tourism, as once ice-bound communities gain access to deepwater vessels, and the trade and tourism they make possible. Stewart et al (2007) forecast greater risks through their research undertaken in the Northwest Passage.

They anticipate accidents, similar to the *Explorer*, as sea ice expands. This may also be true for Alaska's northern waters as the Arctic ice melts and sea ice expands.

Whichever scenario ultimately proves true, it is clear that cruise tourism is undergoing a transformation as passenger interests and community preferences change, and conflicts rise over the number and type of cruise ships allowed to operate in Alaska and the Pacific Northwest region. The governments of the US and Canada, through their respective federal and local institutions, have exercised authority and power to regulate travel practices and tourism numbers in the Inland Passage. However, US congressional action has limited the protective scope of some measures in south-east Alaska. Thus, it may be useful to consider how the industry and 'gateway' port communities might encourage practices similar to those outlined in the International Association of Antarctica Tour Operators' (IAATO's) *Guidance for Visitors to the Antarctic*, or the *Guidelines for Visitors to the Arctic*, published by the Association of Arctic Expedition Cruise Operators (AECO). Both guidebooks are intended to 'conduct respectful, environmentally friendly and safe tourism' (AECO, 2009, p9) in biologically rich polar waters.

These regulations, if strictly adopted and uniformly implemented in Alaska and western Canada, would restrict the presence and number of passenger boats in culturally and ecologically sensitive areas, such as Tracy Arm and Glacier Bay National Park. Cruise companies would also be motivated, through government subsidies and favourable business credits, to contract with local guides and business owners to charter their add-on programmes. This action would help to deconstruct the vertical integration common to the industry and thereby reduce leakage of tourist spending outside the destination.

The creation of cruise policies and practices that voluntarily limit the number of ships in port each day is also recommended, as is a greater emphasis on smaller boats and ports: 'Smaller ports can offer as attractive features their size, authentic cultural heritage, nature experiences and eco-tourism' (Klein, 2005, p20). Such assets, if properly managed and marketed, would offer an economic and environmental boon for communities that preserve their heritage. Research undertaken among cruise visitors to a marine park in Vietnam found that self-described 'eco-tourists' spent approximately US$171 per day. In contrast, tourists interested only in leisure spent approximately US$128. The implications, thus, are clear for cruise ports that maintain their natural and historic environments: the same income may be gained – with less human impact – by focusing on the quality of the visitor experience, rather than the quantity of tourists alone (Ringer, 2002).

This emphasis on the ecological and cultural integrity of the area can be accomplished most effectively through programmes offered in partnership with service providers and non-profit organizations, such as the North West Cruise Ship Association (NWCA). The NWCA represents the eight major cruise lines operating in the Pacific Northwest, Alaska and British Columbia:

In Juneau, Alaska, the NWCA is helping to engage and educate the community about the cruise industry with an environmental education programme for students from local schools. The programme includes tours of ships docked in port, where students learn about the ships' recycling, emissions and wastewater programmes. Princess Cruises shows students to its lower deck recycling centre, while Celebrity Cruises includes the engine room on its tours, to show students where emissions are monitored on video cameras and to teach them about gas turbines. HAL [Holland American Line] has provided oceanography classes to local high school students, including environmental tours of their ships' wastewater systems. (Mittermeier, 2007, p4)

Another environmentally friendly and informative programme worth replicating region-wide is Holland American Line's Whale Protection Programme, operated in partnership with the US National Park Service and the National Oceanic and Atmospheric Administration: 'This program helps mariners recognize and avoid whales as part of its regular employee environmental awareness training' (Mittermier, 2007, p4).

On the regulatory side, new rules should be enacted immediately to prohibit discharges of sewage, waste, and greywater within 12 miles (19.3km) of US shores, with 'maximum limits for levels of faecal coliform and chlorine in treated sewage and greywater' set by the US Coast Guard and Environmental Protection Agency beyond 12 miles, and a goal of zero pollutants by 2015 (Alaska Oceans Program, 2009, p3). To fund these recommendations, a combination of additional fees and taxes should be targeted at both cruise and non-cruise segments of the Alaskan tourism industry, with a significant portion of the revenue dedicated to 'green' port planning and sustainable cruise development (AWRTA, 2005).

Finally, what is needed most are messages from Alaska's port communities to cruise tourists highlighting their natural and human heritage, and inviting them to help protect it through sustainable travel and a lighter 'footprint'. The linkage of cruise terminals, native communities and national parks could provide a powerful image for passengers in search of indigenous peoples and authentic places, motivating visitors to become more engaged in conservation and sustainable travel practices. Even more hopeful, these connections would allow cruise officials and destination stakeholders to better comprehend and, thus, respond to and sustain the multiple socio-economic dimensions of cruise tourism in Alaska's Inland Passage in the 21st century (Research Resolutions and Consulting, 2004; Nanos, 2008).

Note

1   A 'mixing zone' is defined as any surface water body 'in which pollution discharges are allowed to exceed [Alaska's] water-quality standards. They are used by sewage plants, mines, seafood plants and other industries to dilute their discharges. The mixing ban for cruise lines goes into effect' in 2010 (Bluemink, 2009, p1).

References

Adventure Green Alaska (2009) 'Frequently asked questions or help with filling out your application!', Adventure Green Alaska website, www.adventuregreenalaska.org/faqs.html, accessed 31 March 2010

AECO (Association of Arctic Expedition Cruise Operators) (2009) *Guidelines for Visitors to the Arctic*, AECO, Longyearbyen, Norway

Alaska Oceans Program (2009) *Clean Cruise Ships Act: Legislation To Be Introduced by Senator Richard J. Dubin*, Save Alaska's Oceans, 4 March

Anderson, B. (2005) *Air Quality and Cruise Ships*, Presented to the American Association of Port Authorities Cruise Workshop, New Orleans, Louisiana, 16–18 February

Arsenault, N. (2009) *The Cruise Sector and the Environment: Responding to Current Concerns*, Presented to the 2009 Tourism Educators Conference, Vancouver, British Columbia

Associated Press (2009a) 'Alaska tourism summit planned', *KTUU.com: Alaska's News Source*, 8 July, www.ktuu.com/Global/story.asp?S=10665145, accessed 2 August 2009

Associated Press (2009b) 'Cruise ships cited for air quality violations in Alaska', *Fairbanks Daily News-Miner*, 15 February, www.newsminer.com/news/2009/feb/15/cruise-ships-cited-air-quality-violations-alaska, accessed 11 May 2009

Associated Press (2009c) 'Tourist season forecast for Southeast Alaska uncertain; Cruise ships: Business try to lure consumers with discounts, but will they spend once in port?', *Anchorage Daily News*, 4 April, www.adn.com/money/industries/ tourism/story/ 748802.html, accessed 2 August 2009

AWRTA (Alaska Wilderness Recreation and Tourism Association) (2005) 'Ecotourism guidelines', www.awrta.org/index.cfm?section=about, accessed 31 March 2010

Bluemink, E. (2009) 'Critics seek champion to kill cruise pollution law', *Anchorage Daily News*, www.adn.com/money/industries/tourism/story/685219.html, accessed 11 May 2009

BREA (Business Research and& Economic Advisors) (2008) *The Economic Contribution of the International Cruise Industry in Canada 2007: A Survey-Based Analysis of the Impacts of Passenger, Crew and Cruise Line Spending*, North West Cruise Ship Association, Cruise Newfoundland and Labrador, St Lawrence Cruise Association, Atlantic Canada Cruise Association, and Cruise BC, Exton, PA

Brida, J. and Zapata-Aguirre, S. (2008) 'The impacts of the cruise industry on tourism destinations: Sustainable tourism as a factor of local development', 9 November, ssrn.com/abstract=1298403, accessed 19 May 2009

Brida, J. and Zapata-Aguirre, S. (2009) 'Cruise tourism: Economic, socio-cultural and environmental impacts', 25 January, www.papers.ssrn.com/sol3/papers.cfm?abstract_id=1332619, accessed 27 May 2009

Browne, M. (2009) 'Alaska fights back', *Travel Agent Central*, 23 February

Carlock, M. (2006) *The Impact of Air Quality Issues on the Cruise Industry*, Presented to the American Association of Port Authorities, New Orleans, 9 February

Carnival Corporation (2005) *Cruise Ship Pollution Prevention: What Works? ... And What Doesn't?*, Presented to the American Association of Port Authorities, 17 February

Carnival Corporation (2006) *Carnival Comments on Potential Impact of Recently Passed Alaska Cruise Tax Initiative*, Press release, 25 August

CELB (Center for Environmental Leadership in Business) (2008) *From Ship to Shore: Sustainable Stewardship in Cruise Destinations*, Conservation International, Washington, DC

Cerveny, L. K. (2004) *Tourism and its Effects on Southeast Alaska Communities and Resources: Case Studies from Haines, Craig, and Hoonah, Alaska*, Research Paper PNW-RP-566, US Department of Agriculture, Forest Service, Pacific Northwest Research Station, Portland, OR

Chafe, Z. (2008) *Globetrotting with a Conscience*, Worldwatch Institute, Washington, DC

Chicago Sun-Times (2009) 'Economy sinks cruise prices in Alaska', 18 January, www.suntimes.com/lifestyles/travel/northamerica/1382714,TRA-News-alaska18.stng,   accessed 2 August 2009

Cohen, G. (2008) 'California and Alaska charting a new course for the cruise industry', *California Progress Report*, pp1–2

Crannell, Jr. P. (2008) *Trends in Cruise Ship Deployment*, Presented to the American Association of Port Authorities Cruise Conference, San Francisco, 7 February

Cruise BC Association (2008) 'Cruise in British Columbia grows by 21% in four years', *Cruise BC*, 19 March, pp 1–4

Cruise BC Association (2009) 'Cruise in British Columbia remained strong in 2008', *Cruise BC*, 15 April, pp 1–4

CruiseLineFans.com (2009) 'Sustainable Alaska cruise tourism', www.cruiselinefans.com/friday- discussion/39629-cruise-tourism-its-impact-ecology-environment.html, accessed 20 May 2009

de Place, E. (2008) 'Should cruise ships pay for Puget Sound?', *The Daily Score*, 18 November, daily.sightline.org/daily_score/archive/2008/11/18/should-cruise-ships-pay-for-puget-sound, accessed 15 April 2009

Dean, C. (2009) 'As Alaska's glaciers melt, it's land that's rising', *The New York Times*, 17 May, www.nytimes.com/2009/05/18/science/earth/18juneau.html?scp=1&sq=juneau%20glacier&st=cse, accessed 20 May 2009

Environmental Leader (2008) 'Cruise ships worse for environment than planes', *The Executive's Daily Green Briefing*, 22 January

Environmental Leader (2009) 'Alaska cruise industry wants strict water-pollution rule abolished', *The Executive's Daily Green Briefing*, 11 February

Gibson, P. (2006) 'Resource guide in cruise management', *Hospitality, Leisure, Sport and Tourism Network*, 6 January, pp1–13

Gil, A. (2008) *Destination, Port and Cruise Industry*, Presented to the American Association of Port Authorities, San Francisco, 13 January

Green Meeting (2008) 'Exclusive: Eco-activist explains cruise lawsuit', *The Green Meeting*, 4 July

Greve, M. (2006) *Marketing and Branding Cruise Destinations: Potential to Move the Market?*, Presented to the American Association of Port Authorities, 8 February

Hansen, J. (2008) *NW Cruise Update*, Presented to the American Association of Port Authorities, San Francisco, 13 February

Horak, S., Marusic, Z. and Favro, S. (2006) 'Competitiveness of Croatian nautical tourism', *Tourism in Marine Environments*, vol 3, no 2, pp145–161

Jackson, C. (2009) 'Alaska fights a tourist cold front: Cruise lines and resorts offer steep discounts', *The Wall Street Journal – Travel*, 24 April, http://online.wsj.com/article/SB124053310240050877.html, accessed 2 August 2009

Johnson, D. (2002) 'Environmentally sustainable cruise tourism: A reality check', *Marine Policy*, vol 26, pp261–279

Joling, D. (2009) 'Royal Caribbean shifts ship out of Alaska for 2010 tourism season', *The Fairbanks (Alaska) Daily Newsminer.com*, 27 January, www.newsminer.com/news/ 2009/jan/ 27/royal-caribbean-shifts-ship-out-alaska, accessed 20 May 2009

Karantzavelou, V. (2006) 'Carnival comments on potential impact of recently passed Alaska cruise tax initiative', *International TravelDailyNews.com*, 25 August, www.traveldailynews.com/pages/show_page/14881-Carnival-comments-on-potential-impact-of-recently-passed-Alaska-cruise-tax-initiative, accessed 19 May 2009

Klein, R. A. (2005) *Playing Off the Ports: BC and the Cruise Tourism Industry*, Canadian Centre for Policy Alternatives, Vancouver, British Columbia

Kmet, M. (2008) 'Smooth eco sailing: These cruise lines have made major strides in selling sustainable sailings', *Vacation Agent Magazine*, vol 12, no 4, December, pp1–3

Koumelis, T. (2008) 'Bleak tourism year forecast for Alaska's tourism industry: Decreases in business of 30 percent', *International TravelDailyNews.com*, 29 December, www.traveldailynews.com/pages/show_page/28670-   Bleak-tourism-year-forecast-for-Alaska%27s-tourism-industry, accessed 19 May 2009

Lighthouse Foundation (2008) 'Sustainable tourism and cruises', www.lighthouse-foundation.net/index.php?id=113&L=1, accessed 23 May 2009

Lück, M. (ed) (2007) *Nautical Tourism: Concepts and Issues*, Cognizant Communication Corporation, New York, NY

Marquez, J. van Oordt (2006) *An Analysis of Cruise Ship Management Policies in Parks and Protected Areas in the Eastern Canadian Arctic*, MA thesis, Recreation and Leisure Studies, University of Waterloo, Ontario, Canada

Marsh, J. and Staple, S. (1995) 'Cruise tourism in the Canadian Arctic and its implications', in C. M. Hall and M. E. Johnston (eds) *Polar Tourism: Tourism in the Arctic and Antarctic Regions*, John Wiley and Sons, West Sussex, UK

Mittermeier, R. (2007) 'Sustainable stewardship', *Worldcruise-network.com*, 1 March, www.worldcruise-network.com/features/feature950, accessed 19 May 2009

Nanos, J. (2008) 'Cozumel's cruise ships go eco', *Intelligent Travel: Cultural, Authentic and Sustainable*, 25 January, www.blogs.nationalgeographic.com/blogs/intelligenttravel/2008/01 /cozumels-cruise-ships- go-eco.html, accessed 27 May 2009

Neto, F. (2003) *A New Approach to Sustainable Tourism Development: Moving Beyond Environmental Protection*, UN Department of Economic and Social Affairs, New York, NY

North West Cruise Ship Association (2009) 'Welcome to NWCA', www.nwcruiseship.org, accessed 16 May 2009

Park, J. S. (2005) *Sustainable Management of Marine Litter in the Northwest Pacific Region*, Presented to the United Nations Environment Programme, Northwest Pacific Action Plan, 11 November

Peck, R. (2009) 'My turn: Rough seas ahead for Alaska tourism', *Juneau Empire.com*, 28 January, www.juneauempire.com/stories/012809/opi_382463652.shtml, accessed 2 August 2009

Pedrick, D. (2005) *Sustainable Cruise Ports*, Presented to the American Association of Port Authorities Cruise Committee, New Orleans, 17 February

Peisley, T. (2006) *The Future of Cruising – Boom or Bust*, Seatrade Research Report, Colchester, UK

Ray, R. and Williams, P. (2003) *Potential Spatial and Management Implications of Cruise Ship Passenger Activity on the Development of the North Coast LRMP*, Centre for Tourism Policy and Research, School of Resource and Environmental Management, Simon Fraser University, Vancouver, British Columbia

Research Resolutions and Consulting (2004) *Opportunities for British Columbia: Activity-Based Tourists in Canada*, Tourism British Columbia, Victoria, British Columbia

Rice, D. (2006) *California Green Port: Implications for the Cruise Industry*, Presented to the American Association of Port Authorities Cruise Seminar, 9 February

Ringer, G. (2002) 'Convicts and conservation: Con Dao National Park, Vietnam', in R. Harris, T. Griffin and P. Williams (eds) *Sustainable Tourism: A Global Perspective*, Butterworth-Heinemann, London, pp221–237

Ringer, G. (2006) 'Cruising north to Alaska: The new "gold rush"', in R. Dowling (ed) *Cruise Tourism: Issues, Impacts, Cases*, CABI Publishing/Butterworth-Heinemann, Oxford, UK, pp 270–279

Ringer, G. (2007) 'Cruise tourism in the Pacific and Caribbean: Possibilities for Montenegro and the Adriatic', *Selective Tourism: The Journal for Tourist Theory and Practice*, vol 1, no 1, pp29–39

Robertson, G. (2008) 'Cruise tourism in the Antarctic', *Lighthouse Foundation*, www.lighthouse- foundation.de/index.php?id=252&L=1, accessed 19 May 2009

Romero, E. and Castaneda, A. (2008*) Comments and Observations on Cruise Ship Tourism in Belize*, Presented to the Forum on Cruise Tourism, Belize City, 28–29 September

Ruff, E. (2008) *2008 Cruise Industry Outlook*, Presented to the Cruise Lines International Association, 13 February

Seattletimes.NWsource.com (2009) 'Cruise lines slash prices', *eTurboNews*, 12 January, www.eturbonews.com/7168/cruise-lines-slash-prices, accessed 2 August 2009

Servos, P. (2007) *Sustainable Growth Projected for Victoria's Cruise Services Industry*, Press release, Greater Victoria Harbour Authority, 14 March

Sheppard, V. (2005) *Ethics, Tourists and the Environmental Practices of the North American Cruise Ship Industry: A Comparison Study of the Ethical Standards of Alaskan and Caribbean Cruise Ship Tourists*, MA thesis, Brock University, Ontario, Canada

Stewart, E. J. and Draper, D. (2006) 'Sustainable cruise tourism in Arctic Canada: An integrated coastal management approach', *Tourism in Marine Environments*, vol 3, no 2, pp77–88

Stewart, E. J. and Draper, D. (2008) 'The sinking of the *MS Explorer*: Implications for cruise tourism in Arctic Canada', *Arctic InfoNorth*, vol 61, no 2, June, pp224–228

Stewart, E. J., Howell, S. E. L., Draper, D., Yackel, J. and Tivy, A. (2007) 'Sea ice in Canada's Arctic: Implications for cruise tourism', *Arctic*, vol 4, no 1, December, www.articlearchives. com /travel-hospitality-tourism/destinations/1621278-1.html, accessed 15 April 2009

Teixeria, J. (2006) '*From Ship to Shore* report details how cruise industry is serving its passengers while protecting the precious places it visits', Press release, 14 March, Center for Environmental Leadership (CELB), Conservation International, Washington, DC

Valenti, J. (2006) *Key Cruise Issues and Their Relevance to the Port Industry*, Presented to the American Association of Port Authorities Cruise Panel, 13 February

Véronneau, S. and Roy, J. (2009) 'Global service supply chains: An empirical study of current practices and challenges of a cruise line corporation', *Tourism Management*, vol 30, no 1, February, pp128–139

Western Economic Diversification Canada (2008) *Government of Canada and Western Provinces to Negotiate New Economic Development Agreements*, 25 April, WEDC, Banff, Alberta

Westoby, P. (2008) *Current North Coast Industries: Cruise Tourism*, Presented to Together on the Coast: North Coast Sustainable Community Development Forum, Prince Rupert, British Columbia, 20 November

World Expeditions (2009) 'Alaska: The dramatic northwest', www.worldexpeditions.com/index.php?section=trips&id=29955, accessed 11 May 2009

World Tourism Organization (2004) 'Sustainable tourism', www.world-tourism.org/sustainable/concepts.htm, accessed 19 May 2009

World Travel and Tourism Council (2002) *Industry as a Partner for Sustainable Development: Tourism*, WTTC, International Hotel and Restaurant Association, International Federation of Tour Operators, International Council of Cruise Lines and United Nations Environment Programme, London

Part V
CONCLUSIONS

14

Moving Forward

Patrick T. Maher, Emma J. Stewart and Michael Lück

Returning to the beginning

To conclude this book, let us revisit where it began. Discussions on the topic began at the *Tourism and Global Change in Polar Regions* conference in November 2007 in Oulu, Finland. Here, buoyed by discussion with colleagues, we thought about how a cruise tourism-specific text was desperately needed, and especially one that examined the sustainability of the industry and one that asked 'tough questions'. The urgency of the book was fuelled by substantial growth in the cruise sector to both the polar regions, and only days before the Oulu conference we learned of the sad fate of the *Explorer*. If this icon of polar cruising (which was a purpose-built and ice-strengthened vessel) could sink in relatively benign conditions, then questions needed to be addressed about the sustainability of the sector.

As mentioned in the introduction, we used the World Commission on Environment and Development (WCED, 1987, p43) report to define sustainability: 'development that meets the needs of the present without compromising the ability of future generations to meet their own needs'. It was one of the WCED's goals to have all forms of tourism develop sustainably, from mass tourism to special interest tourism, of which cruise tourism crosses between the two in many instances. Within tourism, the inclusion of economic sustainability is almost a given as businesses do not stay in business if they are not economically sustainable. Weaver (2008) notes that there is an area of contention with the inclusion of environmental and social sustainability. While there are good intentions to include both in development plans, problems become apparent when the implementation of tourism development provides the basis for conflicts between the two. In that case, the question is which should take priority over the other and, hence, where this book title arose: *Cruise Tourism in Polar Regions: Promoting Environmental and Social Sustainability?*

In Chapter 1 we discussed the definition of polar tourism and the ambiguity of boundaries, especially marine boundaries, as is the case for shipping. The cruise industry has seen phenomenal growth rates all over the world, and the growing trend in the cruise industry is equally reflected in activities in the polar regions. The majority of tourists to these regions are cruise ship based, with Antarctica's tourism almost entirely ship-based. Cruise Lines International Association (CLIA) member lines saw an almost doubling of capacity in nine years (up to 2009) for Alaska-bound cruises. For Antarctic cruises, it was a more than quadrupling of capacity, to 217,000 in 2009 (CLIA, 2009).

Lessons from the book

Given the steadily increasing demand for polar tourism, tour operators are reacting accordingly. The 12 main chapters presented in this book all make important contributions to understanding four dimensions of polar cruise tourism: the market dimension, the human dimension, the environmental dimension, and the policy/governance dimension. Across these chapters a variety of conclusions are drawn.

Market dimensions

Within the first section, Orams (Chapter 2) concluded that increased yacht traffic in the polar regions will continue. The profiles of the destinations (Arctic and Antarctic) are strong and technology makes the destinations ever-more available in a comfortable manner. This market reality changes the image of polar cruising away from 'expeditions' sold as difficult and trying excursions to a much more 'soft adventure' market. A changing market, changes in the activities sought, and changes in the realities the companies operate in are a tremendous shift. Typical expedition cruise operators would not seek to meet other boats in the polar regions, but Orams's note about cruising rallies may have very real management implications for the International Association of Antarctica Tour Operators (IAATO) and the Antarctic Treaty System (ATS). At present, management seems adequate for the medium to large expedition operations; so how will they handle yachts that are a new and largely unknown entity?

Specific to cruising to the North Pole, Headland (Chapter 3) showcased a unique option for the market, one that utilizes nuclear power. Nuclear icebreakers know virtually no geographical constraints in the Arctic because of their enormous power and lack of time-based need to refuel. The economic sustainability is unique because atomic-powered icebreakers moving through the pack ice of the Arctic Ocean will remain essential for other logistics; but the price for tourism is very high (advertised in recent brochures from 16,000 Euros to 28,000 Euros per person, depending on class of cabin selected). While refuelling time is less of an issue, the fuel for these vessels is not cheap. Additionally, Russian nuclear icebreakers plying waters further afield become a sovereignty issue and one which the burgeoning cruise sector may get entangled in. Environmentally, the use of uranium fuel is a global issue, which may be contrasted with the adverse consequences of burning hydrocarbons. Overall, the sustainability of this market (North Pole cruises) is mainly dependent on economics rather than any use of other resources. It is, out of necessity, a specialist operation and a comparatively new one, but an operation not without contention.

Berger's ethnographic piece (Chapter 4) dealt with what might be called the primary cruise market for both poles: expedition vessels and larger, although not huge, cruise ships such as the *Oasis of the Seas*. Focused on Antarctica, Berger concludes that visitors to the continent are the fortunate few, and that this is to Antarctica's good fortune. Thus, sustainability here is almost self-determined. A few visitors willing to pay enough money will keep the economics sustainable. The reality of the costs will keep visitor numbers low enough; thus, the industry is potentially environmentally sustainable and the social reality (lack of an indigenous population and the clout of the government agencies) keeps it relatively socially sustainable in the Antarctic.

Human dimensions

Klein (Chapter 5) is well known for his work worldwide on the social issues of cruising. In the polar regions there have been accidents at sea; but perhaps a larger concern is the huge growth in the number of large cruise ships, many of which are not strengthened for ice and the weather conditions found in these areas. Passengers need to be concerned about safety and security, and be aware of the unique qualities of polar regions so they can choose a cruise ship that is safe and one that allows them to see all that polar cruising has to offer. Policy-makers and port cities also need to be aware of the problem of accidents. In addition, they need to focus on the economics of cruise tourism to ensure that they receive an equitable share of revenues and cover their costs for port facilities and the infrastructure needed for cruise ships.

Sheppard (Chapter 6) concluded that without modifications to the practices and behaviour of all tourism stakeholders, cruise tourism will continue to have ever-increasing impacts upon the natural environment. Highlighted were some of the difficulties in ensuring that tourists adopt the required sustainable behaviour. Sheppard concluded that the only hope there is of ushering tourists into more ethical behaviour is to begin educating tourists about the impacts of tourism and their impacts as tourists. If tourists were asked to take responsibility for their actions – in both the planning of and during their vacation – they might realize that their behaviour is part of the problem, and an even more important part of the solution. Should more tourists make travel decisions based on the sustainability of the tourism businesses, then operations that choose not to adopt sustainable practices would be penalized. Sustainable business practices would be rewarded and become standard operating practices.

The human dimension of education is well illustrated in Green's (Chapter 7) case study of Students on Ice. Green's experience has taught him to follow his dreams, passions and visions, which will then inevitably cause good things to happen. This is the argument furthered by the IAATO in creating a corps of ambassadors, who have the raised awareness noted by Sheppard; thus, it is hoped that this will create a sustainable Antarctic spreading across the globe north of 60°S. Green's vision also speaks to sustainability for future generations – through engagement, inspiration and a vision of the planet as interconnected, and not owned by humankind.

Environmental dimensions

Lück (Chapter 8) reviewed a variety of environmental impacts associated with the cruise industry in polar regions. With rapidly increasing numbers of cruise vessel visits, the primary concern is the potential damage to the fragile environments in these regions. Even if the cruise industry implemented more sustainable practices, there is still an ever-present risk of vessels colliding with icebergs or running aground. This is a particular challenge due to the increase of 'regular' cruise ships visiting the regions – those ships without strengthened hulls. Regulations of the ATS or the IAATO are of limited power since ships operating under flags of convenience are not bound to these rules. The same issues of problematic regulations and 'watered-down' management are found to be applicable for the Arctic and sub-polar regions as well.

More specific to one region, Stewart et al (Chapter 9) showed that current mechanisms to monitor, assess and manage cruise ship activity in Arctic Canada are woefully lacking, which, in turn, hinder the social and environmental sustainability of cruise tourism in the region. The management system for the industry is difficult to navigate and is, at present, unsustainable. Without improved monitoring and surveillance, the variability of the cruise industry creates problems for communities and residents who cannot account for decreases or influxes of visitors, but are then not equipped to manage adverse economic and environmental consequences arising from cruise tourism.

One of the pressing issues for the environmental sustainability of cruise tourism in the polar regions is climate change, and thus Lamers and Amelung's chapter (Chapter 10) gives an excellent overview of this critical issue. The main conclusion of this chapter is that there is very little known about the relationships between the polar climate and polar (cruise) tourism, let alone about the possible implications of climate change.

Policy and governance dimensions

Liggett et al (Chapter 11) revealed that across all stakeholder groups there is the belief that Antarctic tourism regulation, in its current form, lacks effective mechanisms for monitoring operations as well as policing infringements. There is room for improvement on both the side of the ATS parties and the IAATO. Liggett et al provide concrete options put forward by treaty parties and operators alike, all in the name of preserving and protecting the resource. For the time being, much of the work is based on 'goodwill' and much research is still needed.

Hull and Milne (Chapter 12) present a specific series of insights from a Port Readiness Programme in Newfoundland and Labrador. This programme illustrated the importance of a need for proper planning and development to support sustainable tourism efforts through local coordination and cooperation. Such a conclusion is consistent with the thoughts of others who believe we need to take a long-term view towards the adoption of holistic integrated management approaches. The fragility of polar environments and the small size of many communities require that cruise ship industry stakeholders support efforts to protect these resources that are the basis of the industry. Operators need to invest in good environmental practice and the political will needs to help safeguard destinations.

Ringer's chapter on Alaska (Chapter 13) focused on the largest of the cruise ships, in the most visited of the polar regions. The operation of cruise ships in south-east Alaska is already inducing changes in the identity, structure and behaviour of both human and biological systems, and communities throughout the state. There are challenges for state regulators, residents and the cruise lines as to how best to identify and measure the achievement of 'sustainable' indicators, and how to implement these standards agreeably and constructively.

Cross-cutting themes

Across the 12 main chapters of this text there are a number of important cross-cutting themes that link to the initiation of a wider research agenda:

- market change;
- climate change;
- monitoring;
- education.

What sort of implications will the change in the polar cruise sector markets present for the environment? From an economic perspective, will the 'traditional' model of expedition-style cruising remain viable or will new niches become the norm? How will human presence (indigenous, community and scientific) in both regions cope with this change – more ships, smaller ships or bigger ships that can reach further into a destination region? How will this change in the market affect policy-makers and governance issues that are already quite inadequate for a market that has been reasonably stable for decades?

Climate change is notably mentioned by Lamers and Amelung in Chapter 10, but it cuts across many other chapters. The key message appears to be that we simply do not know what it will mean. However, we do know that the climate is changing and there will be effects, and the polar regions are already being seen as the first witnesses to the effects of change. Coordinated data collection is urgently needed, not just on the climate science, but also research into the implications of climate change for polar cruise tourism. There is large societal relevance here as hundreds of thousands of livelihoods in the polar regions and beyond depend on their environment and, in many ways, on the tourism derived from it. Questions arise about the adaptive capacity of small polar communities and how they may fare as climate changes. Not enough is known about how resilient or, conversely, how vulnerable polar communities may be to the uncertainty of climate warming. It is therefore of utmost importance that a long-term approach towards monitoring and management is taken to strive for sustainable cruise tourism development.

Monitoring cruise activity and creating a baseline is rudimentary for credible research. However, in northern polar locations very little consistent data is collected on the cruise sector. By contrast, in Antarctica the valuable data collected by the IAATO, now amassed over almost 20 years, is key to inform policy and governance. Ultimately, it is good data collection that can underpin appropriate decision-making and management. If any nation, or any group for that matter, is to adequately manage the development of cruise tourism in a changing world, then they need to monitor it and act dynamically when issues are noted. The complexity of such governance arrangements across the polar regions should not be underestimated; but as growth continues, for how much longer can the polar cruise industry be quietly ignored?

From the tourist's perspective, sound education is crucial across all phases of their tours: before, during and after. Education is a key component of broadening awareness, which everyone hopes will lead to behavioural action, increased environmental ethics and so forth. However, education must also mean something to policy-makers, communities and industry. For policy-makers, there is the need to have a better education of what is happening now, and what may happen in the future. Again, this is linked to consistent monitoring and, in many ways, modelling as well. With a focus to the future, policy-makers should not simply forget the past. There is no need to 'reinvent the wheel' each time a challenge presents itself. Communities need assistance in understanding the positive and negative aspects of tourism. Tourism is not a 'golden egg'; so community members need to be appropriately informed to make the best possible decisions about how to develop tourism in their locality. Similarly, industry needs to be cognizant of its role in tourism development at the local level.

These cross-cutting themes help to raise the question at the heart of this book: can cruise activities in the polar regions ever be synonymous with environmental and social sustainability?

Research directions

The intention of this volume was to raise awareness of some subjects that have previously been neglected, both in other texts and in research undertaken during the International Polar Year (IPY). The hope is that it will create some action and solutions, and to start that process, we suggest some research directions that may stimulate that action. These research directions have connections to Maher (2007), which were more general to all polar tourism. We have elaborated upon Maher's (2007) directions that were cruise specific or have importance to the cruise industry, and have also expanded upon them to include the Antarctic:

- While the polar regions may be 'high profile' at the present time with renewed interest and political will post IPY, what are the implications if this trend reverses?
- What sort of infrastructure or local partnerships will be required to support the anticipated growth in the sector?
- What are the implications of climate change for both the industry and locations visited (environment, scientific bases and communities)?
- What are the changing dangers associated with cruise ship tourism in the polar regions (bigger ships, bigger infrastructure, bigger cultural shifts, leakage of money, etc.)?
- What is the social impact of cruise ship tourism, and can methods found in participatory action research offer a new approach to understanding community-level impacts of cruise tourism?

- For areas such as parks and protected areas, what are or should be the management goals to provide appropriate programmes to help visitors protect and enjoy these areas versus destroying them?

From the work of *Cruise Tourism in Polar Regions: Promoting Environmental and Social Sustainability?*, future research directions should be dynamic; thus, perhaps some of the questions above have been answered. However, there are still crosscutting concerns that could now also include market changes (see Figure 14.1), climate change (see Figure 14.2), monitoring (see Figure 14.3) and education (see Figure 14.4).

Figure 14.1 *Market changes: How will market forces due to, and pressuring changes in, vessel size redefine the polar cruise sector?*
Source: Emma J. Stewart

Figure 14.2 *Climate change: What are the implications of a summertime ice-free Northwest Passage for the cruise sector in Arctic Canada? What are the implications elsewhere in the polar world?*
Source: Emma J. Stewart

Figure 14.3 *Monitoring: Who should take responsibility for overcoming the challenges associated with monitoring and policing cruise tourism activities and development in the polar regions – national programmes, operators?*

Source: Patrick T. Maher

Figure 14.4 *Education: With so much faith placed upon the role of education, how can we take positive steps to ensure that it is implemented, but also evaluated, in an appropriate and critical manner? The tough question really is: how do we know it is working?*

Source: Patrick T. Maher

At the end of this book we hope that the reader has been informed of some of the issues occurring within cruise tourism in the polar regions. The chapters have likely raised more questions than they have provided answers; but that is healthy for debate, for stimulating future research, and for encouraging all stakeholders to take action.

References

CLIA (Cruise Lines International Association) (2009) *2009 CLIA Cruise Market Overview: Statistical Cruise Industry Data Through 2008*, Cruise Lines International Association (CLIA), Fort Lauderdale, FL

Maher, P. T. (2007) 'Arctic Tourism: A complex system of visitors, communities, and environments', *Polar Geography*, vol 30, no 1–2, pp1–5

WCED (World Commission on Environment and Development) (1987) *Our Common Future*, Oxford University Press, Oxford, UK

Weaver, D. B. (2008) *Ecotourism*, 2nd edition, John Wiley and Sons, Milton, UK

Index